MEMOIRS OF
ALEXANDER HERZEN

PUBLISHED ON THE FOUNDATION
ESTABLISHED IN MEMORY OF
THEODORE L. GLASGOW

THE MEMOIRS

OF

ALEXANDER HERZEN

PARTS I AND II

TRANSLATED FROM THE RUSSIAN BY

J. D. DUFF

FELLOW OF TRINITY COLLEGE, CAMBRIDGE

LVX ET VERITAS

GREENWOOD PRESS, PUBLISHERS
WESTPORT, CONNECTICUT

92
H576m

Library of Congress Cataloging in Publication Data

Hertzen, Aleksandr Ivanovich, 1812-1870.
  The memoirs of Alexander Herzen, parts I and II.

  Translation of Byloe i dumy.
  Reprint of the 1923 ed. published by Yale University
Press, New Haven.
  1. Hertzen, Aleksandr Ivanovich, 1812-1870--Biogra-
phy. 2. Revolutionists--Russia--Biography. 3. Social-
ists--Russia--Biography. 4. Authors, Russian--
Biography. I. Title.
DK209.6.H4A325 1976   947'.07'0924 [B]   76-48971
ISBN 0-8371-9319-2

m.R

Originally published in 1923 by Yale University Press, New Haven

Reprinted in 1976 by Greenwood Press, Inc.

Library of Congress Catalog Card Number   76-48971

ISBN 0-8371-9319-2

Printed in the United States of America

THE THEODORE L. GLASGOW MEMORIAL
PUBLICATION FUND

The present volume is the seventh work published by the
Yale University Press on the Theodore L. Glasgow Memorial
Publication Fund. This foundation was established September
17, 1918, by an anonymous gift to Yale University in memory
of Flight Sub-Lieutenant Theodore L. Glasgow, R.N. He was
born in Montreal, Canada, and was educated at the University
of Toronto Schools and at the Royal Military College, Kingston.
In August, 1916, he entered the Royal Naval Air Service and
in July, 1917, went to France with the Tenth Squadron attached
to the Twenty-second Wing of the Royal Flying Corps. A
month later, August 19, 1917, he was killed in action on the
Ypres front.

CONTENTS

INTRODUCTION

I

ALEXANDER HERZEN was born in Moscow on March 25,* 1812, six months before Napoleon arrived at the gates of the city with what was left of his Grand Army. He died in Paris on January 9, 1870. Down to his thirty-fifth year he lived in Russia, often in places selected for his residence by the Government; he left Russia, never to return, on January 10, 1847.

He was the elder son of Iván Yákovlev, a Russian noble, and Luise Haag, a German girl from Stuttgart. It was a runaway match; and as the Lutheran marriage ceremony was not supplemented in Russia, the child was illegitimate. "Herzen" was a name invented for him by his parents. Surnames, however, are little used in Russian society; and the boy would generally be called, from his own Christian name and his father's, Alexander Ivánovich. His parents lived together in Moscow, and he lived with them and was brought up much like other sons of rich nobles. It was quite in Herzen's power to lead a life of selfish ease and luxury; but he early chose a different path and followed it to the end. Yet this consistent champion of the poor and humble was himself a typical aristocrat—

*The dates given here are those of the Russian calendar.

generous, indeed, and stoical in misfortune, but bold to rashness and proud as Lucifer.

The story of his early life is told fully in these pages—his solitary boyhood and romantic friendship with his cousin, Nikolai Ogaryóv; his keen enjoyment of College life, and the beginning of his long warfare with the police of that other aristocrat, Nicholas, Tsar of all the Russias, who was just as much in earnest as Herzen but kept a different object in view.

Charged with socialistic propaganda, Herzen spent nine months of 1834-1835 in a Moscow prison and was then sent, by way of punishment, to Vyatka. The exiles were often men of exceptional ability, and the Government made use of their talents. So Herzen was employed for three years in compiling statistics and organizing an exhibition at Vyatka. He was then allowed to move to Vladímir, near Moscow, where he edited the official gazette; and here, on May 9, 1838, he married his cousin, Natálya Zakhárin, a natural daughter of one of his uncles. Receiving permission in 1839 to live, under supervision of the police, where he pleased, he spent some time in Moscow and Petersburg, but he was again arrested on a charge of disaffection and sent off this time to Nóvgorod, where he served in the Government offices for nearly three years. In 1842 he was allowed to retire from his duties and to settle with his wife and family in Moscow. In 1846 his father's death made him a rich man.

For twelve years past, Herzen, when he was not in prison, had lived the life of a ticket-of-leave man. He was naturally anxious to get away from Russia; but a passport was indispensable, and the Government would not give him a passport. At last the difficulties were overcome; and in the beginning of 1847 Herzen, with his wife and children and widowed mother, left Russia for ever.

Twenty-three years, almost to a day, remained for him to live. The first part of that time was spent in France, Italy, and Switzerland; but the suburbs of London, Putney and Primrose Hill, were his most permanent place of residence. He was safe there from the Russian police; but he did not like London. He spoke English very badly;* he made few acquaintances there; and he writes with some asperity of the people and their habits.

His own family party was soon broken up by death. In November, 1851, his mother and his little son, Nikolai (still called Kólya) were drowned in an accident to the boat which was bringing them from Marseilles to Nice, where Herzen and his wife were expecting them. The shock proved fatal to his wife: she died at Nice in the spring of 1852. The three surviving children were not of an age to be companions to him.

For many years after the *coup d'état* of Louis Napoleon, Herzen, who owned a house in Paris, was forbidden to live in France. He settled in London and was joined there by Ogaryóv, the friend of his childhood. Together they started a printing press, in order to produce the kind of literature which Nicholas and his police were trying to stamp out in Russia. In 1857, after the death of the great Autocrat, they began to issue a fortnightly paper, called Kólokol (*The Bell*); and this *Bell*, probably inaudible in London, made an astonishing noise in Russia. Its circulation and influence there were unexampled: it is said that

*Herzen is mentioned in letters of Mrs. Carlyle. She notes (1) that his English was unintelligible; and (2) that of all the exiles who came to Cheyne Walk he was the only one who had money.

the new Tsar, Alexander, was one of its regular readers. Alexander and Herzen had met long before, at Vyatka. February 19, 1861, when Alexander published the edict abolishing slavery throughout his dominions, must have been one of the brightest days in Herzen's life. There was little brightness in the nine years that remained. When Poland revolted in 1863, he lost his subscribers and his popularity by his courageous refusal to echo the prevailing feeling of his countrymen; and he gave men inferior to himself, such as Ogaryóv and Bakúnin, too much influence over his journal.

He was on a visit to Paris, when he died rather suddenly of inflammation of the lungs on January 9, 1870. At Nice there is a statue of Herzen on the grave where he and his wife are buried.

II

The collected Russian edition of Herzen's works—no edition was permitted by the censorship till 1905—extends to seven thick volumes. These are: one volume of fiction; one of letters addressed to his future wife; two of memoirs; and three of what may be called political journalism.

About 1842 he began to publish articles on scientific and social subjects in magazines whose precarious activity was constantly interrupted or arrested by the censorship. His chief novel, *Who Was To Blame?* was written in 1846. From the time when he left Russia he was constantly writing on European politics and the shifting fortunes of the cause which he had at heart. When he was publishing his Russian newspapers in London, first *The Pole-Star* and then *The Bell*, he wrote most of the matter himself.

To readers who are not countrymen or contemporaries of Herzen's, the *Memoirs* are certainly the most interesting part of his production. They paint for us an astonishing picture of Russian life under the grim rule of Nicholas, the life of the rich man in Moscow, and the life of the exile near the Ural Mountains; and they are crowded with figures and incidents which would be incredible if one were not convinced of the narrator's veracity. Herzen is a supreme master of that superb instrument, the Russian language. With a force of intellect entirely out of Boswell's reach, he has Boswell's power of dramatic presentation: his characters, from the Tsar himself to the humblest old woman, live and move before you on the printed page. His satire is as keen as Heine's, and he is much more in earnest. Nor has any writer more power to wring the heart by pictures of human suffering and endurance. The *Memoirs* have, indeed, one fault—that they are too discursive, and that successive episodes are not always clearly connected or well proportioned. But this is mainly due to the circumstances in which they were produced. Different parts were written at considerable intervals and published separately. The narrative is much more continuous in the earlier parts: indeed, Part V is merely a collection of fragments. But Herzen's *Memoirs* are among the noblest monuments of Russian literature.

III

The *Memoirs,* called by Herzen himself *Past and Thoughts,* are divided into five Parts. This translation, made six years ago from the Petersburg edition of 1913, contains Parts I and II. These were written in London in 1852-1853, and printed in London, at 36 Regent's Square, in the Russian journal called *The Pole-Star*.

Part I has not, I believe, been translated into English before. A translation of Part II was published in London during the Crimean war;* but this was evidently taken from a German version by someone whose knowledge of German was inadequate. The German translation of the *Memoirs* by Dr. Buek† seems to me very good; but it is defective: whole chapters of the original are omitted without warning.

To make the narrative easier to follow, I have divided it up into numbered sections, which Herzen himself did not use. I have added a few footnotes.

June 5, 1923.   J. D. Duff.

My Exile in Siberia, by Alexander Herzen. (Hurst and Blackett, London, 1855). Herzen was not responsible for the misleading title, which caused him some annoyance.

†*Erinnerungen von Alexander Herzen,* by Dr. Otto Buek (Berlin, 1907).

PART I

NURSERY AND UNIVERSITY

(1812-1834)

CHAPTER I

My Nurse and the *Grande Armée*—Moscow in Flames—My
Father and Napoleon—General Ilovaiski—A Journey with
French Prisoners—Patriotism—Calot—Property Managed in
Common—The Division—The Senator.

§1

"OH, please, Nurse, tell me again how the French
came to Moscow!" This was a constant petition
of mine, as I stretched myself out in my crib
with the cloth border to prevent my falling out, and
nestled down under the warm quilt.

My old nurse, Vyéra Artamónovna, was just as eager
to repeat her favourite story as I was to hear it; but her
regular reply was: "You've heard that old story ever so
often before, and besides it's time for you to go to sleep;
you had better rise earlier to-morrow."

"Oh, but please tell me just a little—how you heard
the news, and how it all began."

"Well, it began this way. You know how your papa
puts off always. The packing went on and on till at
last it was done. Everyone said it was high time to be
off; there was nothing to keep us and hardly a soul left in
Moscow. But no! He was always discussing with your

uncle Paul* about travelling together, and they were never both ready on the same day. But at last our things were packed, the carriage was ready, and the travellers had just sat down to lunch, when the head cook came into the dining-room as white as a sheet and reported that the enemy had entered the city at the Dragomirovsky Gate. Our hearts went down into our boots, and we prayed that the power of the Cross might be on our side. All was confusion, and, while we were bustling to and fro and crying out, suddenly we saw a regiment of dragoons galloping down the street; they wore strange helmets with horses' tails tied on behind. They had closed all the city gates; so there was your papa in a pretty mess, and you with him! You were still with your foster-mother, Darya; you were very small and weak then."

And I smiled, with pride and pleasure at the thought that I had taken a part in the Great War.

"At first, all went reasonably well, during the first days at least. From time to time two or three soldiers would come into the house and ask for something to drink; of course we gave them a glass apiece, and then they would go away and salute quite politely as well. But then, you see, when the fires began and got worse and worse, there was terrible disorder, and pillage began and every sort of horror. We were living in a wing of the Princess's house, and the house caught fire. Then your uncle Paul invited us to move to his house, which was built of stone and very strong and stood far back in a court-yard. So we all set off, masters and servants together—there was no thought of distinctions at such a time. When we got

*Paul Ivanovitch Golochvastov, who had married my father's youngest sister.

into the boulevard, the trees on each side were beginning
to burn. At last we reached your uncle's house, and it
was actually blazing, with the fire spouting out of every
window. Your uncle could not believe his eyes; he stood
rooted to the ground.

"Behind the house, as you know, there is a big garden,
and we went there, hoping to be safe. We sat down sadly
enough on some benches there were there, when suddenly
a band of drunken soldiers came in and one of them
began to strip your uncle of a fur coat he had put on for
the journey. But the old gentleman resisted, and the
soldier pulled out his dirk and struck him in the face;
and your uncle kept the scar to his dying day. The other
soldiers set upon us, and one of them snatched you from
the arms of your foster-mother, and undid your clothes,
to see if there were any notes or jewels hidden there;
when he found nothing, the mean fellow tore the clothes
on purpose and then left you alone.

"As soon as they had gone, a great misfortune happened. You remember our servant Platon, who was sent
to serve in the Army? He was always fond of the bottle
and had had too much to drink that day. He had got hold
of a sword and was walking about with it tied round his
waist. The day before the enemy came, Count Rostopchín distributed arms of all kinds to the people at the
Arsenal, and Platon had provided himself with a sword.
Towards evening, a dragoon rode into the court-yard and
tried to take a horse that was standing near the stable;
but Platon flew at him, caught hold of the bridle, and
said: 'The horse is ours; you shan't have it.' The dragoon
pointed a pistol at him, but it can't have been loaded.
Your father saw what was happening and called out:

'Leave that horse alone, Platon! Don't you interfere.' But it was no good: Platon pulled out his sword and struck the soldier over the head; the man reeled under the blow, and Platon struck him again and again. We thought we were doomed now; for, if his comrades saw him, they would soon kill us. When the dragoon fell off, Platon caught hold of his legs and threw him into a lime-pit, though the poor wretch was still breathing; the man's horse never moved but beat the ground with its hoof, as if it understood; our people shut it up in the stable, and it must have been burnt to death there.

"We all cleared out of the court as soon as we could; the fires everywhere grew worse and worse. Tired and hungry, we went into a house that had not caught fire, and threw ourselves down to rest; but, before an hour had passed, our servants in the street were calling out: 'Come out! come out! Fire, fire!' I took a piece of oil-cloth off the billiard table, to wrap you up from the night air. We got as far as the Tversky Square, and the French-men were putting out the fires there, because one of their great generals was living in the Governor's house in the square; we sat down as we were on the street; there were sentries moving all about and other soldiers on horseback. You were crying terribly; your foster-mother had no more milk, and none of us had even a piece of bread. But Natálya Konstantínovna was with us then, and she was afraid of nothing. She saw some soldiers eating in a corner; she took you in her arms and went straight off, and showed you to them. 'The baby wants *manger*,' she said. At first they looked angrily at her and said, '*Allez, allez!*' Then she called them every bad name she could think of; and they did not understand a word, but they laughed heartily and gave her some bread soaked in water for you and a crust for herself. Early next morning an officer came and collected all the men, and your father too, and took them off to put out the fires round about; he left the women only, and your uncle who had been wounded. We stayed there alone till evening; we just sat there and cried. But at dark your father came back, and an officer with him."

§2

BUT allow me to take the place of my old nurse and to continue her story.

When my father had finished his duties as a fireman, he met a squadron of Italian cavalry near the Monastery of the Passion. He went up to the officer in command, spoke to him in Italian, and explained the plight of his family. When the Italian heard his native language—*la sua dolce favella*—he promised to speak to the Duc de Trévise,* and to post a sentinel at once, in order to prevent a repetition of the wild scenes which had taken place in my uncle's garden. He gave orders to this effect to an officer, and sent him off with my father. When he heard that none of the party had eaten any food for two days, the officer took us all off to a grocer's shop; it had been wrecked and the floor was covered with choice tea and coffee, and heaps of dates, raisins, and almonds; our servants filled their pockets, and of dessert at least we had abundance. The sentinel proved to be of no little service: again and again, bands of soldiers were inclined to give trouble to the wretched party of women and serv-

*Mortier (1768-1835), one of Napoleon's marshals, bore this title.

ants, camping in a corner of the square; but an order from our protector made them pass on at once.

Mortier, who remembered having met my father in Paris, reported the facts to Napoleon, and Napoleon ordered him to be presented the next day. And so my father, a great stickler for propriety and the rules of etiquette, presented himself, at the Emperor's summons, in the throne-room of the Kremlin, wearing an old blue shooting-jacket with brass buttons, no wig, boots which had not been cleaned for several days, grimy linen, and a beard of two days' growth.

Their conversation—how often I heard it repeated!— is reproduced accurately enough in the French history of Baron Fain and the Russian history of Danilevski.

Napoleon began with those customary phrases, abrupt remarks, and laconic aphorisms to which it was the custom for thirty-five years to attribute some profound significance, until it was discovered that they generally meant very little. He then abused Rostopchín for the fires, and said it was mere vandalism; he declared, as always, that he loved peace above all things and that he was fighting England, not Russia; he claimed credit for having placed a guard over the Foundling Hospital and the Uspenski Cathedral; and he complained of the Emperor Alexander. "My desire for peace is kept from His Majesty by the people round him," he said.

My father remarked that it was rather the business of the conqueror to make proposals of peace.

"I have done my best. I have sent messages to Kutúzov,* but he will hear of no discussions whatever and does not acquaint his master with my proposals. I

*The Russian commander-in-chief.

am not to blame—if they want war they shall have it!"

When this play-acting was done, my father asked for a safe-conduct to leave Moscow.

"I have ordered that no passes be given. Why do you want to go? What are you afraid of? I have ordered the markets to be opened."

Apparently the Emperor did not realise that, though open markets are a convenience, so is a shut house, and that to live in the open street among French soldiers was not an attractive prospect for a Russian gentleman and his family.

When my father pointed this out, Napoleon thought for a little and then asked abruptly:

"Will you undertake to hand to the Tsar a letter from me? On that condition, I will order a pass to be made out for you and all your family."

"I would accept Your Majesty's proposal," said my father, "but it is difficult for me to guarantee success."

"Will you give me your word of honour, that you will use all possible means to deliver my letter with your own hands?"

"I pledge you my honour, Sir."

"That is enough. I shall send for you. Is there anything you need?"

"Nothing, except a roof to shelter my family till we leave."

"The Duc de Trévise will do what he can." Mortier did in fact provide a room in the Governor's palace, and ordered that we should be supplied with provisions; and his *maître d'hôtel* sent us wine as well. After several days Mortier summoned my father at four in the morning, and sent him off to the Kremlin.

By this time the conflagration had spread to a frightful extent; the atmosphere, heated red-hot and darkened by smoke, was intolerable. Napoleon was dressed already and walking about the room, angry and uneasy; he was beginning to realise that his withered laurels would soon be frozen, and that a jest would not serve, as it had in Egypt, to get him out of this embarrassment. His plan of campaign was ill-conceived, and all except Napoleon knew it—Ney, Narbonne, Berthier, and even officers of no mark or position; to all criticisms his reply was the magic word "Moscow"; and, when he reached Moscow, he too discovered the truth.

When my father entered the room, Napoleon took a sealed letter from a table, gave it to him, and said by way of dismissal, "I rely upon your word of honour." The address on the envelope ran thus: *À mon frère l'empereur Alexandre.*

The safe-conduct given to my father is preserved to this day; it is signed by the Duc de Trévise and counter-signed below by Lesseps, chief of police at Moscow. Some strangers, hearing of our good fortune, begged my father to take them with him, under the pretext that they were servants or relations; and they joined our party. An open carriage was provided for my mother and nurse, and for my wounded uncle; the rest walked. A party of cavalry escorted us; when the rear of the Russian Army came in sight, they wished us good fortune and galloped back again to Moscow. The strange party of refugees was surrounded a moment later by Cossacks, who took us to head-quarters. The generals in command were Wintzen-gerode and Ilovaiski.

When the former was told of the letter, he told my

father that he would send him at once, with two dragoons, to see the Tsar at Petersburg.

"What is to become of your party?" asked the Cossack general, Ilovaiski; "They can't possibly stay here, within rifle-shot of the troops; there may be some hot fighting any day." My father asked that we might be sent, if possible, to his Yaroslavl estate; and he added that he was absolutely penniless at the time.

"That does not matter: we can settle accounts later," said the General; "and don't be uneasy: I give you my promise that they shall be sent."

While my father was sent off to Petersburg on a courier's cart, Ilovaiski procured an old rattle-trap of a carriage for us, and sent us and a party of French prisoners to the next town, under an escort of Cossacks; he provided us with money for posting as far as Yaroslavl, and, in general, did all that he could for us in a time of war and confusion.

This was my first long journey in Russia; my second was not attended by either French cavalry or Ural Cossacks or prisoners of war; the whole party consisted of myself and a drunk police-officer sitting beside me in the carriage.

§3

My father was taken straight to Arakchéyev's* house and detained there. When the Minister asked for the letter, my father said that he had given his word of honour to deliver it in person. The Minister then promised to consult the Tsar, and informed him next day in

*This minister was the real ruler of Russia till the death of Alexander in 1825.

writing, that he himself was commissioned by the Tsar to receive the letter and present it at once. For the letter he gave a receipt, which also has been preserved. For about a month my father was under arrest in Arakché-yev's house; no friend might see him, and his only visitor was S. Shishkóv, whom the Tsar sent to ask for details about the burning of Moscow, the entry of the French, and the interview with Napoleon. No eye-witness of these events had reached Petersburg except my father. At last he was told that the Tsar ordered him to be set at liberty; he was excused, on the ground of necessity, for having accepted a safe-conduct from the French authorities; but he was ordered to leave Petersburg at once, without having communication with anyone, except that he was allowed to say good-bye to his elder brother.

When he reached at nightfall the little village where we were, my father found us in a peasant's cottage; there was no manor-house on that estate. I was sleeping on a settle near the window; the window would not shut tight, and the snow, drifting through the crack, had covered part of a stool, and lay, without melting, on the window-sill.

All were in great distress and confusion, and especially my mother. One morning, some days before my father arrived, the head man of the village came hurriedly into the cottage where she was living, and made signs to her that she was to follow him. My mother could not speak a word of Russian at that time; she could only make out that the man was speaking of my uncle Paul; she did not know what to think; it came into her head that the people had murdered him or wished to murder first him and then her. She took me in her arms and followed the head man, more dead than alive, and shaking all over. She entered the cottage occupied by my uncle; he was actually dead, and his body lay near a table at which he had begun to shave; a stroke of paralysis had killed him instantly.

My mother was only seventeen then, and her feelings may be imagined. She was surrounded by half-savage bearded men, dressed in sheepskins and speaking a language to her utterly incomprehensible; she was living in a small, smoke-grimed peasant's cottage; and it was the month of November in the terrible winter of 1812. My uncle had been her one support, and she spent days and nights in tears for his loss. But those "savages" pitied her with all their heart; their simple kindness never failed her, and their head man sent his son again and again to the town, to fetch raisins and gingerbread, apples and biscuits, to tempt her to eat.

Fifteen years later, this man was still living and sometimes paid us a visit at Moscow. The little hair he had left was then white as snow. My mother used to give him tea and talk over that winter of 1812; she reminded him how frightened she was of him, and how the pair of them, entirely unintelligible to one another, made the arrangements about my uncle's funeral. The old man continued to call my mother Yulíza Ivánovna (her name was Luise); and he always boasted that I was quite willing to go to him and not in the least afraid of his long beard.

We travelled by stages to Tver and finally to Moscow, which we reached after about a year. At the same time, a brother of my father's returned from Sweden and settled down in the same house with us. Formerly ambassador in Westphalia, he had been sent on some mission to the court of Bernadotte.

§4

I STILL remember dimly the traces of the great fire, which were visible even in the early twenties—big houses with the roof gone and window-frames burnt out, heaps of fallen masonry, empty spaces fenced off from the street, remnants of stoves and chimneys sticking up out of them.

Stories of the Great Fire, the battle of Borodino, the crossing of the Berezina, and the taking of Paris—these took the place of cradle-song and fairy-tale to me, they were my Iliad and Odyssey. My mother and our servants, my father and my old nurse, were never tired of going back to that terrible time, which was still so recent and had been brought home to them so painfully. Later, our officers began to return from foreign service to Moscow. Men who had served in former days with my father in the Guards and had taken a glorious part in the fierce contest of the immediate past, were often at our house; and to them it was a relief from their toils and dangers to tell them over again. That was indeed the most brilliant epoch in the history of Petersburg: the consciousness of power breathed new life into Russia; business and care were, so to speak, put off till the sober morrow, and all the world was determined to make merry to-day and celebrate the victory.

At this time I heard even more than my old nurse could tell me about the war. I liked especially to listen to the stories of Count Milorádovitch;* I often lay at his back

*Michael Milorádovitch (1770-1825), a famous commander who lost his life in suppressing the Decembrist revolution, December, 1825.

on the long sofa, while he described and acted scenes of the campaign, and his lively narrative and loud laugh were very attractive to me. More than once I fell asleep in that position.

These surroundings naturally developed my patriotic feeling to an extreme degree, and I was resolved to enter the Army. But an exclusive feeling of nationality is never productive of good, and it landed me in the following scrape. One of our guests was Count Quinsonet, a French *émigré* and a general in the Russian army. An out-and-out royalist, he had been present at the famous dinner where the King's Body-Guards trampled on the national cockade and Marie Antoinette drank confusion to the Revolution.* He was now a grey-haired old man, tall and slight, a perfect gentleman and the pink of politeness. A peerage was awaiting him at Paris; he had been there already to congratulate Louis XVIII on his accession, and had returned to Russia to sell his estates. As ill luck would have it, I was present when this politest of generals in the Russian service began to speak about the war.

"But you, surely, were fighting against us," I said very innocently.

"Non, mon petit, non! J'étais dans l'armée russe."

"What!" said I, "you a Frenchman and fighting on our side! That's impossible."

My father gave me a reproving look and tried to talk of something else. But the Frenchman saved the situation nobly: he turned to my father and said, "I like to see such patriotic feeling." But my father did not like to see it, and scolded me severely when our guest had gone. "You see what comes of rushing into things which you

*This dinner took place at Versailles, on October 1, 1789.

don't and can't understand: the Count served *our* Emperor out of loyalty to *his own* sovereign." That was, as my father said, beyond my powers of comprehension.

§5

My father had lived twelve years abroad, and his brother still longer; and they tried to organise their household, to some extent, on a foreign plan; yet it was to retain all the conveniences of Russian life and not to cost much. This plan was not realised; perhaps their measures were unskilful, or perhaps the old traditions of Russian country life were too strong for habits acquired abroad. They shared their land in common and managed it jointly, and a swarm of servants inhabited the ground floor of their house in town; in fact, all the elements of disorder were present.

I was under the charge of two nurses, one Russian and the other German. Vyéra Artamónovna and Mme. Provo were two very good-natured women, but I got weary of watching them all day, as they knitted stockings and wrangled together. So, whenever I could, I escaped to the part of the house occupied by the Senator—my uncle, the former ambassador, was now a Senator* and was generally called by this title—and there I found my only friend, my uncle's valet, Calot.

I have seldom met so kind and gentle a creature as this man. Utterly solitary in Russia, separated from all his own belongings, and hardly able to speak our language, he had a woman's tenderness for me. I spent whole hours in his room, and, though I was often mischievous

*The Senate was not a deliberative body but a Supreme Court of Justice.

and troublesome, he bore it all with a good-natured smile. He cut out all kinds of marvels for me in cardboard, and carved me many toys of wood; and how I loved him in return! In the evenings he used to take picture-books from the library and bring them up to my nursery—*The Travels* of Gmelin and Pallas, and another thick book called *The World in Pictures,* which I liked so much and looked at so long, that the leather binding got worn out: for two hours together Calot would show me the same pictures and repeat the same explanations for the thousandth time.

Before my birthday party, Calot shut himself up in his room, and I could hear mysterious sounds of a hammer and other tools issuing from it. He often walked quickly through the passage, carrying a glue-pot or something wrapped up in paper, but each time he left his room locked. I knew he was preparing some surprise for me, and my curiosity may be imagined. I sent the servants' children to act as spies, but Calot was not to be caught napping. We even managed to make a small hole in the staircase, through which we could look down into the room; but we could see nothing but the top of the window and the portrait of Frederick the Great, with his long nose and a large star on his breast, looking like a sick vulture. At last the noises stopped, and the room was unlocked—but it looked just as before, except for snippings of gilt and coloured paper on the floor. I was devoured by curiosity; but Calot wore a pretence of solemnity on his features and never touched the ticklish subject.

I was still suffering agonies of impatience when the great day arrived. I awoke at six, to wonder what Calot had in store for me; at eight Calot himself appeared, wearing a white tie and white waistcoat under his blue livery, but his hands were empty! I wondered how it would all end, and whether he had spoilt what he was making. The day went on, and the usual presents were forthcoming: my aunt's footman had brought me an expensive toy wrapped up in a napkin, and my uncle, the Senator, had been generous also, but I was too restless, in expectation of the surprise, to enjoy my happiness.

Then, when I was not thinking of it, after dinner or perhaps after tea, my nurse said to me: "Go downstairs for a moment, there is someone there asking for you." "At last!" I thought, and down the bannisters I slid on my arms. The drawing-room door flew open; I heard music and saw a transparency representing my initials; then some little boys, disguised as Turks, offered me sweets; and this was followed by a puppet-show and parlour fireworks. Calot was very hot and very busy; he kept everything going and was quite as excited as I was myself.

No presents could rank with this entertainment. I never cared much for *things*; the bump of acquisitiveness was never, at any age, highly developed in me. The satisfaction of my curiosity, the abundance of candles, the silver paper, the smell of gunpowder—nothing was wanting but a companion of my own age. But I spent all my childhood in solitude and consequently was not exacting on that score.

§6

My father had another brother, the oldest of the three; but he was not even on speaking terms with his two

juniors. In spite of this, they all took a share in the management of the family property, which really meant that
they combined to ruin it. This triple management by
owners at variance with one another was the height of
absurdity. Two of them were always thwarting their
senior's plans, and he did the same for them. The head
men of the villages and the serfs were utterly bamboozled:
one landlord required carts to convey his household, the
second demanded hay, and the third, firewood; each of
the three issued orders, and sent his man of business to
see that they were carried out. If the eldest brother appointed a bailiff, the other two dismissed the man in a
month on some absurd pretext, and appointed another,
who was promptly disowned by their senior. As a natural
result, there were spies and favourites, to carry slanders
and false reports, while, at the bottom of this system, the
wretched serfs, finding neither justice nor protection and
harassed by a diversity of masters, were worked twice
as hard and found it impossible to satisfy such unreasonable demands.

As a consequence of this quarrel between brothers, they
lost a great lawsuit in which the law was on their side.
Though their interests were identical, they could never
settle on a common course of procedure, and their opponents naturally took advantage of this state of affairs.
They lost a large and valuable property in this way; and
the Court also condemned each brother to pay damages
to the amount of 30,000 *roubles*. This lesson opened their
eyes for the first time, and they determined to divide the
family estates between them. Preliminary discussions
went on for nearly a year; the land was divided into three
fairly even parts, and chance was to decide to whom each

should fall. My father and the Senator paid a visit to
their brother, whom they had not seen for several years,
in order to talk things over and be reconciled; and then
it was noised abroad that he would return the visit and
the business would be finally settled on that occasion. The
report of this visit spread uneasiness and dismay throughout our household.

§7

MY uncle was one of those monsters of eccentricity
which only Russia and the conditions of Russian society
can produce. A man of good natural parts, he spent his
whole life in committing follies which often rose to the
dignity of crimes. Though he was well educated after the
French fashion and had read much, his time was spent
in profligacy or mere idleness, and this went on till his
death. In youth he served, like his brothers, in the Guards
and was *aide-de-camp* in some capacity to Potemkin;*
next, he served on a diplomatic mission, and, on his return to Petersburg, was appointed to a post in the Ecclesiastical Court. But no association either with diplomatists
or priests could tame that wild character. He was dismissed from his post, for quarrelling with the Bishops;
and he was forbidden to reside in Petersburg, because
he gave, or tried to give, a box on the ear to a guest at
an official dinner given by the Governor of the city. He
retired to his estate at Tambóv; and there he was nearly
murdered by his serfs for interference with their daughters
and for acts of cruelty; he owed his life to his coachman
and the speed of his horses.

*Grigóri Potemkin (pronounce Pat-yóm-kin), b. 1736, d. 1791; minis-
ter and favourite of the Empress Catherine.

After this experience he settled in Moscow. Disowned by his relations and by people in general, he lived quite alone in a large house on the Tver Boulevard, bullying his servants in town and ruining his serfs in the country. He collected a large library and a whole harem of country girls, and kept both these departments under lock and key. Totally unoccupied and inordinately vain, he sought distraction in collecting things for which he had no use, and in litigation, which proved even more expensive. He carried on his lawsuits with passionate eagerness. One of these suits was about an Amati fiddle; it lasted thirty years, and he won it in the end. He won another case for the possession of a party-wall between two houses: it cost him extraordinary exertions, and he gained nothing by owning the wall. After his retirement, he used to follow in the Gazette the promotions of his contemporaries in the public service; and, whenever one of them received an Order, he bought the star and placed it on his table, as a painful reminder of the distinctions he might have gained.

His brothers and sisters feared him and had no intercourse with him of any kind; our servants would not walk past his house, for fear of meeting him, and turned pale at the sight of him; the women dreaded his insolent persecution, and the domestic servants had prayer offered in church that they might never serve him.

§8

SUCH was the alarming character of our expected visitor. From early morning all the inmates of our house were keenly excited. I had never seen the black sheep myself, though I was born in his house, which was occupied by my father on his return from foreign parts; I was very anxious to see him, and I was also afraid, though I don't know what I was afraid of.

Other visitors came before him—my father's oldest nephew, two intimate friends, and a lawyer, a stout good-natured man who perspired freely. For two hours they all sat in silent expectation, till at last the butler came in, and, with a voice that seemed somehow unnatural, announced the arrival of our kinsman. "Bring him in," said the Senator, in obvious agitation; my father began to take snuff, the nephew straightened his tie, and the lawyer turned to one side and cleared his throat. I was told to go upstairs, but I remained in the next room, shaking all over.

The uncle advanced at a slow and dignified pace, and my father and the Senator went to meet him. He was carrying an *ikon** with both arms stretched out before him, in the way that *ikons* are carried at weddings and funerals; he turned towards his brothers and in a nasal drawl addressed them as follows:

"This is the *ikon* with which our father blessed me on his deathbed, and he then charged me and my late brother, Peter, to take his place and care for you two. If our father could know how you have behaved to your elder brother . . . "

"Come, *mon cher frère*," said my father, in his voice of studied indifference, "you have little to boast about on that score yourself. These references to the past are painful for you and for us, and we had better drop them."

"What do you mean? Did you invite me here for this?" shouted the pious brother, and he dashed the *ikon* down

*A sacred picture.

with such violence that the silver frame rang loudly on the floor. Now the Senator began, and he shouted still louder; but at this point I rushed upstairs, just waiting long enough to see the nephew and the lawyer, as much alarmed as I was, beating a retreat to the balcony.

What then took place, I cannot tell. The servants had all hid for safety and could give no information; and neither my father nor the Senator ever alluded to the scene in my presence. The noise grew less by degrees, and the division of the land was carried out, but whether then or later, I do not know.

What fell to my father was Vasílevskoë, a large estate near Moscow. We spent all the following summer there; and during that time the Senator bought a house for himself in the Arbat quarter of Moscow, so that, when we returned alone to our big house, we found it empty and dead. Soon after, my father also bought a new house in Moscow.

When the Senator left us, he took with him, in the first place, my friend Calot, and, in the second place, all that gave life in our establishment. He alone could check my father's tendency to morbid depression, which now had room to develop and assert itself fully. Our new house was not cheerful: it reminded one of a prison or hospital. The ground-floor rooms were vaulted; the thick walls made the windows look like the embrasures of a fortress; and the house was surrounded on all sides by a uselessly large court-yard.

The real wonder was, not that the Senator left us, but that he was able to stay so long under one roof with my father. I have seldom seen two men more unlike in character.

§9

My uncle was a kind-hearted man, who loved movement and excitement. His whole life was spent in an
artificial world, a world of diplomats and lords-in-waiting,
and he never guessed that there is a different world which
comes nearer to the reality of things. And yet he was not
merely a spectator of all that happened between 1789 and
1815, but was personally involved in that mighty drama.
Count Vorontsov sent him to England, to learn from Lord
Grenville what "General Buonaparte" was up to, after he
left the army of Egypt. He was in Paris at the time of
Napoleon's coronation. In 1811 Napoleon ordered him to
be detained and arrested at Cassel, where he was minister
at the court of King Jérôme*—"Emperor Jérôme," as
my father used to say when he was annoyed. In fact, he
witnessed each scene of that tremendous spectacle; but,
somehow, it seemed not to impress him in the right way.

When captain in the Guards, he was sent on a mission
to London. Paul, who was then Tsar, noticed this when
he read the roster, and ordered that he should report himself at once in Petersburg. The attaché sailed by the first
ship and appeared on parade.

"Do you want to stay in London?" Paul asked in his
hoarse voice.

"If Your Majesty is graciously pleased to allow it,"
answered the captain.

"Go back at once!" the hoarse voice replied; and the
young officer sailed, without even seeing his family in
Moscow.

While he served as ambassador, diplomatic questions

*Jérôme Bonaparte (1784-1860) was King of Westphalia from 1807
to 1813.

were settled by bayonets and cannon-balls; and his diplomatic career came to an end at the Congress of Vienna, that great field-day for all the diplomats of Europe. On his return to Russia, he was created a lord-in-waiting at Moscow—a capital which has no Court. Then he was elected to the Senate, though he knew nothing of law or Russian judicial procedure; he served on the Widows' and Orphans' Board, and was a governor of hospitals and other public institutions. All these duties he performed with a zeal that was probably superfluous, a love of his own way that was certainly harmful, and an integrity that passed wholly unnoticed.

He was never to be found at home. He tired out a team of four strong horses every morning, and another in the afternoon. He never missed a meeting of the Senate; twice a week he attended the Widows' Board; and there were also his hospitals and schools. Besides all this, he was never absent from the theatre when a French play was given, and he was driven to the English Club on three days of every week. He had no time to be bored —always busy with one of his many occupations, perpetually on the way to some engagement, and his life rolled along on easy springs in a world of files and official envelopes.

To the age of seventy, he kept the health of youth. He was always to be seen at every great ball or dinner; he figured at speech-days and meetings of public bodies; whatever their objects might be—agriculture or medicine, fire insurance or natural science—it was all one to him; and, besides all this (perhaps because of this), he kept to old age some measure of humanity and warmth of heart.

§10

IT is impossible to conceive a greater contrast to all
this than my father. My uncle was perpetually active and
perpetually cheerful, an occasional visitor at his own
house. But my father hardly ever went out of doors, hated
all the world of official business, and was always hard to
please and out of humour. We had our eight horses too,
but our stable was a kind of hospital for cripples; my
father kept them partly for the sake of appearance, and
partly that the two coachmen and two postilions might
have some other occupation, as well as going to fetch
newspapers and arranging cock-fights, which last amusement they carried on with much success in the space between the coach-house and the neighbours' yard.

My father did not remain long in the public service.
Brought up by a French tutor in the house of a pious
aunt, he entered the Guards as a serjeant at sixteen and
retired as a captain when Paul became Tsar. In 1801
he went abroad and wandered about from one foreign
country to another till the end of 1811. He returned to
Russia with my mother three months before I was born;
the year after the burning of Moscow he spent in the
Government of Tver, and then settled down permanently
in Moscow, where he led by choice a solitary and monotonous life. His brother's lively temperament was distasteful to him.

After the Senator had left it, the whole house assumed
a more and more gloomy aspect. The walls, the furniture,
the servants—every thing and person had a furtive and
dissatisfied appearance; and of course my father himself
was more dissatisfied than anyone else. The artificial still-
ness, the hushed voices and noiseless steps of the servants,

were no sign of devotion, but of repression and fear. Nothing was ever moved in the rooms: the same books lay on the same tables, with the same markers in them, for five or six years together. In my father's bedroom and study the furniture was never shifted and the windows never opened, not once in a twelvemonth. When he went to the country, he regularly took the key of his rooms in his pocket, lest the servants should take it into their heads to scour the floors or to clean the walls in his absence.

CHAPTER II

Gossip of Nurses and Conversation of Generals—A False Position—Boredom—The Servants' Hall—Two Germans—Lessons and Reading—Catechism and the Gospel.

§1

UNTIL I was ten, I noticed nothing strange or peculiar in my position.* To me it seemed simple and natural that I was living in my father's house, where I had to be quiet in the rooms inhabited by him, though in my mother's part of the house I could shout and make a noise to my heart's content. The Senator gave me toys and spoilt me; Calot was my faithful slave; Vyéra Artamónovna bathed me, dressed me, and put me to bed; and Mme. Provo took me out for walks and spoke German to me. All went on with perfect regularity; and yet I began to feel puzzled.

My attention was caught by some casual remarks incautiously dropped. Old Mme. Provo and the household in general were devoted to my mother, but feared and disliked my father. The disputes which sometimes took place between my parents were often the subject of dis-

*Herzen's parents were never married with the Russian rites, and he bore throughout life a name which was not his father's.

cussion between my nurses, and they always took my mother's side.

It was true that my mother's life was no bed of roses. An exceedingly kind-hearted woman, but not strong-willed, she was utterly crushed by my father; and, as often happens with weak characters, she was apt to carry on a desperate opposition in matters of no importance. Unfortunately, in these trifles my father was almost always in the right, and so he triumphed in the end.

Mme. Provo would start a conversation in this style: "In her place, I declare I would be off at once and go back to Germany. The dulness of the life is fit to kill one; no enjoyment and nothing but grumbling and un-pleasantness."

"You're quite right," said Vyéra Artamónovna; "but she's tied hand and foot by someone"—and she would point her knitting-needles at me. "She can't take him with her, and to leave him here alone in a house like ours would be too much even for one not his mother."

Children in general find out more than people think. They are easily put off, and forget for a time, but they persist in returning to the subject, especially if it is mys-terious or alarming; and by their questions they get at the truth with surprising perseverance and ingenuity.

Once my curiosity was aroused, I soon learned all the details of my parents' marriage—how my mother made up her mind to elope, how she was concealed in the Rus-sian embassy at Cassel by my uncle's connivance, and then crossed the frontier disguised as a boy; and all this I found out without asking a single question.

The first result of these discoveries was to lessen my attachment to my father, owing to the disputes of which

I have spoken already. I had witnessed them before, but had taken them as a matter of course. The whole household, not excluding the Senator, were afraid of my father, and he spared no one his reproofs; and I was so accustomed to this, that I saw nothing strange in these quarrels with my mother. But now I began to take a different view of the matter, and the thought that I was to some extent responsible threw a dark shadow sometimes over my childhood.

A second thought which took root in my mind at that time was this—that I was much less dependent on my father than most children are on their parents; and this independence, though it existed only in my own imagination, gave me pleasure.

§2

Two or three years after this, two old brother-officers of my father's were at our house one evening—General Essen, the Governor of Orenburg, and General Bakhmétyev, who lost a leg at Borodino and was later Lieutenant-Governor of Bessarabia. My room was next the drawing-room where they were sitting. My father happened to mention that he had been speaking to Prince Yusúpov with regard to my future; he wished me to enter the Civil Service. "There's no time to lose," he added; "as you know, he must serve a long time before he gets any decent post."

"It is a strange notion of yours," said Essen good-humouredly, "to turn the boy into a clerk. Leave it to me; let me enroll him in the Ural Cossacks; he will soon get his commission, which is the main thing, and then he can forge ahead like the rest of us."

But my father would not agree: he said that everything military was distasteful to him, that he hoped in time to get me a diplomatic post in some warm climate, where he would go himself to end his days.

Bakhmétyev had taken little part in the conversation; but now he got up on his crutches and said:

"In my opinion, you ought to think twice before you reject Essen's advice. If you don't fancy Orenburg, the boy can enlist here just as well. You and I are old friends, and I always speak my mind to you. You will do no good to the young man himself and no service to the country by sending him to the University and on to the Civil Service. He is clearly in a false position, and nothing but the Army can put that right and open up a career for him from the first. Any dangerous notions will settle down before he gets the command of a regiment. Discipline works wonders, and his future will depend on himself. You say that he's clever; but you don't suppose that all officers in the Army are fools? Think of yourself and me and our lot generally. There is only one possible objection —that he may have to serve some time before he gets his commission; but that's the very point in which we can help you."

This conversation was as valuable to me as the casual remarks of my nurses. I was now thirteen; and these lessons, which I turned over and over and pondered in my heart for weeks and months in complete solitude, bore their fruit. I had formerly dreamt, as boys always do, of military service and fine uniforms, and had nearly wept because my father wished to make a civilian of me; but this conversation at once cooled my enthusiasm, and by degrees—for it took time—I rooted out of my mind every atom of my passion for stripes and epaulettes and aiguillettes. There was, it is true, one relapse, when a cousin, who was at school in Moscow and sometimes came to our house on holidays, got a commission in a cavalry regiment. After joining his regiment, he paid a visit to Moscow and stayed some days with us. My heart beat fast, when I saw him in all his finery, carrying his sabre and wearing the shako held at a becoming angle by the chin-strap. He was sixteen but not tall for his age; and next morning I put on his uniform, sabre, shako, and all, and looked at myself in the glass. How magnificent I seemed to myself, in the blue jacket with scarlet facings! What a contrast between this gorgeous finery and the plain cloth jacket and duck trousers which I wore at home!

My cousin's visit weakened for a time the effect of what the generals had said; but, before long, circumstances gave me a fresh and final distaste for a soldier's uniform.

By pondering over my "false position," I was brought to much the same conclusions as by the talk of the two nurses. I felt less dependence on society (of which, however, I knew nothing), and I believed that I must rely mainly on my own efforts. I said to myself with childish arrogance that General Bakhmétyev and his brother-officers should hear of me some day.

In view of all this, it may be imagined what a weary and monotonous existence I led in the strange monastic seclusion of my home. There was no encouragement for me, and no variety; my father, who showed no fondness for me after I was ten, was almost always displeased with me; I had no companions. My teachers came and went; I saw them to the door, and then stole off to play with the servants' children, which was strictly forbidden. At other times I wandered about the large gloomy rooms, where the windows were shut all day and the lights burnt dim in the evening; I either did nothing or read any books I could lay hands on.

My only other occupation I found in the servants' hall and the maids' room; they gave me real live pleasure. There I found perfect freedom; I took a side in disputes; together with my friends downstairs, I discussed their doings and gave my advice; and though I knew all their secrets, I never once betrayed them by a slip of the tongue in the drawing-room.

§3

THIS is a subject on which I must dwell for a little. I should say that I do not in general mean to avoid digressions and disquisitions; every conversation is full of them, and so is life itself.

As a rule, children are attached to servants. Parents, especially Russian parents, forbid this intimacy, but the children do not obey orders, because they are bored in the drawing-room and happy in the pantry. In this case, as in a thousand others, parents don't know what they are doing. I find it impossible to imagine that our servants' hall was a worse place for children than our morning-room or smoking-room. It is true that children pick up coarse expressions and bad manners in the company of servants; but in the drawing-room they learn coarse ideas and bad feelings.

The mere order to keep at a distance from people with whom the children are in constant relations, is in itself revolting.

Much is said in Russia about the profound immorality of servants, especially of serfs. It is true that they are not distinguished by exemplary strictness of conduct. Their low stage of moral development is proved by the mere fact that they put up with so much and protest so seldom. But that is not the question. I should like to know what class in Russia is less depraved than the servant class. Certainly not the nobles, nor the officials. The clergy, perhaps?

What makes the reader laugh?

Possibly the peasants, but no others, might have some claim to superiority.

The difference between the class of nobles and the class of servants is not great. I hate, especially since the calamities of the year 1848, democrats who flatter the mob, but I hate still more aristocrats who slander the people. By representing those who serve them as profligate animals, slave-owners throw dust in the eyes of others and stifle the protests of their own consciences. In few cases are we better than the common people, but we express our feelings with more consideration, and we are cleverer at concealing selfish and evil passions; our desires are not so coarse or so obvious, owing to the easiness of satisfying them and the habitual absence of self-restraint; we are merely richer, better fed, and therefore more difficult to please. When Count Almaviva named to the barber of Seville all the qualifications he required in a servant, Figaro said with a sigh, "If a servant must possess all these merits, it will be hard to find masters who are fit for a servant's place."

In Russia in general, moral corruption is not deep. It might truly enough be called savage, dirty, noisy, coarse, disorderly, shameless; but it is mainly on the surface. The clergy, in the concealment of their houses, eat and drink to excess with the merchant class. The nobles get drunk in the light of day, gamble recklessly, strike their men-servants and run after the maids, mismanage their affairs, and fail even worse as husbands and fathers. The official class are as bad in a dirtier way; they curry favour, besides, with their superiors and they are all petty thieves. The nobles do really steal less: they take openly what does not belong to them, though without prejudice to other methods, when circumstances are favourable.

All these amiable weaknesses occur in a coarser form among servants—that class of "officials" who are beneath the fourteenth grade—those "courtiers" who belong, not to the Tsar, but to the landowners.* But how they, as a class, are worse than others, I have no idea.

When I run over my recollections on the subject—and for twenty-five years I was well acquainted, not only with our own servants, but with those of my uncle and several neighbours—I remember nothing specially vicious in their conduct. Petty thefts there were, no doubt; but it is hard to pass sentence in this case, because ordinary ideas are perverted by an unnatural status: the human chattel is on easy terms with the chattels that are inanimate, and shows no particular respect for his master's property. One ought, in justice, to exclude exceptional cases—casual favourites, either men or women, who bask in their master's smiles and carry tales against the rest; and besides, *their* behaviour is exemplary, for they never

---

* In Russia civil-service officials (*chinóvniki*) are divided into fourteen classes. Nobles are called *dvoryáne,* and servants attached to a landowner's house *dvoróvïe;* Herzen plays on the likeness of the two names.

get drunk in the daytime and never pawn their clothes at the public-house.

The misconduct of most servants is of a simple kind and turns on trifles—a glass of spirits or a bottle of beer, a chat over a pipe, absence from the house without leave, quarrels which sometimes proceed as far as blows, or deception of their master when he requires of them more than man can perform. They are as ignorant as the peasants but more sophisticated; and this, together with their servile condition, accounts for much that is perverted and distorted in their character; but, in spite of all this, they remain grown-up children, like the American negroes. Trifles make them laugh or weep; their desires are limited and deserve to be called simple and natural rather than vicious.

Spirits and tea, the public-house and the tea-shop—these are the invariable vices of a servant in Russia. For them he steals; because of them he is poor; for their sake he endures persecution and punishment and leaves his wife and children to beggary. Nothing is easier than to sit, like Father Matthew,* in the seat of judgement and condemn drunkenness, while you are yourself intoxicated with sobriety; nothing simpler than to sit at your own tea-table and marvel at servants, because they *will* go to the tea-shop instead of drinking their tea at home, where it would cost them less.

Strong drink stupefies a man and makes it possible for him to forget; it gives him an artificial cheerfulness, an artificial excitement; and the pleasure of this state is increased by the low level of civilisation and the narrow

*An Irish priest who preached temperance in the middle of the nineteenth century.

empty life to which these men are confined. A servant is a slave who may be sold, a slave condemned to perpetual service in the pantry and perpetual poverty: how can such a man do otherwise than drink? He drinks too much when he gets the chance, because he cannot drink every day; this was pointed out by Senkovsky in one of his books fifteen years ago. In Italy and the south of France, there are no drunkards, because there is abundance of wine. And the explanation of the savage drunkenness among English workmen is just the same. These men are broken in a hopeless and ill-matched struggle against hunger and beggary; after all their efforts, they have found everywhere a leaden vault above their heads, and a sullen opposition which has cast them down into the nether darkness of society and condemned them to a life of endless toil—toil without an object and equally destructive of mind and body. What wonder that such a man, after working six days as a lever or wheel or spring or screw, breaks out on Saturday night, like a savage, from the factory which is his prison, and drinks till he is dead drunk? His exhaustion shortens the process, and it is complete in half an hour. Moralists would do better to order "Scotch" or "Irish" for themselves, and hold their tongues; or else their inhuman philanthropy may evoke formidable replies.

To a servant, tea drunk in a tea-shop is quite a different thing. Tea at home is not really tea: everything there reminds him that he is a servant—the pantry is dirty, he has to put the *samovár** on the table himself, his cup

*An urn with a central receptacle to hold hot charcoal: tea in Russia is regularly accompanied by a *samovár*.

has lost its handle, his master's bell may ring at any moment. In the tea-shop he is a free man, a master; the table is laid and the lamps lit for *him*; for *him* the waiter hurries in with the tray, the cups shine, and the teapot glitters; he gives orders, and other people obey him; he feels happy and calls boldly for some cheap caviare or pastry to eat with his tea.

In all this there is more of childlike simplicity than of misconduct. Impressions take hold of them quickly but throw out no roots; their minds are continually occupied —if one can call it occupation—with casual objects, trifling desires, and petty aims. A childish belief in the marvellous turns a grown man into a coward, and the same belief consoles him in his darkest hours. I witnessed the death of several of my father's servants, and I was astonished. One could see then that their whole life had been spent, like a child's, without fears for the future, and that no great sins lay heavy on their souls; even if there had been anything of the kind, a few minutes with the priest were enough to put all to rights.

It is on this resemblance between children and servants that their mutual attachment is based. Children resent the indulgent superiority of grown-up people; they are clever enough to understand that servants treat them with more respect and take them seriously. For this reason, they enjoy a game of bézique with the maids much more than with visitors. Visitors play out of indulgence and to amuse the child: they let him win, or tease him, and stop when they feel inclined; but the maid plays just as much for her own amusement; and thus the game gains in interest.

Servants have a very strong attachment to children;

and this is not servility at all—it is a mutual alliance, with weakness and simplicity on both sides.

§4

IN former days there existed—it still exists in Turkey —a feudal bond of affection between the Russian land-owner and his household servants. But the race of such servants, devoted to the family as a family, is now extinct with us. The reason of this is obvious. The landowner has ceased to believe in his own authority; he does not believe that he will answer, at the dreadful Day of Judgement, for his treatment of his people; and he abuses his power for his own advantage. The servant does not believe in his inferiority; he endures oppression, not as a punishment or trial inflicted by God, but merely because he is defenceless.

But I knew, in my young days, two or three specimens of that boundless loyalty which old gentlemen of seventy sometimes recall with a sigh: they speak of the wonderful zeal and devotion of their servants, but they never mention the return which they and their fathers made to that faithfulness.

There was Andréi Stepánov, whom I knew as a decrepit old man, spending his last days, on very short commons, on an estate belonging to my uncle, the Senator.

When my father and uncle were young men in the Army, he was their valet, a kind, honest, sober man, who guessed what his young masters wanted—and they wanted a good deal—by a mere look at their faces; I know this from themselves. Later he was in charge of an estate near Moscow. The war of 1812 cut him off at once from all communications; the village was burnt down, and he lived on there alone and without money, and finally sold some wood, to save himself from starvation. When my uncle returned to Russia, he went into the estate accounts and discovered the sale of wood. Punishment followed: the man was disgraced and removed from his office, though he was old and burdened with a family. We often passed through the village where he lived and spent a day or two there; and the old man, now paralysed and walking on crutches, never failed to visit us, in order to make his bow to my father and talk to him.

I was deeply touched by the simple devotion of his language and by his miserable appearance; I remember the tufts of hair, between yellow and white, which covered both sides of his bare scalp.

"They tell me, Sir," he said once to my father, "that your brother has received another Order. I am getting old, *bátyushka,* and shall soon give back my soul to God; but I wish God would suffer me to see your brother wearing his Order; just once before I die, I would like to see him with his ribbon and all his glory."

My eyes were on the old man, and everything about him showed that he was speaking the truth—his expression as frank as a child's, his bent figure, his crooked face, dim eyes, and feeble voice. There was no falsehood or flattery there: he did really wish to see, once more before he died, the man who, for fourteen years, had never forgiven him for that wood! Should I call him a saint or a madman? Are there any who attain to sanctity, except madmen?

But this form of idolatry is unknown to the rising generation; and, if there are cases of serfs who refuse emancipation, it is due either to mere indolence or selfish considerations. This is a worse condition of things, I admit, but it brings us nearer the end. The serfs of to-day may wish to see something round their master's neck; but you may feel sure that it is not the ribbon of any Order of Chivalry!

§5

THIS seems an opportunity to give some general account of the treatment shown to servants in our household.

Neither my father nor my uncle was specially tyrannical, at least in the way of corporal punishment. My uncle, being hot-tempered and impatient, was often rough and unjust to servants; but he thought so little about them and came in contact with them so seldom, that each side knew little of the other. My father wore them out by his fads: he could never pass over a look or a word or a movement without improving the occasion; and a Russian often resents this treatment more than blows or bad language.

Corporal punishment was almost unknown with us; and the two or three cases in which it was resorted to were so exceptional, that they formed the subject of conversation for whole months downstairs; it should also be said that the offences which provoked it were serious.

A commoner form of punishment was compulsory enlistment in the Army, which was intensely dreaded by all the young men-servants. They preferred to remain serfs, without family or kin, rather than carry the knapsack for twenty years. I was strongly affected by those horrible scenes: at the summons of the landowner, a file of military police would appear like thieves in the night and seize their victim without warning; the bailiff would explain that the master had given orders the night before for the man to be sent to the recruiting office; and then the victim, through his tears, tried to strike an attitude, while the women wept, and all the people gave him presents, and I too gave what I could, very likely a sixpenny necktie.

I remember too an occasion when a village elder spent some money due from peasants to their master, and my father ordered his beard to be shaved off, by way of punishment. This form of penalty puzzled me, but I was impressed by the man's appearance: he was sixty years old, and he wept profusely, bowing to the ground and offering to repay the money and a hundred *roubles* more, if only he might escape the shame of losing his beard.

While my uncle lived with us, there were regularly about sixty servants belonging to the house, of whom nearly half were women; but the married women might give all their time to their own families; there were five or six house-maids always employed, and laundry-maids, but the latter never came upstairs. To these must be added the boys and girls who were being taught housework, which meant that they were learning to be lazy and tell lies and drink spirits.

As a feature of those times, it will not, I think, be superfluous to say something of the wages paid to servants. They got five *roubles* a month, afterwards raised to six, for board-wages; women got a *rouble* less, and children over ten half the amount. The servants clubbed together for their food, and made no complaint of insufficiency, which proves that food cost wonderfully little. The highest wages paid were 100 *roubles* a year; others got fifty, and some thirty. Boys under eighteen got no wages. Then our servants were supplied with clothes, overcoats, shirts, sheets, coverlets, towels, and mattresses of sail-cloth; the boys who got no wages received a sum of money for the bath-house and to pay the priest in Lent—purification of body and soul was thus provided for. Taking everything into account, a servant cost about 300 *roubles* a year; if we add his share of medical attendance and drugs and the articles of consumption which came in carts from the landlord's estates in embarrassing amount, even then the figure will not be higher than 350 *roubles*. In Paris or London a servant costs four times as much.

Slave-owners generally reckon "insurance" among the privileges of their slaves, *i.e.*, the wife and children are maintained by the master, and the slave himself, in old age, will get a bare pittance in some corner of the estate. Certainly this should be taken into account, but the value of it is considerably lessened by the constant fear of corporal punishment and the impossibility of rising higher in the social scale.

My own eyes have shown me beyond all doubt, how the horrible consciousness of their enslaved condition torments and poisons the existence of servants in Russia, how it oppresses and stupefies their minds. The peasants, especially those who pay *obrók*,* are less conscious of personal want of freedom; it is possible for them not to believe, to some extent, in their complete slavery. But in the other case, when a man sits all day on a dirty bench in the pantry, or stands at a table holding a plate, there is no possible room for doubt.

Obrók is money paid by a serf to his master in lieu of personal service; such a serf might carry on a trade or business of his own and was liable to no other burdens than the *obrók*.

There are, of course, people who enjoy this life as if it were their native element; people whose mind has never been aroused from slumber, who have acquired a taste for their occupation, and perform its duties with a kind of artistic satisfaction.

§6

OUR old footman, Bakai, an exceedingly interesting character, was an instance of this kind. A tall man of athletic build, with large and dignified features, and an air of the profoundest reflexion, he lived to old age in the belief that a footman's place is one of singular dignity.

This respectable old man was constantly out of temper or half-drunk, or both together. He idealised the duties of his office and attributed to them a solemn importance. He could lower the steps of a carriage with a peculiarly loud rattle; when he banged a carriage-door he made more noise than the report of a gun. He stood on the rumble surly and straight, and, every time that a hole in the road gave him a jolt, he called out to the coachman, "Easy there!" in a deep voice of displeasure, though the hole was by that time five yards behind the carriage.

His chief occupation, other than going out with the carriage, was self-imposed. It consisted in training the pantry-boys in the standard of manners demanded by the servants' hall. As long as he was sober, this went well enough; but when he was affected by liquor, he was severe and exacting beyond belief. I sometimes tried to protect my young friends, but my authority had little weight with the Roman firmness of Bakai: he would open the door that led to the drawing-room, with the words: "This is not your place. I beg you will go, or I shall carry you out." Not a movement, not a word, on the part of the boys, did he let pass unrebuked; and he often accompanied his words with a smack on the head, or a painful fillip, which he inflicted by an ingenious and spring-like manipulation of his finger and thumb.

When he had at last driven the boys from the room and was left alone, he transferred his attentions to his only friend, a large Newfoundland dog called Macbeth, whom he fed and brushed and petted and loved. After sitting alone for a few minutes, he would go down to the courtyard and invite Macbeth to join him in the pantry. Then he began to talk to his friend: "Foolish brute! What makes you sit outside in the frost, when there's warmth in here? Well, what are you staring at? Can't you answer?" and the questions were generally followed by a smack on the head. Macbeth occasionally growled at his benefactor; and then Bakai reproved him, with no weak fondness: "Do what you like for a dog, a dog it still remains: it shows its teeth at you, with never a thought of who you are. But for me, the fleas would eat you up!" And then, hurt by his friend's ingratitude, he would take snuff angrily and throw what was left on his fingers at Macbeth's nose. The dog would sneeze, make incredibly awkward attempts to get the snuff out of his eyes with his paw, rise in high dudgeon from the bench, and begin scratching at the door. Bakai opened the door and dismissed the dog with a kick and a final word of reproach. At this point the pantry-boys generally came back, and the sound of his knuckles on their heads began again.

We had another dog before Macbeth, a setter called Bertha. When she became very ill, Bakai put her on his bed and nursed her for some weeks. Early one morning

I went into the servants' hall. Bakai tried to say something, but his voice broke and a large tear rolled down his cheek—the dog was dead. There is another fact for the student of human nature. I don't at all suppose that he hated the pantry-boys either; but he had a surly temper which was made worse by drinking bad spirits and unconsciously affected by his surroundings.

§7

SUCH men as Bakai hugged their chains, but there were others: there passes through my memory a sad procession of hopeless sufferers and martyrs. My uncle had a cook of remarkable skill in his business, a hard-working and sober man who made his way upwards. The Tsar had a famous French *chef* at the time and my uncle contrived to secure for his servant admission to the imperial kitchens. After this instruction, the man was engaged by the English Club at Moscow, made money, married, and lived like a gentleman; but, with the noose of serfdom still round his neck, he could never sleep easy or enjoy his position.

Alexyéi—that was his name—at last plucked up courage, had prayers said to Our Lady of Iberia, and called on my uncle and offered 5,000 *roubles* for his freedom. But his master was proud of the cook as his property— he was proud of another man, a painter, for just the same reason—and therefore he refused the money, promising the cook to give him his freedom in his will, without any payment.

This was a frightful blow to the man. He became depressed; the expression of his features changed; his hair turned grey; and, being a Russian, he took to the bottle. He became careless about his work, and the English Club dismissed him. Then he was engaged by the Princess

Trubetskoi, and she persecuted him by her petty meanness. Alexyéi was a lover of fine phrases; and once, when
he was insulted by her beyond bearing, he drew himself
up and said in his nasal voice, "What a stormy soul in-
habits Your Serene Highness's body!" The Princess was
furious: she dismissed the man and wrote, as a Russian
great lady would, to my uncle to complain of his servant.
My uncle would rather have done nothing, but, out of
politeness to the lady, he sent for the cook and scolded
him, and told him to go and beg pardon of the Princess.

But, instead of going there, he went to the public-house.
Within a year he was utterly ruined: all the money he had
saved for his freedom was gone, and even his last kitchen-
apron. He fought with his wife, and she with him, till at
last she went into service as a nurse away from Moscow.
Nothing was heard of him for a long time. At last a policeman brought him to our house, a wild and ragged
figure. He had no place of abode and wandered from one
drink-shop to another. The police had picked him up in
the street and demanded that his master should take him
in hand. My uncle was vexed and, perhaps, repentant:
he received the man kindly enough and gave him a room
to live in. Alexyéi went on drinking; when he was drunk,
he was noisy and fancied he was writing poetry; and he
really had some imaginative gift but no control over it.
We were in the country at the time, and my uncle sent
the man to us, fancying that my father would have some
control over him. But the man was too far gone. His case
revealed to me the concentrated ill-feeling and hatred
which a serf cherishes in his heart against his masters:
he gnashed his teeth as he spoke, and used gestures which,
especially as coming from a cook, were ominous. My

presence did not prevent him from speaking freely; he was fond of me, and often patted my shoulder as he said, "This is a sound branch of a rotten tree!"

When my uncle died, my father gave Alexyéi his freedom at once. But this was too late: it only meant washing our hands of him, and he simply vanished from sight.

§8

THERE was another victim of the system whom I cannot but recall together with Alexyéi. My uncle had a servant of thirty-five who acted as a clerk. My father's oldest brother, who died in 1813, intending to start a cottage hospital, placed this man, Tolochanov, when he was a boy, with a doctor, in order to learn the business of a dresser. The doctor got permission for him to attend lectures at the College of Medicine; the young man showed ability, learned Latin and German, and practised with some success. When he was twenty-five, he fell in love with the daughter of an officer, concealed his position from her, and married her. The deception could not be kept up for long: my uncle died, and the wife was horrified to discover that she, as well as her husband, was a serf. The "Senator," their new owner, put no pressure on them at all—he had a real affection for young Tolochanov —but the wife could not pardon the deception: she quarrelled with him and finally eloped with another man. Tolochanov must have been very fond of her: he fell into a state of depression which bordered on insanity; he spent his nights in drunken carouses, and, having no money of his own, made free with what belonged to his master. Then, when he saw he could not balance his accounts, he took poison, on the last day of the year 1821.

My uncle was away from home. I was present when Tolochanov came into the room and told my father he had come to say good-bye; he also gave me a message for my uncle, that he had spent the missing money.

"You're drunk," said my father; "go and sleep it off."

"My sleep will last a long time," said the doctor; "I only ask you not to think ill of my memory."

The man's composure frightened my father: he looked at him attentively and asked: "What's the matter with you? Are you wandering?"

"No, Sir; I have only swallowed a dose of arsenic."

The doctor and police were summoned, milk and emetics were administered. When the vomiting began, he tried to keep it back and said: "You stop where you are! I did not swallow you, to bring you up again." When the poison began to work more strongly, I heard his groans and the agonised voice in which he said again and again, "It burns, it burns like fire!" Someone advised that the priest should be sent for; but he refused, and told Calot that he knew *too much anatomy* to believe in a life beyond the grave. At twelve at night he spoke to the doctor: he asked the time, in German, and then said, "Time to wish you a Happy New Year!" and then he died.

In the morning I went hastily to the little wing, used as a bath-house, where Tolochanov had been taken. The body was lying on a table in the attitude in which he died; he was wearing a coat, but the necktie had been removed and the chest was bare; the features were terribly distorted and even blackened. It was the first dead body I had ever seen; and I ran out, nearly fainting. The toys and picture-book which I had got as New Year's presents could not comfort me: I still saw before me the blackened features of Tolochanov, and heard his cry, "It burns like fire!"

To end this sad subject, I shall say only one thing more: the society of servants had no really bad influence on me. On the contrary, it implanted in me, in early years, a rooted hatred for slavery and oppression in all their manifestations. When I had been naughty as a child and my nurse, Vyéra Artamónovna, wished to be very cutting, she used to say, "Wait a bit, and you will be exactly like the rest, when you grow up and become a master!" I felt this to be a grievous insult. Well, the old woman may rest in peace—whatever I became, I did not become "exactly like the rest."

§9

I HAD one other distraction, as well as the servants' hall, and in this I met at least with no opposition. I loved reading as much as I disliked my lessons. Indeed, my passion for desultory reading was one of the main difficulties in the way of serious study. For example, I detested, then as now, the theoretical study of languages; but I was very quick in making out the meaning more or less and acquiring the rudiments of conversation; and there I stopped, because that was all I needed.

My father and my uncle had a fairly large library, consisting of French books of the eighteenth century. The books lay about in heaps in a damp unused room on the ground-floor of the house. Calot kept the key and I was free to rummage as much as I pleased in this literary lumber-room. I read and read with no interruptions. My father approved for two reasons: in the first place, I would learn French quicker; and besides I was kept occupied, sitting quietly in a corner. I must add that I did not display all the books I read openly on the table: some of them I kept secreted in a cupboard.

But what books did I read? Novels, of course, and plays. I read through fifteen volumes, each of which contained three or four plays, French or Russian. As well as French novels, my mother had novels by Auguste Lafontaine and Kotzebue's comedies; and I read them all twice over. I cannot say that the novels had much effect on me. As boys do, I pounced on all the ambiguous passages and disorderly scenes, but they did not interest me specially. A far greater influence was exercised over my mind by a play which I loved passionately and read over twenty times, though it was in a Russian translation— *The Marriage of Figaro.* I was in love with Cherubino and the Countess; nay more, I myself was Cherubino; I felt strong emotion as I read it and was conscious of some new sensation which I could not at all understand. I was charmed with the scene where the page is dressed up as a woman, and passionately desired to have a ribbon belonging to someone, in order to hide it in my breast and kiss it when no one was looking. As a matter of fact, no female society came in my way at that age.

I only remember two school-girls who paid us occasional Sunday visits. The younger was sixteen and strikingly beautiful. I became confused whenever she entered the room; I never dared to address her, or to go beyond stolen glances at her beautiful dark eyes and dark curls. I never spoke a word of this to anyone, and my first love-pangs passed off unknown even to her who caused them.

When I met her years afterwards, my heart beat fast

and I remembered how I had worshipped her beauty at twelve years old.

I forgot to say that *Werther* interested me almost as much as *The Marriage of Figaro*; half of the story I could not understand and skipped, in my eagerness to reach the final catastrophe; but over that I wept quite wildly. When I was at Vladímir in 1839, the same book happened to come into my hands, and I told my wife how I used to cry over it as a boy. Then I began to read the last letters to her; and when I reached the familiar passage, the tears flowed fast and I had to stop.

I cannot say that my father put any special pressure upon me before I was fourteen; but the whole atmosphere of our house was stifling to a live young creature. Side by side with complete indifference about my moral welfare, an excessive degree of importance was attached to bodily health; and I was terribly worried by precautions against chills and unwholesome food, and the fuss that was made over a trifling cold in the head. In winter I was kept indoors for weeks at a time, and, if a drive was permitted, I had to wear warm boots, comforters, and so on. The rooms were kept unbearably hot with stoves. This treatment must have made me feeble and delicate, had I not inherited from my mother the toughest of constitutions. She, on her part, shared none of these prejudices, and in her part of the house I might do all the things which were forbidden when I was with my father.

Without rivalry and without encouragement or approval, my studies made little progress. For want of proper system and supervision, I took things easy and thought to dispense with hard work by means of memory and a lively imagination. My teachers too, as a matter of course, were under no supervision; when once the fees were settled, provided they were punctual in coming to the house and leaving it, they might go on for years, without giving any account of what they were doing.

§10

ONE of the queerest incidents of my early education was when a French actor, Dalès, was invited to give me lessons in elocution.

"People pay no attention to it nowadays," my father said to me, "but your brother Alexander practised *le recit de Théramène** every evening for six months with Aufraine, the actor, and never reached the perfection which his teacher desired."

So I began to learn elocution.

"I suppose, M. Dalès," my father once said to him, "you could give lessons in dancing too."

Dalès was a stout old gentleman of over sixty; with a profound consciousness of his own merits but an equally profound sense of modesty, he answered that he could not judge of his own talents, but that he often gave hints to the ballet-dancers at the Opera.

"Just as I supposed," remarked my father, offering him his snuff-box open—a favour he would never have shown to a Russian or German tutor. "I should be much obliged if you would make him dance a little after the declamation; he is so stiff."

"Monsieur le comte peut disposer de moi."

And then my father, who was a passionate lover of Paris, began to recall the *foyer* of the Opera-house as it was in 1810, the *début* of Mlle. George and the later

* From Racine's *Phèdre*.

years of Mlle. Mars,* and asked many question about
cafés and theatres.

And now you must imagine my small room on a dismal
winter evening, with the water running down the frozen
windows over the sandbags, two tallow candles burning on the table, and us two face to face. On the stage
Dalès spoke in a fairly natural voice, but, in giving a
lesson, he thought himself bound to get away as far as
possible from nature. He recited Racine in a sing-song
voice, and made a parting, like the parting of an Englishman's back hair, at the caesura of each line, so that
every verse came out in two pieces like a broken stick.

Meanwhile he made the gestures of a man who had
fallen into the water and cannot swim. He made me repeat each verse several times and constantly shook his
head: "Not right at all! Listen to me! *'Je crains Dieu,
cher Abner'*—now came the parting; he closed his eyes,
shook his head slightly, and added, repelling the waves
with a languid movement of the arm, *'et n'ai point d'autre
crainte.'* "†

Then the old gentleman, who "feared nothing but God,"
would look at his watch, put away his books, and take
hold of a chair. This chair was my partner.

Is it surprising that I never learned to dance? These
lessons did not last long: within a fortnight they were
brought to an end by a very tragic event.

I was at the theatre with my uncle, and the overture
was played several times without the curtain rising. The
front rows, wishing to show their familiarity with Paris

*George (1787-1867) was the chief actress in tragedy, and Mars
(1779-1847) the chief actress in comedy, on the Paris stage of their
time.

†From Racine's *Athalie*.

customs, began to make the noise which is made in Paris by the back rows only. A manager came out in front of the curtain; he bowed to the left, he bowed to the right, he bowed to the front, and then he said: "We ask for all the indulgence of the audience; a terrible misfortune has befallen us: Dalès, a member of our company,"— and here the manager's speech was interrupted by genuine tears,—"has been found dead in his room, poisoned by the fumes from the stove."

Such were the forcible means by which the Russian system of ventilation delivered me from lessons in elocution, from spouting Racine, and from dancing a solo with the partner who boasted four legs carved in mahogany.

§11

WHEN I was twelve, I was transferred from the hands of women to those of men; and, about that time, my father made two unsuccessful attempts to put a German in charge of me.

"A German in charge of children" is neither a tutor nor a *dyádka**—it is quite a profession by itself. He does not teach or dress the children himself, but sees that they are dressed and taught; he watches over their health, takes them out for walks, and talks whatever nonsense he pleases, provided that it is in German. If there is a tutor in the house, the German is his inferior; but he takes precedence of the *dyádka*, if there is one. The visiting teachers, if they come late from unforeseen causes, or leave too early owing to circumstances beyond their control, are polite to the German; and, though quite unedu-

*A *dyádka* (literally "uncle") is a man-servant put in charge of his young master.

cated, he begins to think himself a man of learning. The governesses make use of the German to do all sorts of errands for them, but never permit any attentions on his part, unless they suffer from positive deformity and see no prospect of any other admirers. When boys are fourteen they go off to the German's room to smoke on the sly, and he allows it, because he needs powerful assistance if he is to keep his place. Indeed, the common practice is to dismiss him at this period, after thanking him in the presence of the boys and presenting him with a watch. If he is tired of taking children out and receiving reprimands when they catch cold or stain their clothes, then the "German in charge of children" becomes a German without qualification: he starts a small shop where he sells amber mouth-pieces, eau-de-cologne, and cigars to his former charges, and performs secret services for them of another kind.

The first German attached to my person was a native of Silesia, and his name was Iokisch; in my opinion, his name alone was a sufficient disqualification. He was a tall, bald man, who professed a knowledge of agriculture, and I believe that this fact induced my father to take him; but his chief distinction was his extreme need of soap and water. I looked with aversion at the Silesian giant, and only consented to walk about with him in the parks and gardens on condition that he told me improper stories, which I retailed in the servants' hall. He did not survive more than a year; he was guilty of some misconduct on our country estate, and a gardener tried to kill him with a scythe; and this made my father order him to clear out.

His successor was Theodore Karlovitch, a soldier (probably a deserter) from Brunswick-Wolfenbüttel, who was remarkable for his beautiful handwriting and excessive stupidity. He had filled a similar post twice already, and had gained some experience, so that he gave himself the airs of a tutor; also, he spoke French, mispronouncing *j* as *sh* and misplacing the accents.*

I had no kind of respect for him, but poisoned every moment of his existence, especially after I was convinced that, in spite of all my efforts, he was unable to understand either decimal fractions or the rule of three. In most boys' hearts there is a good deal that is ruthless and even cruel; and I persecuted the Jäger of Wolfenbüttel unmercifully with sums in proportion. I was so much interested by this, that, though I did not often speak on such subjects to my father, I solemnly informed him of the stupidity of Theodore Karlovitch.

He once boasted to me of a new frock-coat, dark blue with gold buttons, and I actually saw him once wearing it; he was going to a wedding, and the coat, though it was too large for him, really had gold buttons. But the boy who waited on the German informed me that the garment was borrowed from a friend who kept a perfumer's shop. Without the least feeling of pity, I attacked my victim, and asked bluntly where his blue coat was.

"There is a great deal of moth in this house, and I have given it to a tailor whom I know to keep it safe for me."

"Where does the tailor live?"

"What business is that of yours?"

"Why not say?"

---

*The English speak French even worse than the Germans; but they merely mutilate the language, whereas the German vulgarises it. (Author's note.)

"People should mind their own business."

"Oh, very well. But my birthday is next week, and, to please me, you might get the blue coat from the tailor for that day."

"No, I won't; you don't deserve it, after your rudeness."

I held up a threatening finger at him. But the final blow to the German's position took place as follows. He must needs boast one day, in the presence of Bouchot, my French tutor, that he had fought at Waterloo and that the Germans had given the French a terrible mauling. Bouchot merely looked at him and took snuff with such a formidable air that the conqueror of Napoleon was rather taken aback. Bouchot left the room, leaning angrily on his knotted stick, and he never afterwards called the man by any other name than *le soldat de Vilain-ton.** I did not know then that this pun is the property of Béranger, and I was exceedingly delighted by Bouchot's cleverness.

At last this comrade of Blücher's left our house, after a quarrel with my father; and I was not troubled further with Germans.

During the time of the warrior from Brunswick-Wolfen-büttel, I sometimes visited a family of boys, who were also under the charge of a German; and we took long walks together. The two Germans were friends. But, when my German departed, I was left once more in complete solitude. I disliked it and tried hard to escape from it, but without success. As I was powerless to overcome my father's wishes, I should, perhaps, have been crushed by this kind of life; but I was soon saved by a new form of

*I.e., Wellington.

mental activity, and by two new acquaintances, of whom I shall speak in the next chapter. I am sure that it never once occurred to my father what sort of life he was forcing me to lead; or else he would not have vetoed my very innocent wishes and the very natural requests which I put to him.

He let me go occasionally to the French Theatre with my uncle. This was a supreme enjoyment to me. I was passionately fond of the theatre; but even this treat cost me as much pain as pleasure. My uncle often arrived when the play was half over; and, as he was always engaged for some party, he often took me out before the end. The theatre was quite close to our house; but I was strictly forbidden by my father to come home alone.

§12

I was about fifteen when my father summoned a priest to the house to teach me as much Divinity as was required for entrance at the University. I had read Voltaire before I ever opened the Catechism. In the business of education, religion is less obtrusive in Russia than in any other country; and this is, of course, a very good thing. A priest is always paid half the usual fee for lessons in Divinity; and, if the same priest also teaches Latin, he actually gets more for a Latin lesson than for instruction in the Catechism.

My father looked upon religion as one of the indispensable attributes of a gentleman. It was necessary to accept Holy Scripture without discussion, because mere intellect is powerless in that department, and the subject is only made darker by human logic. It was necessary to submit to such rites as were required by the Church into which you were born; but you must avoid excessive piety, which is suitable for women of advanced age but improper for a man. Was he himself a believer? I imagine that he believed to some extent, from habit, from a sense of decency, and just in case—. But he never himself observed any of the rules laid down by the Church, excusing himself on the plea of bad health. He hardly ever admitted a priest to his presence, or asked him to repeat a psalm while waiting in the empty drawing-room for the five-*rouble* note which was his fee. In winter he excused himself on the plea that the priest and his clerk brought in so much cold air with them that he always caught cold in consequence. In the country, he went to church and received the priest at his house; but this was not due to religious feeling but rather a concession to the ideas of society and the wishes of Government.

My mother was a Lutheran, and, as such, a degree more religious. Once or twice a month she went on Sundays to her place of worship—her *Kirche,* as Bakai persisted in calling it, and I, for want of occupation, went with her. I learned there to imitate with great perfection the flowery style of the German pastors, and I had not lost this art when I came to manhood.

My father always made me keep Lent. I rather dreaded confession, and church ceremonies in general were impressive and awful to me. The Communion Service caused me real fear; but I shall not call that religious feeling: it was the fear which is always inspired by the unintelligible and mysterious, especially when solemn importance is attached to the mystery. When Easter brought the end of the Fast, I ate all the Easter dishes—dyed

eggs, currant loaf, and consecrated cakes, and thought
no more about religion for the rest of the year.

Yet I often read the Gospel, both in Slavonic and in
Luther's translation, and loved it. I read it without notes
of any kind and could not understand all of it, but I felt
a deep and sincere reverence for the book. In my early
youth, I was often attracted by the Voltairian point of
view—mockery and irony were to my taste; but I don't
remember ever taking up the Gospel with indifference
or hostility. This has accompanied me throughout life:
at all ages and in all variety of circumstances, I have
gone back to the reading of the Gospel, and every time
its contents have brought down peace and gentleness into
my heart.

When the priest began to give me lessons, he was astonished, not merely at my general knowledge of the
Gospel but also at my power of quoting texts accurately.
"But," he used to say, "the Lord God, who has opened
the mind, has not yet opened the heart." My theological
instructor shrugged his shoulders and was surprised by
the inconsistency he found in me; still he was satisfied
with me, because he thought I should be able to pass my
examination.

A religion of a different kind was soon to take possession of my heart and mind.

CHAPTER III

Death of Alexander I—The Fourteenth of December—Moral Awakening—Bouchot—My Cousin—N. Ogaryóv.

§1

ONE winter evening my uncle came to our house at an unusual hour. He looked anxious and walked with a quick step to my father's study, after signing to me to stay in the drawing-room.

Fortunately, I was not obliged to puzzle my head long over the mystery. The door of the servants' hall opened a little way, and a red face, half hidden by the wolf-fur of a livery coat, invited me to approach; it was my uncle's footman, and I hastened to the door.

"Have you not heard?" he asked.

"Heard what?"

"The Tsar is dead. He died at Taganrog."

I was impressed by the news: I had never before thought of the possibility of his death. I had been brought up in great reverence for Alexander, and I thought with sorrow how I had seen him not long before in Moscow. We were out walking when we met him outside the Tver Gate; he was riding slowly, accompanied by two or three high officers, on his way back from manœuvres. His face was attractive, the features gentle and rounded, and his expression was weary and sad. When he caught us up, I took off my hat; he smiled and bowed to me.

Confused ideas were still simmering in my head; the shops were selling pictures of the new Tsar, Constantine; notices about the oath of allegiance were circulating; and good citizens were making haste to take the oath—when suddenly a report spread that the Crown Prince had abdicated. Immediately afterwards, the same footman, a great lover of political news, with abundant opportunities for collecting it from the servants of senators and lawyers —less lucky than the horses which rested for half the day, he accompanied his master in his rounds from morning till night—informed me that there was a revolution in Petersburg and that cannon were firing in the capital.

On the evening of the next day, Count Komarovsky, a high officer of the police, was at our house, and told us of the band of revolutionaries in the Cathedral Square, the cavalry charge, and the death of Milorádovitch.*

Then followed the arrests—"They have taken so-and-so"; "They have caught so-and-so"; "They have arrested so-and-so in the country." Parents trembled in fear for their sons; the sky was covered over with black clouds.

During the reign of Alexander, political persecution was rare: it is true that he exiled Púshkin for his verses, and Labzin, the secretary of the Academy of Fine Arts, for proposing that the imperial coachman should be elected a member;† but there was no systematic persecu-

*When Nicholas became Emperor in place of his brother Constantine, the revolt of the Decembrists took place in Petersburg on December 14, 1825. Five of the conspirators were afterwards hanged, and over a hundred banished to Siberia.

†The president had proposed to elect Arakchéyev, on the ground of

tion. The secret police had not swollen to its later proportions: it was merely an office, presided over by De Sanglin,
a freethinking old gentleman and a sayer of good things,
in the manner of the French writer, Etienne de Jouy.
Under Nicholas, De Sanglin himself came under police
supervision and passed for a liberal, though he remained
precisely what he had always been; but this fact alone
serves to mark the difference between the two reigns.

The tone of society changed visibly; and the rapid de-
moralisation proved too clearly how little the feeling of
personal dignity is developed among the Russian aristocracy. Except the women, no one dared to show sympathy or to plead earnestly in favour of relations and
friends, whose hands they had grasped yesterday but who
had been arrested before morning dawned. On the contrary, men became zealots for tyranny, some to gain their
own ends, while others were even worse, because they had
nothing to gain by subservience.

Women alone were not guilty of this shameful denial
of their dear ones. By the Cross none but women were
standing; and by the blood-stained guillotine there were
women too—a Lucile Desmoulins, that Ophelia of the
French Revolution, wandering near the fatal axe and
waiting her turn, or a George Sand holding out, even on
the scaffold, the hand of sympathy and friendship to the
young fanatic, Alibaud.*

The wives of the exiles were deprived of all civil rights;

his nearness to the Tsar. Labzin then proposed the election of Ilyá
Baikov, the Tsar's coachman. "He is not only near the Tsar but sits
in front of him," he said.

*Camille Desmoulins was guillotined, with Danton, April 5, 1794;
his wife, Lucile, soon followed him. Alibaud was executed July 11, 1836,
for an attempt on the life of Louis Philippe.

abandoning their wealth and position in society, they faced a whole lifetime of slavery in Eastern Siberia, where the terrible climate was less formidable than the Siberian police. Sisters, who were not permitted to accompany their condemned brothers, absented themselves from Court, and many of them left Russia; almost all of them retained in their hearts a lively feeling of affection for the sufferers. But this was not so among the men: fear devoured this feeling in their hearts, and none of them dared to open their lips about "the unfortunate."

As I have touched on this subject, I cannot refrain from giving some account of one of these heroic women, whose history is known to very few.

§2

IN the ancient family of the Ivashevs a French girl was living as a governess. The only son of the house wished to marry her. All his relations were driven wild by the idea; there was a great commotion, tears, and entreaties. They succeeded in inducing the girl to leave Petersburg and the young man to delay his intention for a season. Young Ivashev was one of the most active conspirators, and was condemned to penal servitude for life. For this was a form of *mésalliance* from which his relations did not protect him. As soon as the terrible news reached the young girl in Paris, she started for Petersburg, and asked permission to travel to the Government of Irkutsk, in order to join her future husband. Benkendorf tried to deter her from this criminal purpose; when he failed, he reported the case to Nicholas. The Tsar ordered that the position of women who had remained faithful to their exiled husbands should be explained to her. "I don't keep her back," he added; "but she ought to realise that if wives, who have accompanied their husbands out of loyalty, deserve some indulgence, she has no claim whatever to such treatment, when she intends to marry one whom she knows to be a criminal."

In Siberia nothing was known of this permission. When she had found her way there, the poor girl was forced to wait while a correspondence went on with Petersburg. She lived in a miserable settlement peopled with released criminals of all kinds, unable to get any news of her lover or to inform him of her whereabouts.

By degrees she made acquaintances among her strange companions. One of these was a highwayman who was now employed in the prison, and she told him all her story. Next day he brought her a note from Ivashev; and soon he offered to carry messages between them. All day he worked in the prison; at nightfall he got a scrap of writing from Ivashev and started off, undeterred by weariness or stormy weather, and returned to his daily work before dawn.

At last permission came for their marriage. A few years later, penal servitude was commuted to penal settlement, and their condition was improved to some extent. But their strength was exhausted, and the wife was the first to sink under the burden of all she had undergone. She faded away, as a flower from southern climes was bound to fade in the snows of Siberia. Ivashev could not survive her long: just a year later he too died. But he had ceased to live before his death: his letters (which impressed even the inquisitors who read them) were evidence not only of intense sorrow, but of a distracted brain; they were full of a gloomy poetry and a crazy piety; after her death he never really lived, and the process of his death was slow and solemn.

This history does not end with their deaths. Ivashev's father, after his son's exile, transferred his property to an illegitimate son, begging him not to forget his unfortunate brother but to do what he could. The young pair were survived by two children, two nameless infants, with a future prospect of the roughest labour in Siberia— without friends, without rights, without parents. Ivashev's brother got permission to adopt the children. A few years later he ventured on another request: he used influence, that their father's name might be restored to them, and this also was granted.

§3

I was strongly impressed by stories of the rebels and their fate, and by the horror which reigned in Moscow. These events revealed to me a new world, which became more and more the centre of my whole inner life; I don't know how it came to pass; but, though I understood very dimly what it was all about, I felt that the side that possessed the cannons and held the upper hand was not my side. The execution of Pestel* and his companions finally awakened me from the dreams of childhood.

Though political ideas occupied my mind day and night, my notions on the subject were not very enlightened: indeed they were so wide of the mark that I believed one of the objects of the Petersburg insurrection to consist in placing Constantine on the throne as a constitutional monarch.

It will easily be understood that solitude was a greater

*One of the Decembrists.

burden to me than ever: I needed someone, in order to impart to him my thoughts and ideals, to verify them, and to hear them confirmed. Proud of my own "disaffection," I was unwilling either to conceal it or to speak of it to people in general.

My choice fell first on Iván Protopópov, my Russian tutor.

This man was full of that respectable indefinite liberalism, which, though it often disappears with the first grey hair, marriage, and professional success, does nevertheless raise a man's character. He was touched by what I said, and embraced me on leaving the house. "Heaven grant," he said, "that those feelings of your youth may ripen and grow strong!" His sympathy was a great comfort to me. After this time he began to bring me manuscript copies, in very small writing and very much frayed, of Púshkin's poems—*Ode to Freedom, The Dagger,* and of Ryléev's *Thoughts.* These I used to copy out in secret; and now I print them as openly as I please!

As a matter of course, my reading also changed. Politics for me in future, and, above all, the history of the French Revolution, which I knew only as described by Mme. Provo. Among the books in our cellar I unearthed a history of the period, written by a royalist; it was so unfair that, even at fourteen, I could not believe it. I had chanced to hear old Bouchot say that he was in Paris during the Revolution; and I was very anxious to question him. But Bouchot was a surly, taciturn man, with spectacles over a large nose; he never indulged in any needless conversation with me: he conjugated French verbs, dictated examples, scolded me, and then took his departure, leaning on his thick knotted stick.

The old man did not like me: he thought me a mere idler, because I prepared my lessons badly; and he often said, "You will come to no good." But when he discovered my sympathy with his political views, he softened down entirely, pardoned my mistakes, and told me stories of the year '93, and of his departure from France when "profligates and cheats" got the upper hand. He never smiled; he ended our lesson with the same dignity as before, but now he said indulgently, "I really thought you would come to no good, but your feelings do you credit, and they will save you."

§4

To this encouragement and approval from my teachers there was soon added a still warmer sympathy which had a profound influence upon me.

In a little town of the Government of Tver lived a granddaughter of my father's eldest brother. Her name was Tatyana Kuchin. I had known her from childhood, but we seldom met: once a year, at Christmas or Shrovetide, she came to pay a visit to her aunt at Moscow. But we had become close friends. Though five years my senior, she was short for her age and looked no older than myself. My chief reason for getting to like her was that she was the first person to talk to me in a reasonable way: I mean, she did not constantly express surprise at my growth; she did not ask what lessons I did and whether I did them well; whether I intended to enter the Army, and, if so, what regiment; but she talked to me as most sensible people talk to one another, though she kept the little airs of superiority which all girls like to show to boys a little younger than themselves.

We corresponded, especially after the events of 1824;

but letters mean paper and pen and recall the school-
room table with its ink-stains and decorations carved
with a penknife. I wanted to see her and to discuss our
new ideas; and it may be imagined with what delight I
heard that my cousin was to come in February (of 1826)
and to spend several months with us. I scratched a calendar on my desk and struck off the days as they passed,
sometimes abstaining for a day or two, just to have the
satisfaction of striking out more at one time. In spite of
this, the time seemed very long; and when it came to an
end, her visit was postponed more than once; such is the
way of things.

One evening I was sitting in the school-room with
Protopópov. Over each item of instruction he took, as
usual, a sip of sour broth; he was explaining the hexame-
ter metre, ruthlessly hashing, with voice and hand, each
verse of Gnyéditch's translation of the Iliad into its separate feet. Suddenly, a sound unlike that of town sledges
came from the snow outside; I heard the faint tinkle of
harness-bells and the sound of voices out-of-doors. I
flushed up, lost all interest in the hashing process and the
wrath of Achilles, and rushed headlong to the front hall.
There was my cousin from Tver, wrapped up in furs,
shawls, and comforters, and wearing a hood and white
fur boots. Blushing red with frost and, perhaps, also with
joy, she ran into my arms.

§5

MOST people speak of their early youth, its joys and
sorrows, with a slightly condescending smile, as if they
wished to say, like the affected lady in Griboyédov's play,
"How childish!" Children, when a few years are past, are

ashamed of their toys, and this is right enough: they
want to be men and women, they grow so fast and change
so much, as they see by their jackets and the pages of
their lesson-books. But adults might surely realise that
childhood and the two or three years of youth are the
fullest part of life, the fairest, and the most truly our
own; and indeed they are possibly the most important
part, because they fix all that follows, though we are not
aware of it.

So long as a man moves modestly forwards, never stopping and never reflecting, and until he comes to the edge
of a precipice or breaks his neck, he continues to believe
that his life lies ahead of him; and therefore he looks
down upon his past and is unable to appreciate the present. But when experience has laid low the flowers of
spring and chilled the glow of summer—when he dis-
covers that life is practically over, and all that remains
a mere continuance of the past, then he feels differently
towards the brightness and warmth and beauty of early
recollections.

Nature deceives us all with her endless tricks and de-
vices: she makes us a gift of youth, and then, when we
are grown up, asserts her mastery and snares us in a web
of relations, domestic and public, most of which we are
powerless to control; and, though we impart our personal
character to our actions, we do not possess our souls in
the same degree; the lyric element of personality is
weaker, and, with it, our feelings and capacity for enjoyment—all, indeed, is weaker, except intelligence and will.

§6

My cousin's life was no bed of roses. She lost her mother
in childhood; her father was a passionate gambler, who,

like all men who have gambling in their blood, was constantly rich and poor by turns and ended by ruining himself. What was left of his fortune he devoted to his stud, which now became the object of all his thoughts and desires. His only son, a good-natured cavalry officer, was taking the shortest road to ruin: at the age of nineteen, he was a more desperate gambler than his father.

When the father was fifty, he married, for no obvious reason, an old maid who was a teacher in the Smolny Convent. She was the most typical specimen of a Petersburg governess whom I had ever happened to meet: thin, blonde, and very shortsighted, she looked the teacher and the moralist all over. By no means stupid, she was full of an icy enthusiasm in her talk, she abounded in commonplaces about virtue and devotion, she knew history and geography by heart, spoke French with repulsive correctness, and concealed a high opinion of herself under an artificial and Jesuitical humility. These traits are common to all pedants in petticoats; but she had others peculiar to the capital or the convent. Thus she raised tearful eyes to heaven, when speaking of the visit of "the mother of us all" (the Empress, Márya Fyódorovna*); she was in love with Tsar Alexander, and carried a locket or ring containing a fragment of a letter from the Empress Elizabeth†—*"il a repris son sourire de bienveillance!"*

It is easy to imagine the harmonious trio that made up this household: a card-playing father, passionately devoted to horses and racing and noisy carouses in disreputable company; a daughter brought up in complete independ-

---

*The wife of Paul and mother of Alexander I and Nicholas.
†Elizabeth, daughter of Peter the Great, reigned from 1741 to 1762. Probably *il* refers to her father.

ence and accustomed to do as she pleased in the house; and a middle-aged blue-stocking suddenly converted into a bride. As a matter of course, no love was lost between the stepmother and stepdaughter. In general, real friendship between a woman of thirty-five and a girl of seventeen is impossible, unless the former is sufficiently unselfish to renounce all claim to sex.

The common hostility between stepmothers and stepdaughters does not surprise me in the least: it is natural and even moral. A new member of the household, who usurps their mother's place, provokes repulsion on the part of the children. To them the second marriage is a second funeral. The child's love is revealed in this feeling, and whispers to the orphan, "Your father's wife is not your mother." At one time the Church understood that a second marriage is inconsistent with the Christian conception of marriage and the Christian dogma of immortality; but she made constant concessions to the world, and went too far, till she came up against the logic of facts—the simple heart of the child who revolts against the absurdity and refuses the name of mother to his father's second choice.

The woman too is in an awkward situation when she comes away from the altar to find a family of children ready-made: she has nothing to do with them, and has to force feelings which she cannot possess; she is bound to convince herself and the world, that other people's children are just as attractive to her as her own.

Consequently, I don't blame either the convent-lady or my cousin for their mutual dislike; but I understand how a young girl unaccustomed to control was eager to go wherever she could be free. Her father was now getting old and more submissive to his learned wife; her brother, the officer, was behaving worse and worse; in fact, the atmosphere at home was oppressive, and she finally induced her stepmother to let her go on a visit to us, for some months or possibly for a year.

§7

THE day after her arrival, my cousin turned my usual routine, with the exception of my lessons, upside down. With a high hand she fixed hours for us to read together, advised me to stop reading novels, and recommended Ségur's *General History* and *The Travels of Anacharsis.** From the ascetic point of view she opposed my strong inclination to smoke on the sly—cigarettes were then unknown, and I rolled the tobacco in paper myself: in general, she liked to preach to me, and I listened meekly to her sermons, if I did not profit by them. Fortunately, she was not consistent: quite forgetting her own arrangements, she read with me for amusement rather than instruction, and often sent out a secret messenger in the shape of a pantry-boy to buy buckwheat cakes in winter or gooseberries in summer.

I believe that her influence on me was very good. She brought into my monastic life an element of warmth, and this may have served to keep alive the enthusiasms that were beginning to stir in my mind, when they might easily have been smothered by my father's ironical tone. I learned to be attentive, to be nettled by a single word, to care for a friend, and to feel affection; I learned also to talk about feelings. In her I found support for my

Voyage du jeune Anacharsis, by the Abbé Barthélemy, published in 1779. Ségur was a French historian (1753-1830).

political ideas; she prophesied a remarkable future and reputation for me, and I, with a child's vanity, believed her when she said I would one day be a Brutus or Fabricius.

To me alone she confided the secret of her love for a cavalry officer in a black jacket and dolman. It was really a secret; for the officer, as he rode at the head of his squadron, never suspected the pure little flame that burnt for him in the breast of this young lady of eighteen. Whether I envied him, I can't say; probably I did, a little; but I was proud of being chosen as her confidant, and I imagined (under the influence of *Werther*) that this was a tragic passion, fated to end in some great catastrophe involving suicide by poison or the dagger. I even thought at times of calling on the officer and telling him the whole story.

My cousin brought shuttlecocks with her from home. One of them had a pin stuck into it, and she always used it in playing; if anyone else happened to get hold of it, she took it away and said that no other suited her as well. But the demon of mischief, which was always whispering its temptations in my ear, tempted me to take out this pin and stick it into another shuttlecock. The trick was entirely successful: my cousin always chose the shuttle-cock with the pin in it. After a fortnight I told her what I had done: she changed colour, burst out crying, and ran to her own room. I was frightened and distressed; after waiting half an hour I went to find her. Her door was locked, and I asked her to open it. She refused, say-ing that she was not well, and that I was an unkind, heart-less boy. Then I wrote a note in which I begged her to forgive me, and after tea we made it up: I kissed her hand, and she embraced me and explained the full importance of the incident. A year before, the officer had dined at their house and played battledore with her afterwards; and the marked shuttlecock had been used by him. I felt very remorseful, as if I had committed a real act of sacrilege.

My cousin stayed with us till October, when her father summoned her home, promising to let her spend the next summer with us in the country. We looked forward with horror to the separation; and soon there came an autumn day when a carriage arrived to fetch her, and her maid carried down baskets and band-boxes, while our servants put in provisions of all kinds, to last a week, and crowded to the steps to say their good-byes. We exchanged a close embrace, and both shed tears; the carriage drove out into the street, turned into a side-street close to the very shop where we used to buy the buckwheat cakes, and disappeared. I took a turn in the courtyard, but it seemed cold and unfriendly; my own room, where I went next, seemed empty and cold too. I began to prepare a lesson for Protopópov, and all the time I was thinking, "Where is the carriage now? has it passed the gates or not?"

I had one comfort: we should spend next June together in the country.

§8

I HAD a passionate love for the country, and our visits there gave me new life. Forests, fields, and perfect freedom—all this was a complete change to me, who had grown up wrapped in cotton-wool, behind stone walls, never daring to leave the house on any pretext without asking leave, or without the escort of a footman.

From spring onwards, I was always much exercised by one question—shall we go to the country this year or not? Every year my father said that he wished to see the leaves open and would make an early start; but he was never ready before July. One year he put off so long that we never went at all. He sent orders every winter that the country house was to be prepared and heated, but this was merely a deep device, that the head man and ground-officer, fearing our speedy arrival, might pay more attention to their duties.

It seemed that we were to go. My father said to my uncle, that he should enjoy a rest in the country and must see what was doing on the land; but still weeks went by.

The prospect became brighter by degrees. Food supplies were sent off—tea and sugar, grain of different kinds and wine; then came another delay; but at last the head man was ordered to send a certain number of peasants' horses on a fixed day. Joy! Joy! we are to go!

At that time I never thought of the trouble caused to the peasants by the loss of four or five days at the busiest time of the year. I was completely happy and made haste to pack up my books and notebooks. The horses came, and I listened with inward satisfaction to the sound of their munching and snorting in the court. I took a lively interest in the bustle of the drivers and the wrangles of the servants, as they disputed where each should sit and accommodate his belongings. Lights burnt all night in the servants' quarters: all were busy packing, or dragging about boxes and bags, or putting on special clothes for the journey, though it was not more than eighty *versts*. My father's valet was the most excited of the party: he realised all the importance of packing, pulled out in fury all that others had put in, tore his hair with vexation, and was quite impossible to approach.

On the day itself my father got up no earlier than usual —indeed, it seemed later—and took just as long over his coffee; it was eleven o'clock before he gave the order to put to the horses. First came a coach to hold four, drawn by six of our own horses; this was followed by three or sometimes four equipages—an open carriage, a britzka, and either a large waggon or two carts; all these were filled by the servants and their baggage, in addition to the carts which had preceded us; and yet there was such a squeeze that no one could sit in comfort.

§9

WE stopped half-way, to dine and feed the horses, at a large village, whose name of Perkhushkov may be found in Napoleon's bulletins. It belonged to a son of the uncle, of whom I spoke in describing the division of the property. The neglected manor-house stood near the high road, which had dull flat fields on each side of it; but to me even this dusty landscape was delightful after the confinement of a town. The floors of the house were uneven, and the steps of the staircase shook; our tread sounded loud, and the walls echoed the noise, as if surprised by visitors. The old furniture, prized as a rarity by its former owner, was now spending its last days in banishment here. I wandered, with eager curiosity, from room to room, upstairs and downstairs, and finally into the kitchen. Our cook was preparing a hasty meal for us, and looked discontented and scornful; the bailiff was generally sitting in the kitchen, a grey-haired man with a lump on his head. When the cook turned to him and complained of the kitchen-range, the bailiff listened and said from time to time, "Well, perhaps you're right"; he looked uneasily at all the stir in the house and clearly hoped we should soon go away.

Dinner was served on special plates, made of tin or Britannia metal, and bought for the purpose. Meanwhile the horses were put to; and the hall was filled with those who wished to pay their respects—former footmen, spending their last days in pure air but on short commons, and old women who had been pretty house-maids thirty years ago, all the creeping and hopping population of great houses, who, like the real locusts, devour the peasants' toil by no fault of their own. They brought with them flaxen-haired children with bare feet and soiled clothes; the children kept pushing forward, and the old women kept pulling them back, and both made plenty of noise. The women caught hold of me when they could and expressed surprise at my growth in the same terms every year. My father spoke a few words to them; some tried to kiss his hand, but he never permitted it; others made their bow; and then we went away.

By the edge of a wood our bailiff was waiting for us, and he rode in front of us the last part of the way. A long lime avenue led up to our house from the vicarage; at the house we were met by the priest and his wife, the sexton, the servants, and some peasants. An idiot, called Pronka, was there too, the only self-respecting person; for he kept on his dirty old hat, stood a little apart and grinned, and started away whenever any of the newcomers tried to approach him.

§10

I HAVE seen few more charming spots than this estate
of Vasílevskoë. On one side, where the ground slopes,
there is a large village with a church and an old manor-
house; on the other side, where there is a hill and a
smaller village, was a new house built by my father.
From our windows there was a view for many miles: the
endless corn-fields spread like lakes, ruffled by the breeze;
manor-houses and villages with white churches were
visible here and there; forests of varying hues made a
semicircular frame for the picture; and the ribbon of the
Moscow River shone blue outside it. In the early morning
I used to push up my window as high as it would go, and
look, and listen, and drink in the air.

Yet I had a tenderness for the old manor-house too,
perhaps because it gave me my first taste of the country;
I had a passion for the long shady avenue which led up
to it, and the neglected garden. The house was falling
down, and a slender shapely birch-tree was growing out
of a crack in the hall floor. A willow avenue went to the
left, followed by reed-beds and white sand, all the way
to the river; about my twelfth year, I used to play the
whole morning on this sand and among the reeds. An
old gardener, bent and decrepit, was generally sitting in
front of the house, boiling fruit or straining mint-wine;
and he used to give me peas and beans to eat on the sly.
There were a number of rooks in the garden; they nested
in the tree-tops and flew round and round, cawing; sometimes, especially towards evening, they rose up in hundreds at a time, rousing others by their noise; sometimes
a single bird would fly quickly from tree to tree, amid
general silence. When night came on, some distant owl

would cry like a child or burst out laughing; and, though I feared those wild plaintive noises, yet I went and listened.

The years when we did not stay at Vasílevskoë were few and far between. On leaving, I always marked my height on the wall near the balcony, and my first business on arriving was to find out how much I had grown. But I could measure more than mere bodily growth by this place: the regular recurrence to the same surroundings enabled me to detect the development of my mind. Different books and different objects engaged my attention. In 1823 I was still quite a child and took childish books with me; and even these I left unread, taking more interest in a hare and a squirrel that lived in a garret near my room. My father allowed me, once every evening, to fire off a small cannon, and this was one of my chief delights. Of course, all the servants bore a hand in this occupation, and grey-haired men of fifty were no less excited than I was. In 1827 my books were Plutarch and Schiller; early in the morning I sought the remotest part of the wood, lay down under a tree, and read aloud, fancying myself in the forests of Bohemia. Yet, all the same, I paid much attention to a dyke which I and another boy were making across a small stream, and I ran there ten times a day to look at it and repair it. In 1829 and the next year, I was writing a "philosophical" review of Schiller's *Wallenstein,* and the cannon was the only one of my old amusements that still maintained its attraction.

But I had another pleasure as well as firing off the cannon—the evenings in the country haunted me like a passion, and I feel them still to be times of piety and peace and poetry. . . . One of the last bright hours of my life also recalls to me an evening in the country. I was in Italy, and *she* was with me. The sun was setting, solemn and bright, in an ocean of fire, and melting into it. Suddenly the rich crimson gave place to a sombre blue, and smoke-coloured vapour covered all the sky; for in Italy darkness comes on fast. We mounted our mules; riding from Frascati to Rome, we had to pass through a small village; lights were twinkling already here and there, all was peace, the hoofs of the mules rang out on the stone, a fresh dampish wind blew from the Apennines. At the end of the village there was a small Madonna in a niche, with a lamp burning before her; the village girls, coming home from work with white kerchiefs over their heads, knelt down and sang a hymn, and some begging *pifferari* who were passing by added their voices. I was profoundly impressed and much moved by the scene. We looked at each other, and rode slowly on to the inn where our carriage was waiting. When we got home, I described the evenings I had spent at Vasílevskoë. What was it I described?

The shepherd cracks his long whip and plays on his birch-bark pipe. I hear the lowing and bleating of the returning animals, and the stamping of their feet on the bridge. A barking dog scurries after a straggling sheep, and the sheep breaks into a kind of wooden-legged gallop. Then the voices of the girls, singing on their way from the fields, come nearer and nearer; but the path takes a turn to the right, and the sound dies away again. House-doors open with creaking of the hinges, and the children come out to meet their cows and sheep. Work is over. Children play in the street or by the river, and their voices come penetrating and clear over the water through the evening glow. The smell of burning passes from the corn-kilns through the air; the soaking dew begins to spread like smoke over the earth, the wind seems to walk audibly over the trees, the sunset glow sends a last faint light over the world—and Vyéra Artamónovna finds me under a lime-tree, and scolds me, though she is not seriously angry.

"What's the meaning of this? Tea has long been served, and everyone is there. I have looked and looked for you everywhere till I'm tired out. I'm too old for all this running. And what *do* you mean by lying on the wet grass? You'll have a cold to-morrow, I feel sure."

"Never mind, never mind," I would answer laughing; "I shan't have a cold, and I want no tea; but you must steal me some cream, and mind you skim off the top of the jug!"

"Really, I can't find it in my heart to be angry with you! But how dainty you are! I've got cream ready for you, without your asking. Look how red the sky is! That's a sign of a good harvest."

And then I made off home, jumping and whistling as I went.

§11

WE never went back to Vasílevskoë after 1832, and my father sold it during my banishment. In 1843 we were staying in the country within twenty *versts* of the old home and I could not resist paying it a visit. We drove along the familiar road, past the pine-wood and the hill covered with nut bushes, till we came to the ford which had given me such delight twenty years ago—I remembered the splashing water, the crunching sound of the pebbles, the coachmen shouting at the jibbing horses. At last we reached the village and the priest's house; there was the bench where the priest used to sit, wearing his brown cassock—a simple kindly man who was always chewing something and always in a perspiration; and then the estate-office where Vassíli Epifánov made out his accounts; never quite sober, he sat crouching over the paper, holding his pen very low down and tucking his third finger away behind it. The priest was dead, and Vassíli Epifánov, not sober yet, was making out accounts somewhere else. The village head man was in the fields, but we found his wife at their cottage.

Changes had taken place in the interval. A new manor-house had been built on the hill, and a new garden laid out round it. Returning past the church and churchyard, we met a poor deformed object, creeping, as it seemed, on all-fours. It signed to me, and I went close to it. It was an old woman, bent, paralysed, and half-crazy; she used to live on charity and work in the old priest's garden; she was now about seventy, and her, of all people, death had spared! She knew me and shed tears, shaking her head and saying: "How old you have grown! I only knew you by your walk. And me—but there's no use talking about me."

As we drove home, I saw the head man, the same as in our time, standing in a field some way off. He did not recognise me at first; but when we were past, he made out who I was, took off his hat, and bowed low. A little further on, I turned round, and Grigóri Gorski—that was the head man's name—was standing on the same spot and watching our carriage. That tall bearded figure, bowing in the harvest field, was a link with the past; but Vasílevskoë had ceased to be ours.

CHAPTER IV

My Friend Niko and the Sparrow Hills.

§1

SOME time in the year 1824 I was walking one day with my father along the Moscow River, on the far side of the Sparrow Hills; and there we met a French tutor whom we knew. He had nothing on but his shirt, was obviously in great alarm, and was calling out, "Help! Help!" Before our friend had time to pull off his shirt or pull on his trousers, a Cossack ran down from the Sparrow Hills, hurled himself into the water, and disappeared. In another moment he reappeared, grasping a miserable little object, whose head and hands shook like clothes hung out to dry; he placed this burden on the bank and said, "A shaking will soon bring him round."

The bystanders collected fifty *roubles* for the rescuer. The Cossack made no pretences but said very honestly, "It's a sin to take money for a thing like that; for he gave me no trouble, no more than a cat, to pull him out. But," he added, "though I don't ask for money, if I'm offered it, I may as well take it. I'm a poor man. So thank you kindly." Then he tied up the money in his handker-chief and went back to his horses grazing on the hill.

My father asked the man's name and wrote next day to tell his commanding officer of his gallantry; and the Cossack was promoted to be a corporal. A few months later the Cossack appeared at our house and brought a companion, a German with a fair curling wig, pock-marked, and scented. This was the drowning man, who had come to return thanks on behalf of the Cossack; and he visited us afterwards from time to time.

Karl Sonnenberg had taught boys German in several families, and was now employed by a distant relation of my father's, who had confided to him the bodily health and German pronunciation of his son. This boy, Nikolai Ogaryóv, whom Sonnenberg always called Niko, attracted me. There was something kind, gentle, and thoughtful about him; he was quite unlike the other boys whom I was in the way of seeing. Yet our intimacy ripened slowly: he was silent and thoughtful, I was lively and feared to trouble him by my liveliness.

Niko had lost his mother in infancy, and his grand-mother died about the time when my cousin Tatyana left us and went home. Their household was in confusion, and Sonnenberg, who had really nothing to do, made out that he was terribly busy; so he brought the boy to our house in the morning and asked if we would keep him for the whole day. Niko was frightened and sad; I sup-pose he loved his grandmother.

After sitting together for some time, I proposed that we should read Schiller. I was soon astonished by the similarity of our tastes: he knew by heart much more than I did, and my favourite passages were those he knew best; we soon shut the book, and each began to explore the other's mind for common interests.

He too was familiar with the unprinted poems of Púshkin and Ryléev;* the difference from the empty-headed boys whom I sometimes met was surprising. His heart beat to the same tune as mine; he too had cut the painter that bound him to the sullen old shore of conservatism; our business was to push off with a will; and we decided, perhaps on that very first day, to act in support of the Crown Prince Constantine!

This was our first long conversation. Sonnenberg was always in our way, persistent as a fly in autumn and spoiling all our talk by his presence. He was constantly interfering, criticising without understanding, putting the collar of Niko's shirt to rights, or in a hurry to go home; in short, he was thoroughly objectionable. But, before a month was over, it was impossible for my friend and me to pass two days without meeting or writing; I, who was naturally impulsive, became more and more attached to Niko, and he had a less demonstrative but deep love for me.

From the very first, our friendship was bound to take a serious turn. I cannot remember that we thought much of amusement, especially when we were alone. I don't mean that we sat still always; after all, we were boys, and we laughed and played the fool and teased Sonnenberg and shot with a bow in our court-yard. But our friendship was not founded on mere idle companionship: we were united, not only by equality of age and "chemical" affinity, but by a common religion. Nothing in the world

---

*One of the five Decembrists who were hanged when the revolt was suppressed.

has more power to purify and elevate that time of life, nothing preserves it better, than a strong interest in humanity at large. We respected, in ourselves, our own future; we regarded one another as chosen vessels, with a fixed task before us.

We often took walks into the country; our favourite haunts were the Sparrow Hills, and the fields outside the Dragomirovsky Gate. Accompanied by Sonnenberg, he used to come for me at six or seven in the morning; and if I was still asleep, he used to throw sand or pebbles at my window. I woke up joyfully and hastened to join him.

These morning walks had been started by the activity of Sonnenberg. My friend had been brought up under a *dyádka,** in the manner traditional in noble Russian families, till Sonnenberg came. The influence of the *dyádka* waned at once, and the oligarchy of the servants' hall had to grin and bear it: they realised that they were no match for the "accursed German" who was permitted to dine with the family. Sonnenberg's reforms were radical: the *dyádka* even wept when the German took his young master in person to a shop to buy ready-made boots. Just like the reforms of Peter the Great, Sonnenberg's reforms bore a military character even in matters of the least warlike nature. It does not follow from this that Sonnenberg's narrow shoulders were ever covered by epaulettes, plain or laced—nature has constructed the German on such a plan, that, unless he is a philologer or theologian and therefore utterly indifferent to personal neatness, he is invariably military, whatever civilian sphere he may adorn. Hence Sonnenberg liked tight clothes, closely buttoned and belted in at the waist; and

*See note to p. 55.

hence he was a strict observer of rules approved by himself. He had made it a rule to get up at six in the morning; therefore he made his pupil get up one minute before six or, at latest, one minute after it, and took him out into the fresh air every morning.

§2

THE Sparrow Hills, at the foot of which Sonnenberg had been so nearly drowned, soon became to us a Holy Place.

One day after dinner, my father proposed to take a drive into the country, and, as Niko was in the house, invited him and Sonnenberg to join us. These drives were no joke. Though the carriage was made by Iochim, most famous of coachmakers, it had been used, if not severely, for fifteen years till it had become old and ugly, and it weighed more than a siege mortar, so that we took an hour or more to get outside the city-gates. Our four horses, ill-matched both in size and colour, underworked and overfed, were covered with sweat and lather in a quarter of an hour; and the coachman, knowing that this was forbidden, had to keep them at a walk. However hot it was, the windows were generally kept shut. To all this you must add the steady pressure of my father's eye and Sonnenberg's perpetual fussy interference; and yet we boys were glad to endure it all, in order that we might be together.

We crossed the Moscow River by a ferry at the very place where the Cossack pulled Sonnenberg out of the water. My father walked along with gloomy aspect and stooping figure, as always, while Sonnenberg trotted at his side and tried to amuse him with scandal and gossip. We two walked on in front till we had got a good lead;

then we ran off to the site of Vitberg's cathedral* on the Sparrow Hills.

Panting and flushed, we stood there and wiped our brows. The sun was setting, the cupolas of Moscow glittered in his rays, the city at the foot of the hill spread beyond our vision, a fresh breeze fanned our cheeks. We stood there leaning against each other; then suddenly we embraced and, as we looked down upon the great city, swore to devote our lives to the struggle we had undertaken.

Such an action may seem very affected and theatrical on our part; but when I recall it, twenty-six years after, it affects me to tears. That it was absolutely sincere has been proved by the whole course of our lives. But all vows taken on that spot are evidently doomed to the same fate: the Emperor Alexander also acted sincerely when he laid the first stone of the cathedral there, but the first stone was also the last.

We did not know the full power of our adversary, but still we threw down the glove. Power dealt us many a shrewd blow, but we never surrendered to it, and it was not power that crushed us. The scars inflicted by power are honourable; the strained thigh of Jacob was a sign that he had wrestled with God in the night.

From that day the Sparrow Hills became a place of pilgrimage for us: once or twice a year we walked there, and always by ourselves. There, five years later, Ogaryóv asked me with a modest diffidence whether I believed in his poetic gift. And in 1833 he wrote to me from the country:

"Since I left Moscow, I have felt sad, sadder than I

*See part II, chap. IX.

ever was in my life. I am always thinking of the Sparrow Hills. I long kept my transports hidden in my heart; shyness or some other feeling prevented me from speaking of them. But on the Sparrow Hills these transports were not lessened by solitude: you shared them with me, and those moments are unforgettable; like recollections of bygone happiness, they pursued me on my journey, though I passed no hills but only forests."

"Tell the world," he ended, "how our lives (yours and mine) took shape on the Sparrow Hills."

Five more years passed, and I was far from those Hills, but their Prometheus, Alexander Vitberg, was near me, a sorrowful and gloomy figure. After my return to Moscow, I visited the place again in 1842; again I stood by the foundation-stone and surveyed the same scene; and a companion was with me—but it was not my friend.

§3

AFTER 1827 we two were inseparable. In every recollection of that time, whether detailed or general, *he* is always prominent, with the face of opening manhood, with his love for me. He was early marked with that sign of consecration which is given to few, and which, for weal or for woe, separates a man from the crowd. A large oil-painting of Ogaryóv was made about that time and long remained in his father's house. I often stopped in front of it and looked long at it. He was painted with a loose open collar: the artist has caught successfully the luxuriant chestnut hair, the fleeting beauty of youth on the irregular features, and the somewhat swarthy complexion. The canvas preserves the serious aspect which precedes hard intellectual work. The vague sorrow and extreme gentleness which

shine from the large grey eyes, give promise of great
power of sympathy; and that promise was fulfilled. The
portrait was given to me. A lady, not related to Ogaryóv,
afterwards got hold of it; perhaps she will see these lines
and restore it to me.

I do not know why people dwell exclusively on recollections of first love and say nothing about memories of
youthful friendship. First love is so fragrant, just because
it forgets difference of sex, because it is passionate friendship. Friendship between young men has all the fervour
of love and all its characteristics—the same shy reluc-
tance to profane its feeling by speech, the same diffidence
and absolute devotion, the same pangs at parting, and
the same exclusive desire to stand alone without a rival.

I had loved Niko long and passionately before I dared
to call him "friend"; and, when we were apart in summer, I wrote in a postscript, "whether I am your friend
or not, I don't know yet." He was the first to use "thou"
in writing to me; and he called me Damon before I called
him Pythias.

Smile, if you please, but let it be a kindly smile, such
as men smile when recalling their own fifteenth year.
Perhaps it would be better to ask, "Was *I* like that in my
prime?" and to thank your stars, if you ever *had* a prime,
and to thank them doubly, if you had a friend to share it.

The language of that time seems to us affected and
bookish. We have travelled far from its passing enthusiasms and one-sided partisanships, which suddenly give
place to feeble sentimentality or childish laughter. In a
man of thirty it would be absurd, like the famous *Bettina
will schlafen;** but, in its own season, this language of

*This must refer to Bettina von Arnim's first interview with Goethe

adolescence, this *jargon de la puberté,* this breaking of
the soul's voice—all this is quite sincere, and even its
bookish flavour is natural to the age which knows theory
and is ignorant of practice.

Schiller remained our favourite; the characters in his
plays were real for us; we discussed them and loved or
hated them as living beings and not as people in a book.
And more than that—we identified ourselves with them. I
was rather distressed that Niko was too fond of Fiesco,
and wrote to say that behind every Fiesco stands a Verina.
My own ideal was Karl Moor, but I soon deserted him
and adopted the Marquis Posa instead.

§4

THUS it was that Ogaryóv and I entered upon life hand
in hand. We walked in confidence and pride; without
counting the cost, we answered every summons and surrendered ourselves sincerely to each generous impulse.
The path we chose was not easy; but we never once left
it; wounded and broken, we still went on, and no one out-
stripped us on the way. I have reached, not our goal but
the place where the road turns downhill, and I seek instinctively for your arm, my friend, that I may press it
and say with a sad smile as we go down together, "So
this is all!"

Meanwhile, in the wearisome leisure to which I am
condemned by circumstances, as I find in myself neither
strength nor vigour for fresh toil, I am recording *our*
recollections.* Much of what bound us so closely has

at Weimar in April, 1807. She writes that she sprang into Goethe's arms
and slept there. The poet was then 58, and Bettina had ceased to be
a child.

*This was written in 1853.

found a place in these pages, and I give them to you. For you they have a double meaning, the meaning of epitaphs, on which we meet with familiar names.

But it is surely an odd reflection, that, if Sonnenberg had learned to swim or been drowned when he fell into the river, or if he had been pulled out by some ordinary private and not by that Cossack, we should never have met; or, if we had, it would have been at a later time and in a different way—not in the little room of our old house where we smoked our first cigars, and where we drew strength from one another for our first long step on the path of life.

CHAPTER V

Details of Home Life—Men of the Eighteenth Century in Russia—A Day at Home—Guests and Visitors—Sonnenberg—Servants.

§1

THE dulness and monotony of our house became more intolerable with every year. But for the prospect of University life, my new friendship, my interest in politics, and my lively turn of character, I must either have run away or died of the life.

My father was seldom cheerful; as a rule he was dissatisfied with everyone and everything. He was a man of unusual intelligence and powers of observation, who had seen and heard a great deal and remembered it; he was a finished man of the world and could be exceedingly pleasant and interesting; but he did not choose to be so, and sank deeper and deeper into a state of morbid solitude.

What precisely it was that infused so much bile and bitterness into his blood, it is hard to say. No period of passion, of great misfortunes, mistakes, and losses, had ever taken place in his life. I could never fully understand the source of that bitter scorn and irritation which filled his heart, of his distrust and avoidance of mankind, and of the disgust that preyed upon him. Perhaps he took with him to the grave some recollection which he never confided to any ear; perhaps it was merely due to the combination of two things so incongruous as the eighteenth century and Russian life; and there was a third factor, the traditional idleness of his class, which had a terrible power of producing unreasonable tempers.

§2

In Europe, especially in France, the eighteenth century produced an extraordinary type of man, which combined all the weaknesses of the Regency with all the strength of Spartans or Romans. Half like Faublas and half like Regulus, these men opened wide the doors of revolution and were the first to rush into it, jostling one another in their haste to pass out by the "window" of the guillotine. Our age has ceased to produce those strong, complete natures; but last century evoked them everywhere, even in countries where they were not needed and where their development was bound to be distorted. In Russia, men who were exposed to the influence of this powerful European current, did not make history, but they became unlike other men. Foreigners at home and foreigners abroad, spoilt for Russia by European prejudices and for Europe by Russian habits, they were a living contradiction in terms and sank into an artificial life of sensual enjoyment and monstrous· egoism.

Such was the most conspicuous figure at Moscow in those days, Prince Yusúpov, a Tatar prince, a *grand seigneur* of European reputation, and a Russian grandee of brilliant intellect and great fortune. He was surrounded by a whole pleiad of grey-haired Don Juans and freethinkers—such men as Masalski, Santi, and the rest. They were all men of considerable mental development and culture; but they had nothing to do, and they rushed after pleasure, loved and petted their precious selves, genially gave themselves absolution for all transgressions, exalted the love of eating to the height of a Platonic passion, and lowered love for women into a kind of gluttonous epicureanism.

Old Yusúpov was a sceptic and a *bon-vivant*; he had been the friend of Voltaire and Beaumarchais, of Diderot and Casti; and his artistic taste was beyond question. You may convince yourself of this by a single visit to his palace outside Moscow and a glance at his pictures, if his heir has not sold them yet by auction. At eighty, this luminary was setting in splendour, surrounded by beauty in marble and colour, and also in flesh and blood. Púshkin, who dedicated a noble Epistle to him,* used to converse with Yusúpov in his country-house; and Gonzaga, to whom Yusúpov dedicated his theatre, used to paint there.

§3

By his education and service in the Guards, by his birth and connexions, my father belonged to the same circle; but neither temperament nor health allowed him to lead a life of dissipation to the age of seventy, and he went to the opposite extreme. He determined to secure a life of solitude, and found it intensely tedious—all the more tedious because he had sought it merely for his own sake. A strong will was degraded into stubborn wilfulness, and unused powers spoilt his temper and made it difficult.

* *To a Great Man* (1830).

At the time of his education European civilisation was so new in Russia that a man of culture necessarily became less of a Russian. To the end of his life he wrote French with more ease and correctness than Russian, and he literally never read a Russian book, not even the Bible. The Bible, indeed, he did not read even in other languages; he knew, by hearsay and from extracts, the matter of Holy Scripture in general, and felt no curiosity to examine further. He did respect Derzhávin and Krylóv, the first because he had written an ode on the death of his uncle, Prince Meshcherski, and the latter, because they had acted together as seconds in a duel. When my father heard that the Emperor Alexander was reading Karamzín's *History of the Russian Empire,* he tried it himself but soon laid it aside: "Nothing but old Slavonic names! Who can take an interest in all that?"—such was his disparaging criticism.

His contempt for mankind was unconcealed and without exceptions. Never, under any circumstances, did he rely on anyone, and I don't remember that he ever preferred a considerable request in any quarter; and he never did anything to oblige other people. All he asked of others was to maintain appearances: *les apparences, les convenances*—his moral code consisted of these alone. He excused much, or rather shut his eyes to much: but any breach of decent forms enraged him to such a degree that he became incapable of the least indulgence or sympathy. I puzzled so long over this unfairness that I ended by understanding it: he was convinced beforehand that any man is capable of any bad action, and refrains from it only because it does not pay, or for want of opportunity; but in any breach of politeness he found personal

offence, and disrespect to himself, or "middle-class breed-
ing," which, in his opinion, excluded a man from all
decent society.

"The heart of man," he used to say, "is hidden, and
nobody knows what another man feels. I have too much
business of my own to attend to other people, let alone
judging their motives. But I cannot live in the same room
with an ill-bred man: he offends me, *il me froisse*. Otherwise he may be the best man in the world; if so, he will
go to Heaven; but I have no use for him. The most important thing in life, more important than soaring intellect
or erudition, is *savoir vivre*, to do the right thing always,
never to thrust yourself forward, to be perfectly polite to
everyone and familiar with nobody."

All impulsiveness and frankness my father disliked and
called familiarity; and all display of feeling passed with
him for sentimentality. He regularly represented himself
as superior to all such trivialities; but what that higher
object was, for the sake of which he sacrificed his feelings, I have no idea. And when this proud old man, with
his clear understanding and sincere contempt of mankind,
played this part of a passionless judge, whom did he mean
to impress by the performance? A woman whose will he
had broken, though she never tried to oppose him; a boy
whom his own treatment drove from mere naughtiness to
positive disobedience; and a score of footmen whom he
did not reckon as human beings!

And how much strength and endurance was spent for
this object, how much persistence! How surprising the
consistency with which the part was played to the very
end, in spite of old age and disease! The heart of man is
indeed hidden.

At the time of my arrest, and later when I was going into exile, I saw that the old man's heart was much more open than I supposed to love and even to tenderness. But I never thanked him for this; for I did not know how he would have taken my thanks.

As a matter of course, he was not happy. Always on his guard, discontented with everyone, he suffered when he saw the feelings he inspired in every member of the household. Smiles died away and talk stopped whenever he came into the room. He spoke of this with mockery and resented it; but he made no concession whatever and went his own way with steady perseverance. Stinging mockery and cool contemptuous irony were the weapons which he could wield with the skill of an artist, and he used them equally against us and against the servants. There are few things that a growing boy resents more; and, in fact, up to the time of my imprisonment I was on bad terms with my father and carried on a petty warfare against him, with the men and maids for my allies.

§4

For the rest, he had convinced himself that he was dangerously ill, and was constantly under treatment. He had a doctor resident in the house and was visited by two or three other physicians; and at least three consultations took place each year. His sour looks and constant complaints of his health (which was not really so bad) soon reduced the number of our visitors. He resented this; yet he never remonstrated or invited any friend to the house. An air of terrible boredom reigned in our house, especially in the endless winter evenings. The whole suite of drawing-rooms was lit up by a single pair of lamps; and there the old man walked up and down, a stooping figure with his hands behind his back; he wore cloth boots, a velvet skull-cap, and a warm jacket of white lamb-skin; he never spoke a word, and three or four brown dogs walked up and down with him.

As melancholy grew on him, so did his wish to save, but it was entirely misapplied. His management of his land was not beneficial either to himself or to his serfs. The head man and his underlings robbed both their master and the peasants. In certain matters there was strict economy: candle-ends were saved and light French wine was replaced by sour wine from the Crimea; on the other hand, a whole forest was felled without his knowledge on one estate, and he paid the market price for his own oats on another. There were men whom he permitted to steal; thus a peasant, whom he made collector of the *obrók* at Moscow, and who was sent every summer to the country, to report on the head man and the farm-work, the garden and the timber, grew rich enough to buy a house in Moscow after ten years' service. From childhood I hated this factotum: I was present once when he thrashed an old peasant in our court-yard; in my fury I caught him by the beard and nearly fainted myself. From that time I could never bear the sight of him. He died in 1845. Several times I asked my father where this man got the money to buy a house.

"The result of sober habits," he said; "that man never took a drop in his life."

§5

EVERY year about Shrovetide our peasants from the Government of Penza brought their payments in kind to

Moscow. It was a fortnight's journey for the carts, laden with carcasses of pork, sucking-pigs, geese, chickens, rye, eggs, butter, and even linen. The arrival of the peasants was a regular field-day for all our servants, who robbed and cheated the visitors right and left, without any right to do so. The coachman charged for the water their horses drank, and the women charged for a warm place by the fire, while the aristocrats of the servants' hall expected each to get a sucking-pig and a piece of cloth, or a goose and some pounds of butter. While the peasants remained in the court-yard, the servants feasted continuously: soup was always boiling and sucking-pigs roasting, and the servants' hall reeked perpetually of onions, burning fat, and bad whiskey. During the last two days Bakai never came into the hall, but sat in the kitchen-passage, dressed in an old livery overcoat, without jacket or waistcoat underneath it; and other servants grew older visibly and darker in complexion. All this my father endured calmly enough, knowing that it must be so and that reform was impossible.

These provisions always arrived in a frozen condition, and thereupon my father summoned his cook Spiridon and sent him to the markets to enquire about prices. The cook reported astonishingly low figures, lower by half than was actually offered. My father called him a fool and sent for his factotum and a dealer in fruit named Slepushkin. Both expressed horror at the cook's figures, made enquiries, and quoted prices a little higher. Finally Slepushkin offered to take the whole in a lump—eggs, sucking-pigs, butter, rye, and all,—"to save you, *bát-yushka,* from further worry." The price he offered was of course a trifle higher than the cook had mentioned. My

father consented: to celebrate the occasion, Slepushkin
presented him with some oranges and gingerbread, and
the cook with a note for 200 *roubles*. And the most extraordinary part of this transaction was that it was repeated exactly every year.

Slepushkin enjoyed my father's favour and often
borrowed money of him; and the strange way in which
he did it showed his profound knowledge of my father's
character.

He would borrow 500 *roubles* for two months, and two
days before payment was due, he would present himself
at our house, carrying a currant-loaf on a dish and 500
roubles on the top of the loaf. My father took the money,
and the borrower bowed low and begged, though unsuc-
cessfully, to kiss his benefactor's hand. But Slepushkin
would turn up again a week later and ask for a loan of
1,500 *roubles*. He got it and again paid his debt on the
nail; and my father considered him a pattern of honesty.
A week later, Slepushkin would borrow a still larger sum.
Thus in the course of a year he secured 5,000 *roubles* in
ready money to use in his business; and for this he paid,
by way of interest, a couple of currant-loaves, a few
pounds of figs and walnuts, and perhaps a hundred
oranges and Crimean apples.

§6

I SHALL end this subject by relating how my father lost
nearly a thousand acres of valuable timber on one of the
estates which had come to him from his brother, the
Senator.

In the forties Count Orlóv, wishing to buy land for
his sons, offered a price for this estate, which was in the

Government of Tver. The parties came to terms, and it seemed that the transaction was complete. But when the Count went to examine his purchase, he wrote to my father that a forest marked upon the plan of the estate had simply disappeared.

"There!" said my father, "Orlóv is a clever man of course; he was involved in the conspiracy too.* He has written a book on finance; but when it comes to business, he is clearly no good. Necker† over again! I shall send a friend of my own to look at the place, not a conspirator but an honest man who understands business."

But alas! the honest man came back and reported that the forest had disappeared; all that remained was a fringe of trees, which made it impossible to detect the truth from the high-road or from the manor-house. After the division between the brothers, my uncle had paid five visits to the place, but had seen nothing!

§7

THAT our way of life may be thoroughly understood, I shall describe a whole day from the beginning. They were all alike, and this very monotony was the most killing part of it all. Our life went on like an English clock with the regulator put back—with a slow and steady movement and a loud tick for each second.

At ten in the morning, the valet who sat in the room next the bedroom, informed Vyéra Artamónovna, formerly my nurse, that the master was getting up; and she went off to prepare coffee, which my father drank alone in his study. The house now assumed a different

*See p. 207.

†Jacques Necker (1732-1804), Minister of Finance under Louis XVI; the husband of Gibbon's first love, and the father of Mme. de Staël.

aspect: the servants began to clean the rooms or at least to make a pretence of doing something. The servants' hall, empty till then, began to fill up; and even Macbeth, the big Newfoundland dog, sat down before the stove and stared unwinkingly at the fire.

Over his coffee my father read the *Moscow Gazette* and the *Journal de St. Petersbourg*. It may be worth mentioning that the newspapers were warmed to save his hands from contact with the damp sheets, and that he read the political news in the French version, finding it clearer than the Russian. For some time he took in the *Hamburg Gazette,* but could not pardon the Germans for using German print; he often pointed out to me the difference between French and German type, and said that the curly tails of the Gothic letters tried his eyes. Then he ordered the *Journal de Francfort* for a time, but finally contented himself with the native product.

When he had read the newspaper, he noticed for the first time the presence of Sonnenberg in the room. When Niko reached the age of fifteen, Sonnenberg professed to start a shop; but having nothing to sell and no customers, he gave it up, when he had spent such savings as he had in this useful form of commerce; yet he still called himself "a commercial agent." He was then much over forty, and at that pleasant age he lived like the fowls of the air or a boy of fourteen; he never knew to-day where he would sleep or how he would secure a dinner to-morrow. He enjoyed my father's favour to a certain extent: what that amounted to, we shall see presently.

§8

In 1840 my father bought the house next to ours, a

larger and better house, with a garden, which had belonged to Countess Rostopchín, wife of the famous governor of Moscow. We moved into it. Then he bought a
third house, for no reason except that it was adjacent.
Two of these houses stood empty; they were never let
because tenants would give trouble and might cause fires
—both houses were insured, by the way—and they were
never repaired, so that both were in a fair way to fall
down. Sonnenberg was permitted to lodge in one of these
houses, but on conditions: (1) he must never open the
yard-gates after 10 p.m. (as the gates were never shut,
this was an easy condition); (2) he was to provide fire-
wood at his own expense (he did in fact buy it of our
coachman); and (3) he was to serve my father as a kind
of private secretary, coming in the morning to ask for
orders, dining with us, and returning in the evening, when
there was no company, to entertain his employer with conversation and the news.

The duties of his place may seem simple enough; but
my father contrived to make it so bitter that even Sonnenberg could not stand it continuously, though he was familiar with all the privations that can befall a man with no
money and no sense, with a feeble body, a pock-marked
face, and German nationality. Every two years or so, the
secretary declared that his patience was at an end. He
packed up his traps, got together by purchase or barter
some odds and ends of disputable value and doubtful
quality, and started off for the Caucasus. Misfortune
dogged him relentlessly. Either his horse—he drove his
own horse as far as Tiflis and Redut-Kale—came down
with him in dangerous places inhabited by Don Cossacks;
or half his wares were stolen; or his two-wheeled cart

broke down and his French scent-bottles wasted their
sweetness on the broken wheel at the foot of Mount
Elbruz; he was always losing something, and when he
had nothing else to lose, he lost his passport. Nearly a
year would pass, and then Sonnenberg, older, more un-
kempt, and poorer than before, with fewer teeth and less
hair than ever, would turn up humbly at our house, with
a stock of Persian powder against fleas and bugs, faded
silk for dressing-gowns, and rusty Circassian daggers;
and down he settled once more in the empty house, to
buy his own fire-wood and run errands by way of rent.

§9

As soon as he noticed Sonnenberg, my father began a
little campaign at once. He acknowledged by a bow enquiries as to his health; then he thought a little, and
asked (this just as an example of his methods), "Where
do you buy your hair-oil?"

I should say that Sonnenberg, though the plainest of
men, thought himself a regular Don Juan: he was careful about his clothes and wore a curling wig of a golden-
yellow colour.

"I buy it of Buis, on the Kuznetsky Bridge," he answered abruptly, rather nettled; and then he placed one
foot on the other, like a man prepared to defend himself.

"What do you call that scent?"

"Night-violet," was the answer.

"The man is cheating you. Violet is a delicate scent,
but this stuff is strong and unpleasant, the sort of thing
embalmers use for dead bodies. In the weak condition of
my nerves, it makes me feel ill. Please tell them to bring
me some eau-de-cologne."

Sonnenberg made off himself to fetch the bottle.

"Oh, no! you'd better call someone. If you come nearer me yourself, I shall faint." Sonnenberg, who counted on his hair-oil to captivate the maids, was deeply injured.

When he had sprinkled the room with eau-de-cologne, my father set about inventing errands: there was French snuff and English magnesia to be ordered, and a carriage advertised for sale to be looked at—not that my father ever bought anything. Then Sonnenberg bowed and disappeared till dinner-time, heartily glad to get away.

§10

THE next to appear on the scene was the cook. Whatever he had bought or put on the slate, my father always objected to the price.

"Dear, dear! how high prices are! Is nothing coming in from the country?"

"No, indeed, Sir," answered the cook; "the roads are very bad just now."

"Well, you and I must buy less, until they're mended."

Next he sat down at his writing table, where he wrote orders for his bailiff or examined his accounts, and scolded me in the intervals of business. He consulted his doctor also; but his chief occupation was to quarrel with his valet, Nikíta. Nikíta was a perfect martyr. He was a short, red-faced man with a hot temper, and might have been created on purpose to annoy my father and draw down reproofs upon himself. The scenes that took place between the two every day might have furnished material for a comedy, but it was all serious to them. Knowing that the man was indispensable to him, my father often put up with his rudeness; yet, in spite of thirty years of complete failure, he still persisted in lecturing him for his faults. The valet would have found the life unendurable, if he had not possessed one means of relief: he was generally tipsy by dinner-time. My father, though this did not escape him, did not go beyond indirect allusions to the subject: for instance, he would say that a piece of brown bread and salt prevented a man from smelling of spirits. When Nikíta had taken too much, he shuffled his feet in a peculiar way while handing the dishes; and my father, on noticing this, used to invent a message for him at once; for instance, he would send him to the barber's to ask if he had changed his address. Then he would say to me in French: "I know he won't go; but he's not sober; he might drop a soup plate and stain the cloth and give me a start. Let him take a turn; the fresh air will do him good."

On these occasions, the valet generally made some reply, or, if not, muttered to himself as he left the room. Then the master called him back with unruffled composure, and asked him, "What did you say to me?"

"I said nothing at all to you."

"Then who are you talking to? Except you and me, there is nobody in this room or the next."

"I was talking to myself."

"A very dangerous thing: madness often begins in that way."

The valet went off in a fury to his room, which was next to his master's bedroom. There he read the *Moscow Gazette* and made wigs for sale. Probably to relieve his feelings, he took snuff furiously, and the snuff was so strong or the membrane of his nose so weak, that he always sneezed six or seven times after a pinch.

The master's bell rang and the valet threw down the hair in his hands and answered the bell.

"Is that you sneezing?"

"Yes, Sir."

"Then, bless you!"—and a motion of the hand dismissed the valet.

§11

ON the eve of each Ash Wednesday all the servants came, according to the old custom, to ask pardon of their master for offences; and on these solemn occasions my father came into the drawing-room accompanied by his valet. He always pretended that he could not recognise some of the people.

"Who is that decent old man, standing in that corner?" he would ask the valet.

"Danilo, the coachman," was the impatient answer; for Nikíta knew this was all play-acting.

"Dear, dear! how changed he is! I really believe it is drinking too much that ages them so fast. What does he do now?"

"He drives fire-wood."

My father made a face as if he were suffering severe pain. "Drives wood? What do you mean? Wood is not driven, it is conveyed in a cart. Thirty years might have taught you to speak better. . . . Well, Danilo, God in His mercy has permitted me to meet you yet another year. I pardon you all your offences throughout the year, your waste of my oats and your neglect of my horses; and you must pardon me. Go on with your work while strength lasts; and now that Lent is beginning, I advise you to take rather less spirits: at our years it is bad for the health, and the Church forbids it." This was the kind of way in which he spoke to them all on this occasion.

§12

WE dined at four: the dinner lasted a long time and was very tiresome. Spiridon was an excellent cook; but his parsimony as well as my father's made the meal rather unsatisfying, though there were a number of courses. My father used to put bits for the dogs in a red jar that stood beside his place; he also fed them off his fork, a proceeding which was deeply resented by the servants and therefore by myself also; but I do not know why.

Visitors, rare in general, were especially rare at dinner. I only remember one, whose appearance at the table had power at times to smoothe the frown from my father's face, General Nikolai Bakhmétyev. He had given up active service long ago; but he and my father had been gay young subalterns together in the Guards, in the time of Catherine; and, while her son was on the throne, both had been court-martialled, Bakhmétyev for fighting a duel, and my father for acting as a second. Later, the one had gone off to foreign parts as a tourist, the other to Ufá as Governor. Bakhmétyev was a big man, healthy and handsome even in old age: he enjoyed his dinner and his glass of wine, he enjoyed cheerful conversation, and other things as well. He boasted that in his day he had eaten a hundred meat patties at a sitting; and, at sixty, he could eat a dozen buckwheat cakes swimming in a pool of butter, with no fear of consequences. I witnessed his feats of this kind more than once.

He had some faint influence over my father and could

control him to some extent. When he saw that his friend
was in too bad a temper, he would put on his hat and
march away. "I'm off for the present," he would say;
"you're not well, and dull to-night. I meant to dine with
you but I can't stand sour faces at my dinner. *Gehorsamer
Diener!*" Then my father would say to me, by way of
explanation: "What life there is in that old man yet! He
may thank God for his good health; he can't feel for
poor sufferers like me; in this awful frost he rushes about
in his sledge and thinks nothing of it, at this season; but
I thank my Creator every morning for waking up with
the breath still in my body. There is truth in the proverb
—it's ill talking between a full man and a fasting." More
indulgence than this it was impossible to expect from my
father.

Family dinners were given occasionally to near relations, but these entertainments proceeded rather from
deep design than from mere warmth of heart. Thus my
uncle, the Senator, was always invited to a party at our
house for his birthday, February 20, and we were invited
by him for St. John's Day, June 24, which was my
father's birthday; this arrangement not only set an edifying example of brotherly love, but also saved each of
them from giving a much larger entertainment at his own
house.

There were some regular guests as well. Sonnenberg
appeared at dinner *ex officio*; he had prepared himself
by a bumper of brandy and a sardine eaten beforehand,
and declined the tiny glass of stale brandy offered him. My
last French tutor was an occasional guest—an old miser
and scandal-monger, with an impudent face. M. Thirié
constantly made the mistake of filling his glass with wine

instead of beer. My father would say to him, "If you remember that the wine is on your right, you will not make the mistake in future": and Thirié crammed a great pinch of snuff into his large and crooked nose, and spilt the snuff over his plate.

§13

ONE of these visitors was an exceedingly comic figure, a short, bald old man, who always wore a short, tight tail-coat, and a waistcoat which ended where a modern waist-coat begins. His name was Dmitri Pimyónov, and he al-ways looked twenty years out of date, reminding you of 1810 in 1830, and of 1820 in 1840. He was interested in literature, but his natural capacity was small, and he had been brought up on the sentimental phrases of Karamzín, or Marmontel and Marivaux. Dmítriev was his master in poetry; and he had been tempted to make some experi-ments of his own on that slippery track which is trod by Russian authors—his first publication was a translation of La Rochefoucauld's *Pensées,* and his second a treatise on *Female Beauty and Charm.* But his chief distinction was, not that he had once published books which nobody ever read, but that, if he once began to laugh, he could not stop, but went on till he crowed convulsively like a child with whooping-cough. He was aware of this, and therefore took his precautions when he felt it coming on: he pulled out his handkerchief, looked at his watch, buttoned up his coat, and covered his face with both hands; then, when the paroxysm was imminent, he got up, turned his face to the wall, and stood in that position suffering tor-ments, for half an hour or longer; at last, red in the face and worn out by his exertions, he sat down again and mopped his bald head; and for a long time an occasional sob heaved his body.

He was a kindly man, but awkward and poor and a man of letters. Consequently my father attached no importance to him and considered him as "below the salt" in all respects; but he was well aware of this tendency to convulsive laughter, and used to make his guest laugh to such an extent that other people could not help laughing too in an uncomfortable fashion. Then the author of all this merriment, with a slight smile on his own lips, used to look at us as a man looks at puppies when they are rioting.

My father sometimes played dreadful tricks on this unlucky admirer of *Female Beauty and Charm*.

A Colonel of Engineers was announced by the servant one day. "Bring him in," said my father, and then he turned to Pimyónov and said, "Please be careful before him: he is unfortunate enough to have a very peculiar stammer"—here he gave a very successful imitation of the Colonel—"I know you are easily amused, but please restrain yourself."

That was quite enough: before the officer had spoken three words, Pimyónov pulled out his handkerchief, made an umbrella out of his hand, and finally sprang to his feet.

The officer looked on in surprise, while my father said to me with perfect composure: "What can be the matter with our friend? He is suffering from spasms of some kind: order a glass of cold water for him at once, and bring eau-de-cologne."

But in these cases Pimyónov clutched his hat and vanished. Home he went, shouting with laughter for a mile or so, stopping at the crossings, and leaning against the lamp-posts.

For several years he dined at our house every second Sunday, with few exceptions; and my father was equally vexed, whether he came or failed to come. He was not kind to Pimyónov, but the worthy man took the long walk, in spite of that, until he died. There was nothing laughable about his death: he was a solitary old bachelor, and, when his long illness was nearing the end, he looked on while his housekeeper robbed him of the very sheets upon his bed and then left him without attendance.

§14

BUT the real martyrs of our dinner-table were certain old and feeble ladies, who held a humble and uncertain position in the household of Princess Khovanski, my father's sister. For the sake of change, or to get information about our domestic affairs—whether the heads of the family had quarrelled, whether the cook had beaten his wife and been detected by his master, whether a maid had slipped from the path of virtue—these old people sometimes came on a saint's day to spend the day. I ought to mention that these old widows had known my father forty or fifty years earlier in the house of the Princess Meshcherski, where they were brought up for charity. During this interval between their precarious youth and unsettled old age, they had quarrelled for twenty years with husbands, tried to keep them sober, nursed them when paralysed, and buried them. One had fought the battle of life in Bessarabia with a husband on half-pay and a swarm of children; another, together with her husband, had been a defendant for years in the criminal courts; and all these experiences had left on them the traces of life in provincial towns—a dread of those who have power in this world, a spirit of humility and also of blind fanaticism.

Their presence often gave rise to astonishing scenes.

"Are you not well, that you are eating nothing, Anna Yakimovna?" my father would ask.

Then Anna Yakimovna, the widow of some obscure official, an old woman with a worn faded face and a perpetual smell of camphor, apologised with eyes and fingers as she answered: "Excuse me, *bátyushka*—I am really quite ashamed; but, you know, by old custom to-day is a Fast-day."

"What a nuisance! You are too scrupulous, *mátushka*: 'not that which entereth into a man defileth a man but that which cometh out': whatever you eat, the end is the same. But we ought to watch 'what cometh out of the mouth,' and that means scandal against our neighbours. I think you should dine at home on such days. Suppose a Turk were to turn up, he might want pilaus; but my house is not a hotel where each can order what he wants." This terrified the old woman who had intended to ask for some milk pudding; but she now attacked the *kvass* and the salad, and made a pretence of eating enormously.

But if she, or any of them, began to eat meat on a Fast-day, then my father (who never fasted himself) would shake his head sorrowfully and say: "Do you really think it worth while, Anna Yakimovna, to give up the ancient custom, when you have so few years still to live? I, poor sinner, don't fast myself, because I have many diseases; but you may thank God for your health, considering your age, and you have kept the fasts all your life; and now

all of a sudden—think what an example to *them*—"
pointing to the servants. And the poor old woman once
more fell upon the *kvass* and the salad.

These scenes filled me with disgust, and I sometimes
ventured to defend the victim by pointing out the desire
of conformity which he expressed at other times. Then
it was my father's custom to get up and take off his velvet
skull-cap by the tassel: holding it over his head, he would
thank me for my lecture and beg me to excuse his forget-
fulness. Then he would say to the old lady: "These are
terrible times! Little wonder that you neglect the Fast,
when children teach their parents! What are we coming
to? It is an awful prospect; but fortunately you and I
will not live to see it."

§15

AFTER dinner my father generally lay down for an hour
and a half, and the servants at once made off to the
taverns and tea-shops. Tea was served at seven, and we
sometimes had a visitor at that hour, especially my uncle,
the Senator. This was a respite for us; for he generally
brought a budget of news with him and produced it with
much vivacity. Meanwhile my father put on an air of
absolute indifference, keeping perfectly grave over the
most comic stories, and questioning the narrator, as if
he could not see the point, when he was told of any striking fact.

The Senator came off much worse, when he occasionally
contradicted or disagreed with his younger brother, and
sometimes even without contradicting him, if my father
happened to be specially out of humour. In these serio-
comic scenes, the most comic feature was the contrast

between my uncle's natural vehemence and my father's artificial composure. "Oh, you're not well to-day," my uncle would say at last, and then snatch his hat and go off in a hurry. One day he was unable in his anger to open the door. "Damn that door!" he said, and kicked it with all his might. My father walked slowly up to the door, opened it, and said with perfect calmness, "The door works perfectly: but it opens outwards, and you try to open it inwards and get angry with it." I may mention that the Senator, being two years older than my father, always addressed him as "thou," while my father said "you" as a mark of respect for seniority.

When my uncle had gone, my father went to his bedroom; but first he always enquired whether the gates of the court were shut, and expressed some doubt when he was told they were, though he never took any steps to ascertain the facts. And now began the long business of undressing: face and hands were washed, fomentations applied and medicines swallowed; the valet placed on the table near the bed a whole arsenal of phials, nightlights, and pill-boxes. For about an hour the old man read memoirs of some kind, very often Bourrienne's *Memorial de St. Hélène*. And so the day ended.

§16

SUCH was the life I left in 1834, and such I found it in 1840, and such it remained down to my father's death in 1846. When I returned from exile at the age of thirty, I realised that my father was right in many respects, and that he, to his misfortune, knew the world only too well. But did I deserve that he should preach even the truth in a manner so repulsive to the heart of youth? His intelligence, chilled by a long life spent in a corrupt society, made him suspicious of all the world; his feelings were not warm and did not crave for reconciliation; and therefore he remained at enmity with all his fellow-creatures.

In 1839, and still more in 1842, I found him feeble and suffering from symptoms which were not imaginary. My uncle's death had left him more solitary than ever; even his old valet had gone, but he was just the same; his bodily strength had failed him, but his cruel wit and his memory were unaffected; he still carried on the same petty tyranny, and the same old Sonnenberg still pitched his camp in our old house and ran errands as before.

For the first time, I realised the sadness of that life and watched with an aching heart that solitary deserted existence, fading away in the parched and stony desert which he had created around him by his own actions, but was powerless to change. He knew his powerlessness, and he saw death approaching, and held out jealously and stubbornly. I felt intense pity for the old man, but I could do nothing—he was inaccessible.

I sometimes walked past his study and saw him sitting in his deep armchair, a hard, uncomfortable seat; he had his dogs round him and was playing with my three-year-old son, just the two together. It seemed to me that the sight of this child relaxed the clutching fingers and stiffening nerves of old age, and that, when his dying hand touched the cradle of infancy, he could rest from the anxiety and irritable strife in which his whole life had been spent.

CHAPTER VI

The Kremlin Offices—Moscow University—The Chemist—
The Cholera—Philaret—Passek.

§1

IN spite of the ominous prognostications of the one-
legged general, my father entered my name for
service at the Government offices in the Kremlin,
under Prince Yusúpov. I signed some document, and
there the matter ended. I never heard anything more
about my office, except once, three years later, when a
man was sent to our house by Yusúpov, to inform me
that I had gained the first step of official promotion; this
messenger was the court architect, and he always shouted
as if he were standing on the roof of a five-storeyed
house and giving orders from there to workmen in the
cellar. I may remark in passing, that all this hocus-pocus
was useless: when I passed my final examination at the
University, this gave me at once the promotion earned
by service; and the loss of a year or two of seniority was
not serious. On the other hand, this pretence of office-
work nearly prevented me from matriculating; for, when
the University authorities found that I was reckoned as
a Government clerk, they refused me permission to take
the examination.

For the clerks in public offices there were special after-noon lectures, of an elementary kind, which gave the right of admission to a special examination. Rich idlers, young gentlemen whose education had been neglected, men who wished to avoid military service and to get the rank of *assessor* as soon as possible—such were the can-didates for this examination; and it served as a kind of gold-mine to the senior professors, who gave private in-struction at twenty *roubles* a lesson.

To pass through these Caudine Forks to knowledge was entirely inconsistent with my views, and I told my father decidedly that unless he found some other method I should retire from the Civil Service.

He was angry: he said that my wilfulness prevented him from settling my future, and blamed my teachers for filling my head with this nonsense; but when he saw that all this had little effect upon me, he determined to wait on Prince Yusúpov.

The Prince settled the matter in no time; there was no shillyshallying about his methods. He sent for his sec-retary and told him to make out leave of absence for me —for three years. The secretary hummed and hawed and respectfully submitted to his chief that four months was the longest period for which leave could be granted with-out the imperial sanction.

"Rubbish, my friend!" said the Prince; "the thing is perfectly simple: if he can't have leave of absence, then say that I order him to go through the University course and complete his studies."

The secretary obeyed orders, and next day found me sitting in the lecture-theatre of the Faculty of Mathe-matics and Physics.

The University of Moscow and the High School of
Tsárskoë Seló* play an important part in the history of
Russian education and in the life of the last two genera-
tions.

§2

AFTER the year 1812, Moscow University and Moscow
itself rose in importance. Degraded from her position as
an imperial capital by Peter the Great, the city was promoted by Napoleon, partly by his wish but mainly against
it, to be the capital of the Russian nation. The people
discovered the ties of blood that bound them to Moscow
by the pain they felt on hearing of her capture by the
enemy. For her it was the beginning of a new epoch; and
her University became more and more the centre of Russian education, uniting as it did everything to favour its
development—historical importance and geographical
position.

There was a vigorous outburst of intellectual activity
in Petersburg after the death of the Emperor Paul; but
this died away in the darkness that followed the fourteenth of December, 1825.

All was reversed, the blood flowed back to the heart,
and all activity was forced to ferment and burrow underground. But Moscow University stood firm and was the
first visible object to emerge from the universal fog.

The University soon grew in influence. All the youth
and strength of Russia came together there in one common meeting-place, from all parts of the country and all
sections of society; there they cast off the prejudices

*Tsárskoë Seló=The Tsar's Village, near Petersburg. Púshkin was at
this school.

they had acquired at home, reached a common level, formed ties of brotherhood with one another, and then went back to every part of Russia and penetrated every class.

Down to 1848 the constitution of our universities was purely democratic. Their doors were open to everyone who could pass the examination, provided he was not a serf, or a peasant detained by the village community. The Emperor Nicholas limited the number of freshmen and increased the charges to pensioners, permitting poor nobles only to escape from this burden. But all this belongs to the class of measures that will disappear together with the passport system, religious intolerance, and so on.

A motley assemblage of young men, from high to low, from North and South, soon blended into a compact body united by ties of friendship. Among us social distinctions had none of that offensive influence which one sees in English schools and regiments—to say nothing of English universities which exist solely for the rich and well-born. If any student among us had begun to boast of his family or his money, he would have been tormented and sent to Coventry by the rest.

The external distinctions among us were not deep and proceeded from other sources. For instance, the Medical School was across the park and somewhat removed from the other faculties; besides, most of the medical students were Germans or came from theological seminaries. The Germans kept somewhat apart, and the bourgeois spirit of Western Europe was strong in them. The whole education of the divinity students and all their ideas were different from ours; we spoke different languages; they had grown up under the yoke of monastic control and been crammed with rhetoric and theology; they envied our freedom, and we resented their Christian humility.

Though I joined the Faculty of Mathematics and Physics, I never had any great turn or much liking for mathematics. Niko and I were taught the subject by the same teacher, whom we liked because he told us stories; he was very entertaining, but I doubt if he could have developed a special passion in any pupil for his branch of science. He knew as far as Conic Sections, *i.e.,* just what was required from schoolboys entering the University; a true philosopher, he had never had the curiosity to glance at the "University branches" of mathematics. It was specially remarkable that he taught for ten years continuously out of a single book—Francœur's treatise—and always stopped at the same page, having no ambition to go beyond the required minimum.

I chose that Faculty, because it included the subject of natural science, in which I then took a specially strong interest; and this interest was due to a rather odd meeting.

§3

I HAVE described already the remarkable division of the family property in 1822. When it was over, my oldest uncle went to live in Petersburg, and nothing was heard of him for a long time. At last a report got abroad that he intended to marry. He was then over sixty, and it was well known that he had other children as well as a grown-up son. He did, in fact, marry the mother of his eldest son and so made the son legitimate. He might as well have legitimised the other children; but the chief object of these proceedings was well known—he wished to disinherit his brothers; and he fully attained that object by the acknowledgement of his son. In the famous inundation of 1824, the water flooded the carriage in which he was driving. The old man caught cold, took to his bed, and died in the beginning of 1825.

About the son there were strange reports: it was said that he was unsociable and had no friends; he was interested in chemistry and spent his life over the microscope; he read even at meals and disliked women's society.

His uncles transferred to him the grievance they had felt against his father. They always called him "The Chemist," using this as a term of contempt, and giving it to be understood that chemistry was a quite impossible occupation for a gentleman.

He had suffered horrible treatment from his father, who kept a harem in the house and not only insulted him by the spectacle of shameless senile profligacy but was actually jealous of his son's rivalry. From this dishonourable existence The Chemist tried to escape by means of laudanum; but a friend who worked at chemistry with him saved his life by a mere chance. This frightened the father, and he treated his son better afterwards.

When his father died, The Chemist set free the fair captives of the harem, reduced by half the heavy dues levied by his father on the peasants, forgave all arrears, and gave away for nothing the exemptions which his father used to sell, excusing household servants from service in the Army.

When he came to Moscow eighteen months later, I was anxious to see him; for I was inclined to like him for his treatment of his peasants, and also for the dislike which his uncles unjustly felt for him.

He called on my father one morning—a shortish man, with a large nose and half his hair gone; he wore gold spectacles, and his fingers were stained with chemicals. My father's reception was cold and cutting, but the nephew gave just as good as he got; when they had taken each other's measure, they talked on casual topics with a show of indifference and parted politely, but a strong feeling of dislike was concealed on both sides. My father saw that his antagonist would never give way.

They never came closer afterwards. The Chemist very rarely visited his uncles; the last time he and my father met was after the Senator's death—he came to ask a loan of 30,000 *roubles,* in order to buy land. My father refused to lend it; The Chemist was angry, but he rubbed his nose and said with a smile: "What possible risk is there? My estate is entailed, and I want the money for improvements. I have no children, so that you are the heir to my land as I am to yours."* My father, who was then seventy-five, never forgave his nephew this sally.

§4

I BEGAN to visit him from time to time. His was a singular existence. He had a large house on the Tver Boulevard, where he lived in one very small room and used another as a laboratory. His old mother occupied another small room at the end of the passage; and the rest of the house was unused, and left exactly as it was when his father migrated to Petersburg. Tarnished chandeliers, valuable furniture, rarities of all kinds, grandfather's clocks supposed to have been bought by Peter the Great in Amster-

*Herzen himself was excluded from succession by his birth.

dam, armchairs supposed to have belonged to Stanislas Leshchinski,* empty frames, and pictures turned to the wall—all these, in complete disorder, filled three large drawing-rooms which were neither heated nor lighted. In the outer hall the servants were generally playing the banjo and smoking—in the very room where formerly they hardly dared to breathe or say their prayers. One of them lit a candle and escorted me through the long museum; and he never failed to advise me to keep on my overcoat, because it was very cold in the drawing-rooms. Thick layers of dust covered all the projections of the furniture, and the contents of the rooms were reflected in the carved mirrors and seemed to move with the candle; straw, left over from packing, lay comfortably here and there, together with scraps of paper and bits of string.

After passing through these rooms, you came at last to a curtained door which led into the study. The heat in this room was terrific; and here The Chemist was always to be found, wearing a stained dressing-gown trimmed with squirrel-fur, sitting behind a rampart of books, and surrounded by bottles, retorts, crucibles, and other apparatus. A few years earlier, this room had been the scene of shocking vice and cruelty; now it smelt of chlorine and was ruled by the microscope; and in this very room I was born! When my father returned from foreign parts, he had not yet quarrelled with his brother, and spent some months under his roof. Here too my wife was born in the year 1817. After two years The Chemist sold the house, and I spent many evenings there, arguing about Pan-Slavism and losing my temper with Homya-

*King of Poland and father-in-law of Louis XV.

kóv,* though nothing could make him lose his. The chief rooms were altered then, but the outside steps, front hall, and staircase were unchanged; and the little study was left as before.

The Chemist's household arrangements, simple at all times, were even simpler when his mother went to the country in summer and took the cook with her. At four in the afternoon, his valet brought a coffee-pot, made some strong broth in it, and placed it by the fire of the chemical furnace, where all sorts of poisons were brewing; then he fetched half a chicken and a loaf from an eating-house; and that was his master's dinner. When it was eaten, the valet washed the coffee-pot and restored it to its proper functions. The man came again in the evening: he removed from the sofa a heap of books and a tiger-skin which The Chemist had inherited from his father; and when he had spread out a sheet and fetched pillows and a coverlet, the study, which had served as kitchen and drawing-room, was converted just as easily into a bedroom.

§5

At the very beginning of our acquaintance, The Chemist perceived that I was no mere idler; and he urged me to give up literature and politics—the former was mere trifling and the latter not only fruitless but dangerous—and take to natural science. He gave me Cuvier's *Essay on Geological Changes* and *Candolle's Botanical Geography,* and, seeing that I profited by the reading, he placed at my disposal his own excellent collections and

*Alexyéi Homyakóv (1804-1860), poet, theologian, and a leader of the Slavophile party.

preparations, and even offered to direct my studies himself. On his own ground he was very interesting—exceedingly learned, acute, and even amiable, within certain limits. As far as the monkeys, he was at your service: from the inorganic kingdom up to the orang-outang, nothing came amiss to him; but he did not willingly venture farther, and philosophy, in particular, he avoided as mere moonshine. He was no enemy to reform, nor Rip van Winkle: he simply disbelieved in human nature—he believed that selfishness is the one and only motive of our actions, and is limited only by stupidity in some cases and by ignorance in others.

His materialism shocked me. It was quite unlike the superficial and half-hearted scepticism of a previous generation. His views were deliberate, consistent, and definite —one thought of Lalande's famous answer to Napoleon. "Kant accepts the hypothesis of a deity," said Napoleon. "Sir," answered the astronomer, "in the course of my studies I have never found it necessary to make use of that hypothesis."

The Chemist's scepticism did not refer merely to theology. Geoffroy Saint-Hilaire he called a mystic, and Oken a mere lunatic. He felt for the works of natural philosophers the contempt my father had expressed for Karamzín—"They first invent spiritual forces and First Causes, and then they are surprised that they cannot prove them or understand them." In fact, it was my father over again, but differently educated and belonging to a different generation.

His views on social questions were even more disquieting. He believed that men are no more responsible for their actions, good or bad, than beasts: it was all a matter of constitution and circumstances and depended mainly on the state of the nervous system, from which, as he said, people expect more than it is able to give. He disliked family life, spoke with horror of marriage, and confessed frankly that, at thirty years of age, he had never once been in love. This hard temperament had, however, one tender side which showed itself in his conduct towards his mother. Both had suffered much from his father, and common suffering had united them closely. It was touching to see how he did what he could to surround her solitary and sickly old age with security and attention.

He never tried to make converts to his views, except on chemistry: they came out casually or were elicited by my questions. He was even unwilling to answer the objections I urged from an idealistic point of view; his answers were brief, and he smiled as he spoke, showing the kind of considerateness that an old mastiff will show to a lapdog whom he allows to snap at him and only pushes gently from him with his paw. But I resented this more than anything else and returned unwearied to the attack, though I never gained a single inch of ground. In later years I often called to mind what The Chemist had said, just as I recalled my father's utterances; and, of course, he was right in three-fourths of the points in dispute. But, all the same, I was right too. There are truths which, like political rights, cannot be conveyed from one man to another before a certain age.

§6

It was The Chemist's influence that made me choose the Faculty of Mathematics and Physics. Perhaps I should have done better to take up medicine; but it did me no great harm to acquire a partial knowledge of differential and integral equations, and then to lose it absolutely.

Without a knowledge of natural science, there is no salvation for the modern man. This wholesome food, this strict training of the mind by facts, this proximity to the life that surrounds ours, and this acknowledgement of its independence—without these there lurks somewhere in the soul a monastic cell, and this contains a germ of mysticism which may cover like a dark cloud the whole intellect.

Before I had gone through College, The Chemist had moved to Petersburg, and I did not meet him again till my return from exile. A few months after my marriage I paid a half-secret visit of a few days to my father, who was living near Moscow. He was still displeased at my marriage, and the purpose of my journey was to make peace between us once for all. I broke my journey at the village of Perkhushkov, the place where we had so often stayed in my youth. The Chemist was expecting me there; he even had dinner ready for me, and two bottles of champagne. Four or five years had made no change in him, except that he looked a little older. Before dinner he said to me quite seriously: "Please tell me frankly how marriage and domestic life strike you. Do you find it to your taste, or only passable?" I laughed, and he went on: "I am astonished at your boldness; no man in a normal condition could ever decide on so awful a step. More than one good match has been suggested to me; but when I think that a woman would do as she liked in my room, arranging everything in what she thinks order, forbidding me to smoke possibly, making a noise and talking nonsense, I feel such terror of the prospect that I prefer to die in solitude."

"Shall I stop the night here or go on to my father's?" I asked him after dinner.

"There is room enough in the house," he answered, "but for your own sake I advise you to go on; you will get there by ten o'clock. Of course you know he's still angry with you. Well, old people's nerves are generally less active at night, before they get to sleep, and you will probably get a much better reception to-night than to-morrow morning; by then his spurs will be sharp for the fray."

"Ha! ha! ha!" I laughed, "there is my old instructor in physiology and materialism! You remind me of those blissful days, when I used to come to you, like Wagner in *Faust,* to bore you with my idealism and to suffer, with some impatience, the cold water you threw on it."

He laughed too and replied, "You have lived long enough, since then, to find out that all human actions depend merely on the nerves and chemical combination."

Later, we somehow drifted apart; probably we were both to blame. Nevertheless, he wrote me a letter in 1846. I had published the first part of *Whose Fault Is It?* * and was beginning to be the fashion. He wrote that he was sorry to see me wasting my powers on trivial objects. "I made it up with you because of your letters on the study of Nature, in which you made me understand (as far as it is intelligible to the mind of man) the German philosophy. But why, instead of going on with serious work, do you write fairy tales?" I sent a few friendly words in reply, and there our relations ended.

* A novel.

If these lines happen to fall under The Chemist's eyes, I beg that he will read them before going to bed, when the nerves are less active; and I am convinced that he will be able then to pardon this friendly gossip, and all the more because I cherish a real regard for him.

§7

AND SO, at last, the doors of my prison were opened, and I was free. The solitude of my smallish room and the quiet half-secret interviews with my one friend, Ogaryóv, were now exchanged for a noisy family of six hundred members. In a fortnight, I was more at home there than I had ever been, from the day I was born, in my father's house.

But even here my father's house pursued me, in the shape of a footman whom my father sent with me to the University, especially when I walked there. I spent a whole term in trying to dodge this escort, and was formally excused from it at last. I say "formally," because my valet Peter, who was entrusted with this duty, very soon realised, first, that I disliked being escorted, and secondly, that he himself would be much better off in various places of amusement than in the entrance-hall of my lecture-room, where he had no occupation except to exchange gossip and pinches of snuff with the two porters. What was the motive of this precaution? Was it possible that Peter, who had been liable all his life to drinking-bouts that lasted for days, could keep me straight? I don't suppose my father believed that; but, for his own peace of mind, he took measures—ineffective, indeed, but still measures—much in the way that freethinkers keep Lent. This is a characteristic feature of the old system of education in Russia. Till I was seven, I was not allowed to come downstairs alone—the flight was rather steep; and Vyéra Artamónovna went on bathing me till I was eleven. It was of a piece with this system that I should have a serv-ant walking behind me to College, and should not be allowed, before I was twenty-one, to be out later than half-past ten. I was never really free and independent till I was banished; but for that incident, the system would probably have gone on till I was twenty-five or thirty-five.

§8

LIKE most energetic boys who have been brought up alone, I rushed into the arms of my companions with such frank eagerness, made proselytes with such sublime confidence, and was myself so fond of everyone, that I could not but kindle a corresponding warmth in my hearers, who were mostly of the same age as myself. I was then seventeen.

The process of making friends was hastened partly by the advice which worldly wisdom gave me—to be polite to all and intimate with none, to confide in nobody; and there was also the belief which we all took with us to College, the belief that here our dreams would be realised, that here we should sow the seed of a future harvest and lay the foundations of a permanent alliance.

The young men of my time were admirable. It was just the time when ideals were stirring more and more in Rus-sia. The formalism of theological training and Polish indolence had alike disappeared, and had not yet given place to German utilitarianism, which applies culture to the mind, like manure to a field, in the hope of a heavier crop. The best students had ceased to consider learning as a tiresome but indispensable byway to official promotion; and the questions which we discussed had nothing to do with advancement in the Civil Service.

On the other hand, the pursuit of knowledge had not yet become divorced from realities, and did not distract our attention from the suffering humanity around us; and this sympathy heightened the *social* morality of the students. My friends and I said openly in the lecture-room whatever came into our heads; copies of forbidden poems were freely circulated, and forbidden books were read aloud and commented on; and yet I cannot recall a single instance of information given by a traitor to the authorities. There were timid spirits who held aloof and shut their eyes; but even they held their tongues.

One foolish boy made some disclosures to his mother, when she questioned him, under threat of the rod, about the Málov affair. The fond mother—she was a Princess and a leader in society—rushed to the Rector and communicated her son's disclosures, in order to prove his repentance. We found this out, and tormented him so, that he left before his time was up.

But this episode, which led to my confinement within the walls of the University prison, is worth telling.

§9

MÁLOV, though a professor in the University, was a stupid, rude, ill-educated man, an object of contempt and derision to the students. One of them, when asked by a Visitor, how many professors there were in their department, replied that there were nine, not counting Málov.* And this man, who could be spoken of in this way, began

* There is here an untranslatable play on words.

to treat his class with more and more rudeness, till they determined to turn him out of the lecture-room. When their plan was made, they sent two spokesmen to our department, and invited me to bring reinforcements. I raised the fiery cross against the foe at once, and was joined by some adherents. When we entered Málov's lecture-room, he was there and saw us.

One fear only was depicted on the faces of all the audience—that he might refrain for once from rude remarks. But that fear soon passed off. The tightly packed lecture-room was in a fever and gave vent to a low suppressed noise. Málov made some objection, and a scraping of feet began. "You are like horses, expressing your thoughts with your feet," said the professor, imagining, I suppose, that horses think by gallop and trot. Then the storm broke, with hisses and yells. "Turn him out! turn him out! *Pereat!*" Málov turned white as a sheet and made a desperate effort to control the noise, but failed; the students jumped up on the benches. Málov slowly left his chair, hunched himself up, and made his way to the door. The students followed him through the court to the street outside, and threw his goloshes out after him. The last detail was important: if once it reached the street, the proceeding became much more serious; but what lads of seventeen or eighteen would ever take that into account?

The University Council took fright and induced the Visitor to represent the affair as settled, and, with that object, to consign the guilty persons or someone, at least, to the University prison. That was rather ingenious on their part. Otherwise, it was likely enough that the Emperor would send an *aide-de-camp,* and that the *aide-de-*

camp, in order to earn a cross, would have magnified the affair into conspiracy and rebellion; then he would have advised penal servitude for all the offenders, and the Emperor, in his mercy, would have sent them to the colours instead. But seeing vice punished and virtue triumphant, the Emperor merely confirmed the action of the students by dismissing the professor. Though we drove Málov as far as the University gates, it was Nicholas who drove him out of them.

So the fat was in the fire. On the following afternoon, one of the porters hobbled up to me, a white-haired old man who was normally in a state more drunk than sober, and produced from the lining of his overcoat a note from the Rector for me: I was ordered to call on him at seven in the evening. The porter was soon followed by a student, a baron from the Baltic Provinces, who was one of the unfortunate victims enticed by me, and had received an invitation similar to mine. He looked pale and frightened and began by heaping reproaches on me; then he asked me what I advised him to say.

"Lie desperately," I answered; "deny everything, except that there was a row and you were present."

"But if the Rector asks why I was in the wrong lecture-room?"

"That's easy. Say of course that our lecturer did not turn up, and that you, not wishing to waste your time, went to hear someone else."

"He won't believe me."

"That's his affair."

When we entered the University yard, I looked at my baron: his plump cheeks were very pale, and he was obviously feeling uncomfortable. "Listen to me," I said;

"you may be sure that the Rector will deal with me first. Say what I say, with variations; you really took no special part in the affair. But remember one thing: for making a row and for telling lies about it, they will, at most, put you in the prison; but, if you are not careful and involve any other student, I shall tell the rest and we shall poison your existence." The baron promised, and kept his word like a gentleman.

§10

THE Rector at that time was Dvigubski, a survival and a typical specimen of the antediluvian professor—but, for flood I should substitute fire, the Great Fire of 1812.

They are extinct now: the patriarchal epoch of Moscow University ends with the appointment of Prince Obolenski as Visitor. In those days the Government left the University alone: the professors lectured or not, the students attended or not, just as they pleased, and the latter, instead of the kind of cavalry uniform they have now, wore mufti of varying degrees of eccentricity, and very small caps which would hardly stick on over their virgin locks. Of professors there were two classes or camps, which carried on a bloodless warfare against each other—one composed exclusively of Germans, the other of non-Germans. The Germans included some worthy and learned men, such as Loder, Fischer, Hildebrandt, and Heim; but they were distinguished as a rule for their ignorance and dislike of the Russian language, their want of sympathy with the students, their unlimited consumption of tobacco, and the large number of stars and orders which they always wore. The non-Germans, on their side, knew no modern language but Russian; they had the ill-breeding of the theological school and the servile temper of their nation; they were mostly overworked, and they made up for abstention from tobacco by an excessive indulgence in strong drinks. Most of the Germans came from Göttingen, and most of the non-Germans were sons of priests.

Dvigubski belonged to the latter class. He looked so much the ecclesiastic that one of the students—he had been brought up at a priests' school—asked for his blessing and regularly addressed him as "Your Reverence" in the course of an examination. But he was also startlingly like an owl wearing the Order of St. Anne; and as such he was caricatured by another student who had come less under church influences. He came occasionally to our lecture-room, and brought with him the dean, Chumakov, or Kotelnitski, who had charge of a cupboard labelled *Materia Medica,* and kept, for some unknown reason, in the mathematical class-room; or Reiss, who had been imported from Germany because his uncle knew chemistry, and lectured in French with such a pronunciation that *poisson* took the place of *poison* in his mouth, and some quite innocent words sounded unprintable. When these old gentlemen appeared, we stared at them: to us they were a party of "dug-outs," the Last of the Mohicans, representatives of a different age, quite remote from ours —of the time when Knyazhnín and Cheraskov were read, the time of good-natured Professor Dilthey, who had two dogs which he named *Babil* and *Bijou,* because one never stopped barking and the other was always silent.

§11

BUT Dvigubski was by no means a good-natured professor: his reception of us was exceedingly abrupt and discourteous; I talked terrible nonsense and was rude, and the baron played second fiddle to me. Dvigubski was provoked and ordered us to appear before the Council next morning. The Council settled our business in half an hour: they questioned, condemned, and sentenced us, and referred the sentence, for confirmation, to Prince Go- litsyn.

I had hardly had time to give half a dozen performances in the lecture-room, representing the proceedings of the University Court, when the beginning of the lecture was interrupted by the appearance of a party, consisting of our inspector, an army major, a French dancing-master, and a corporal, who carried an order for my arrest and incarceration. Some students escorted me, and there were many more in the court-yard, who waved their hands or caps. Clearly I was not the first victim. The University police tried in vain to push them back.

I found two captives already immured in the dirty cellar which served as a prison, and there were two more in another room; six was the total number of those who suffered for this affair. We were sentenced to a diet of bread and water, and, though we declined some soup which the Rector sent us, we did not suffer; for when the College emptied at nightfall, our friends brought us cheese, game, cigars, wine, and *liqueurs*. The sentry grumbled and scolded, but he took a small bribe, and in- troduced the supplies. After midnight, he moved to some distance and allowed several of our friends to join us. And so we spent our time, feasting by night and sleeping by day.

A certain Panin, a brother of the Minister of Justice and employed under our Visitor, mindful of Army traditions, took it into his head one night to go the rounds and inspect our cellar-prison. We had just lit a candle, keeping it under a chair to betray no light, and were attacking our midnight meal, when a knocking was heard at the outer door, not the meek sound that begs for admittance and fears to be heard more than not to be heard, but a knock of power and authority. The sentry turned rigid, we hid the bottles and our guests in a cupboard, blew out the light, and dropped on our pallet-beds. Panin came in. "You appear to be smoking," he said—the smoke was so thick that Panin and the inspector who were carrying a lantern were hardly visible. "Where do they get a light from? From you?" he asked the sentry. The man swore he was innocent, and we said that we had got tinder of our own. The inspector promised to take it and our cigars away; and Panin went off, without ever noticing that there were twice as many caps in the room as heads.

On Saturday evening the inspector appeared and announced that I and one other might go home; the rest were to stay till Monday. I resented this proposal and asked him whether I might stay. He fell back a step, looked at me with that expression of dignified wrath which is worn by ballet-dancers when representing angry kings or heroes, and said, "By all means, if you want to!" Then he left us; and this sally on my part brought down more paternal wrath on me than any other part of the affair.

Thus the first nights which I spent away from home were spent in prison. I was soon to experience a prison of another kind, and there I spent, not eight days, but nine months; and when these had passed, instead of going home, I went into exile. But much happened before that.

From this time I was a popular hero in the lecture-room. Till then I was considered "all right" by the rest; but, after the Málov affair, I became, like the lady in Gógol, all right in the fullest sense of that term.

§12

BUT did we learn anything, meanwhile, and was study possible under such circumstances? I think we did. The instruction was more limited in quantity and scope than in the forties. But a university is not bound to complete scientific education: its business is rather to put a man in a position to walk by himself; it should raise problems and teach a man to ask questions. And this is exactly what was done by such professors as Pávlov and Kachenovsky, each in his own way. But the collision of young minds, the exchange of ideas, and the discussion of books —all this did more than professors or lectures to develop and ripen the student. Moscow University was a successful institution; and the professors who contributed by their lectures to the development of Lérmontov, Byelínski, Turgénev, Kavélin, and Pirógov, may play cards with an easy conscience, or, with a still easier conscience, rest in their graves.

And what astonishing people some of them were! There was Chumakov, who treated the formulae of Poinsot's *Algebra* like so many serfs—adding letters and subtracting them, mixing up square numbers and their roots, and treating x as the known quantity. There was Myágkov, who, in spite of his name,* lectured on the harshest of sciences, the science of tactics. The constant study of this

Myágki is the Russian for "mild."

noble subject had actually given a martial air to the professor; and as he stood there buttoned up to the throat
and erect behind his stock, his lectures sounded more like
words of command than mere conversation. "Gentlemen,
artillery!" he would cry out. It sounded like the field of
battle, but it only meant that this was the heading of his
next discourse. And there was Reiss, who lectured on
chemistry but never ventured further than hydrogen—
Reiss, who was elected to the Chair for no knowledge of
his own but because his uncle had once studied the
science. The latter was invited to come to Russia towards
the end of Catherine's reign; but the old man did not
want to move, and sent his nephew instead.

My University course lasted four years, the additional
year being due to the fact that a whole session was lost
owing to the cholera. The most remarkable events of that
time were the cholera itself, and the visits of Humboldt
and Uvárov.

§13

WHEN Humboldt* was on his way back from the Ural
Mountains, he was welcomed to Moscow at a formal
meeting of the Society for the Pursuit of Natural Science,
most of whose members were state functionaries of some
kind, not at all interested in science, either natural or unnatural. But the glory of Humboldt—a Privy Councillor
of the Prussian King, a man on whom the Tsar had graciously conferred the Order of St. Anne, with instructions
that the recipient was to be put to no expense in the matter—was a fact of which even they were not ignorant; and

*Alexander Humboldt (1769-1859), born at Berlin, a famous writer
on natural science.

they were determined to show themselves to advantage before a man who had climbed Chimborazo and who lived at Sans-Souci.*

§14

OUR attitude towards Europe and Europeans is still that of provincials towards the dwellers in a capital: we are servile and apologetic, take every difference for a defect, blush for our peculiarities and try to hide them, and confess our inferiority by imitation. The fact is that we are intimidated: we have never got over the sneers of Peter the Great and his coadjutors, or the superior airs of French tutors and Germans in our Civil Service. Western nations talk of our duplicity and cunning; they believe we want to deceive them, when we are only trying to make a creditable appearance and pass muster. A Russian will express quite different political views in talking to different persons, without any ulterior object, and merely from a wish to please: the bump of complaisance is highly developed in our skulls.

"Prince Dmitri Golitsyn," said Lord Durham on one occasion, "is a true Whig, a Whig at heart." Prince Golitsyn was a worthy Russian gentleman, but I do not understand in what sense he was a Whig. It is clear enough that the Prince in his old age wished to be polite to Lord Durham and put on the Whig for that purpose.

§15

HUMBOLDT's reception in Moscow and at the University was a tremendous affair. Everyone came to meet him—the Governor of the city, functionaries military and

*The Prussian palace, near Potsdam.

civil, and the judges of the Supreme Court; and the professors were there wearing full uniform and their Orders, looking most martial with swords and three-cornered hats tucked under their arms. Unaware of all this, Humboldt arrived in a blue coat with gilt buttons and was naturally taken aback. His way was barricaded at every point between the entrance and the great hall: first the Rector stopped him, then the Dean, now a budding professor, and now a veteran who was just ending his career and therefore spoke very slowly; each of them delivered a speech of welcome in Latin or German or French, and all this went on in those terrible stone funnels miscalled passages, where you stopped for a minute at the risk of catching cold for a month. Humboldt listened bare-headed to them all and replied to them all. I feel convinced that none of the savages, either red-skinned or copper-coloured, whom he had met in his travels, made him so uncomfortable as his reception at Moscow.

When he reached the hall at last and could sit down, he had to get up again. Our Visitor, Pisarev, thought it necessary to set forth in a few powerful Russian sentences the merits of His Excellency, the famous traveller; and then a poet, Glinka, in a deep hoarse voice recited a poem of his own which began—

"Humboldt, Prometheus of our time!"

What Humboldt wanted was to discuss his observations on the magnetic pole, and to compare the meteorological records he had taken in the Ural Mountains with those at Moscow; but the Rector preferred to show him some relic plaited out of the hair of Peter the Great. It was

with difficulty that Ehrenberg and Rose found an opportunity to tell him something of their discoveries.*

Even in unofficial circles, we don't do things much
better in Russia. Liszt was received in just the same way
by Moscow society ten years ago. There was folly enough
over him in Germany; but that was quite a different
thing—old-maidish gush and sentimentality and strewing
of roses, whereas in Russia there was servile acknowledgement of power and prim formality of a strictly official type. And Liszt's reputation as a Don Juan was mixed
up in an unpleasant way with it all: the ladies swarmed
around him, just as boys in out-of-the-way places swarm
round a traveller when he is changing horses and stare
at him or his carriage or his hat. Every ear was turned to
Liszt, every word and every reply was addressed to him
alone. I remember one evening when Homyakóv, in his
disgust with the company, appealed to me to start a dispute with him on any subject, that Liszt might discover
there were some people in the room who were not exclusively taken up with him. I can only say one thing to
console our ladies—that Englishwomen treated other ce-
lebrities, Kossuth, Garibaldi, and others, in just the same
way, crowding and jostling round the object of worship;

*Odd views were taken in Russia of Humboldt's travels. There was
a Cossack at Perm who liked describing how he escorted "a mad
Prussian prince called Gumplot." When asked what Gumplot did, he
said: "He was quite childish, picking grasses and gazing at sand. At
one place he told me through the interpreter to wade into a pool and
fish out what was at the bottom—there was nothing but what there
is at the bottom of every pool. Then he asked if the water at the
bottom was very cold. You won't catch me that way, thought I; so I
saluted and said, 'The rules of the service require it, Your Excellency.'"
[Author's Note.]

but woe to him who seeks to learn good manners from Englishwomen, or their husbands!

§16

OUR other distinguished visitor was also "a Prometheus of our time" in a certain sense; only, instead of stealing fire from Zeus, he stole it from mankind. This Prometheus, whose fame was sung, not by Glinka but by Púshkin himself in his *Epistle to Lucullus,* was Uvárov, the Minister of Education.* He astonished us by the number of languages he spoke and by the amount of his miscellaneous knowledge; he was a real shopman behind the counter of learning and kept samples of all the sciences, the elements chiefly, in his head. In Alexander's reign, he wrote reform pamphlets in French; then he had a German correspondence with Goethe on Greek matters. After becoming minister, he discoursed on Slavonic poetry of the fourth century, which made Kochenovsky remark to him that our ancestors were much busier in fighting bears than in hymning their gods and kings. As a kind of patent of nobility, he carried about in his pocket a letter from Goethe, in which Goethe paid him a very odd compliment: "You have no reason to apologise for your style: you have succeeded in doing what I could never do—forgetting German grammar."

This highly placed Admirable Crichton invented a new

---

*Serghéi Uvárov (1786-1855) was both Minister of Education and President of the Academy of Sciences. He used his power to tighten the censorship and suppressed *The Moscow Telegraph,* edited by Polevoi, which was the most independent of Russian journals; in this way he "stole fire from mankind." The reference to Púshkin is malicious: what Púshkin wrote about Uvárov in that poem was the reverse of complimentary. "Lucullus" was Count Sheremétyev and Uvárov was his heir.

kind of torture for our benefit. He gave directions that the best students should be selected, and that each of them should deliver a lecture in his own department of study, in place of the professor. The Deans of course chose the readiest of the students to perform.

These lectures went on for a whole week. The students had to get up all the branches of their subject, and the Dean drew a lot to determine the theme and the speaker. Uvárov invited all the rank and fashion of Moscow. Ecclesiastics and judges, the Governor of the city, and the old poet, Dmitriev—everyone was there.

§17

It fell to me to lecture on a mineralogical subject. Our professor, Lovetski,—he is now dead,—was a tall man with a clumsy figure and awkward gait, a large mouth and a large and entirely expressionless face. He wore a pea-green overcoat, adorned in the fashion of the First Consulate with a variety of capes; and while taking off this garment in the passage outside the lecture-room, he always began in an even and wooden voice which seemed to suit his subject, "In our last lecture we dealt fully with silicon dioxide"—then he took his seat and went on, "We proceed to aluminium . . . " In the definition of each metal, he followed an absolutely identical formula, so that some of them had to be defined by negatives, in this way: "Crystallisation: this metal does not crystallise"; "Use: this metal is never used"; "Service to man: this substance does nothing but harm to the human organism."

Still he did not avoid poetical illustration or edifying comment: whenever he showed us counterfeit gems and explained how they were made, he never failed to add,

"Gentlemen, this is dishonest." When alluding to farm-ing, he found *moral* worth in a cock that was fond of crowing and courting his hens, and blue blood in a ram if he had "bald knees." He had also a touching story about some flies which ran over the bark of a tree on a fine summer day till they were caught in the resin which had turned to amber; and this always ended with the words, "Gentlemen, these things are an allegory."

When I was summoned forth by the Dean, the audience was somewhat weary: two lectures on mathematics had had a depressing effect upon hearers who did not under-stand a word of the subject. Uvárov called for something more lively and a speaker with a ready tongue; and I was chosen to meet the situation.

While I was mounting to the desk, Lovetski sat there motionless, with his hands on his knees, looking like Memnon or Osiris. I whispered to him, "Never fear! I shan't give you away!"—and the worthy professor, with-out looking at me and hardly moving his lips, formed the words, "Boast not, when girding on thine armour!" I nearly laughed aloud, but when I looked in front of me, the whole room swam before my eyes, I felt that I was losing colour, and my mouth grew strangely dry. It was my first speech in public; the lecture-room was full of students, who relied upon me; at a table just below me sat the dignitaries and all the professors of our faculty. I took the paper and read out in a voice that sounded strange to myself, "Crystallisation: its conditions, laws, and forms."

While I was considering how I should begin, a consol-ing thought came into my head—that, if I did make mis-takes, the professors might perhaps detect them but would certainly not speak of them, while the rest of the audience would be quite in the dark, and the students would be quite satisfied if I managed not to break down; for I was a favourite with them. So I delivered my lecture and ended up with some speculative observations, addressing myself throughout to my companions and not to the minister. Students and professors shook me by the hand and expressed their thanks. Uvárov presented me to Prince Golitsyn, who said something, but I could not understand it, as the Prince used vowels only and no consonants. Uvárov promised me a book as a souvenir of the occasion; but I never got it.

My second and third appearances on a public stage were very different. In 1836 I took a chief part in amateur theatricals before the Governor and *beau monde* of Vyatka. Though we had been rehearsing for a month, my heart beat furiously and my hands trembled; when the overture came to an end, dead silence followed, and the curtain slowly rose with an awful twitching. The leading lady and I were in the green-room; and she was so sorry for me, or so afraid that I would break down and spoil the piece, that she administered a full bumper of champagne; but even this was hardly able to restore me to my senses.

This preliminary experience saved me from all nervous symptoms and self-consciousness when I made my third public appearance, which was at a Polish meeting held in London and presided over by the ex-Minister Ledru-Rollin.

§18

But perhaps I have dwelt long enough on College memories. I fear it may be a sign of senility to linger so long over them; and I shall only add a few details on the cholera of 1831.

The word "cholera," so familiar now in Europe and especially in Russia, was heard in the North for the first time in 1831. The dread contagion caused general terror, as it spread up the course of the Volga towards Moscow. Exaggerated rumours filled men's minds with horror. The epidemic took a capricious course, sometimes pausing, and sometimes passing over a district; it was believed that it had gone round Moscow, when suddenly the terrible tidings spread like wildfire, "The cholera is in the city."

A student who was taken ill one morning died in the University hospital on the evening of the next day. We went to look at the body. It was emaciated as if by long illness, the eyes were sunk in their sockets, and the features were distorted. Near him lay his attendant who had caught the infection during the night.

We were told that the University was to be closed. The notice was read in our faculty by Denísov, the professor of technology; he was depressed and perhaps frightened; before the end of the next day he too was dead.

All the students collected in the great court of the University. There was something touching in that crowd of young men forced asunder by the fear of infection. All were excited, and there were many pale faces; many were thinking of relations and friends; we said good-bye to the scholars who were to remain behind in quarantine, and dispersed in small groups to our homes. There we were greeted by the stench of chloride of lime and vinegar, and submitted to a diet which, of itself and without chloride or cholera, was quite enough to cause an illness.

It is a strange fact, but this sad time is more solemn than sad in my recollection of it.

The aspect of Moscow was entirely changed. The city was animated beyond its wont by the feeling of a common life. There were fewer carriages in the streets; crowds stood at the crossings and spoke darkly of poisoners; ambulances, conveying the sick, moved along at a footpace, escorted by police; and people turned aside as the hearses went by. Bulletins were published twice a day. The city was surrounded by troops, and an unfortunate beadle was shot while trying to cross the river. These measures caused much excitement, and fear of disease conquered the fear of authority; the inhabitants protested; and meanwhile tidings followed tidings—that so-and-so had sickened and so-and-so was dead.

The Archbishop, Philaret, ordained a Day of Humiliation. At the same hour on the same day all the priests went in procession with banners round their parishes, while the terrified inhabitants came out of their houses and fell on their knees, weeping and praying that their sins might be forgiven; even the priests were moved by the solemnity of the occasion. Some of them marched to the Kremlin, where the Archbishop, surrounded by clerical dignitaries, knelt in the open air and prayed, "May this cup pass from us!"

§19

PHILARET carried on a kind of opposition to Government, but why he did so I never could understand, unless it was to assert his own personality. He was an able and learned man, and a perfect master of the Russian language, which he spoke with a happy flavouring of Church-

Slavonic; but all this gave him no right to be in opposition. The people disliked him and called him a freemason, because he was intimate with Prince A. N. Golitsyn and preached in Petersburg just when the Bible Society was in vogue there. The Synod forbade the use of his Catechism in the schools. But the clergy who were under his rule trembled before him.

Philaret knew how to put down the secular powers with great ingenuity and dexterity; his sermons breathed that vague Christian socialism to which Lacordaire and other far-sighted Roman Catholics owed their reputation. From the height of his episcopal pulpit, Philaret used to say that no man could be legally the mere instrument of another, and that an exchange of services was the only proper relation between human beings; and this he said in a country where half the population were slaves.

Speaking to a body of convicts who were leaving Moscow on their way to Siberia, he said, "Human law has condemned you and driven you forth; but the Church will not let you go; she wishes to address you once more, to pray for you once again, and to bless you before your journey." Then, to comfort them, he added, "You, by your punishment, have got rid of your past, and a new life awaits you; but, among others" (and there were probably no others present except officials) "there are even greater sinners than you"; and he spoke of the penitent thief at the Crucifixion as an example for them.

But Philaret's sermon on the Day of Humiliation left all his previous utterances in the shade. He took as his text the passage where the angel suffered David to choose between war, famine, and pestilence as the punishment for his sin, and David chose the pestilence. The Tsar came to Moscow in a furious rage, and sent a high Court official to reprove the Archbishop; he even threatened to send him to Georgia to exercise his functions there. Philaret submitted meekly to the reproof; and then he sent round a new rescript to all the churches, explaining that it was a mistake to suppose that he had meant David to represent the Tsar: we ourselves were David, sunk like him in the mire of sin. In this way, the meaning of the original sermon was explained even to those who had failed to grasp its meaning at first.

Such was the way in which the Archbishop of Moscow played at opposition.

The Day of Humiliation was as ineffectual as the chloride of lime; and the plague grew worse and worse.

§20

I WITNESSED the whole course of the frightful epidemic of cholera at Paris in 1849. The violence of the disease was increased by the hot June weather; the poor died like flies; of the middle classes some fled to the country, and the rest locked themselves up in their houses. The Government, exclusively occupied by the struggle against the revolutionists, never thought of taking any active steps. Large private subscriptions failed to meet the requirements of the situation. The working class were left to take their chance; the hospitals could not supply all the beds, nor the police all the coffins, that were required; and corpses remained for forty-eight hours in living-rooms crowded with a number of different families.

In Moscow things were different.

Prince Dmitri Golitsyn was Governor of the city, not a strong man, but honourable, cultured, and highly respected. He gave the line to Moscow society, and everything was arranged by the citizens themselves without much interference on the part of Government. A committee was formed of the chief residents—rich landowners and merchants. Each member of the committee undertook one of the districts of Moscow. In a few days twenty hospitals were opened, all supported by voluntary contributions and not costing one penny to the State. The merchants supplied all that was required in the hospitals —bedding, linen, and warm clothing, and this last might be kept by convalescents. Young people acted gratuitously as inspectors in the hospitals, to see that the free-will offerings of the merchants were not stolen by the orderlies and nurses.

The University too played its part. The whole medical school, both teachers and students, put themselves at the disposal of the committee. They were distributed among the hospitals and worked there incessantly until the infection was over. For three or four months these young men did fine work in the hospitals, as assistant physicians, dressers, nurses, or clerks, and all this for no pecuniary reward and at a time when the fear of infection was intense. I remember one Little Russian student who was trying to get an *exeat* on urgent private affairs when the cholera began. It was difficult to get an *exeat* in term-time, but he got it at last and was just preparing to start when the other students were entering the hospitals. He put his *exeat* in his pocket and joined them. When he left the hospital, his leave of absence had long expired, and he was the first to laugh heartily at the form his trip had taken.

Moscow has the appearance of being sleepy and slack,

of caring for nothing but gossip and piety and fashion-
able intelligence; but she invariably wakes up and rises
to the occasion when the hour strikes and when the
thunder-storm breaks over Russia.

She was wedded to Russia in blood in 1612, and she
was welded to Russia in the fire of 1812.

She bent her head before Peter, because he was the
wild beast whose paw contained the whole future of
Russia.

Frowning and pouting out his lips, Napoleon sat outside
the gates, waiting for the keys of Moscow; impatiently
he pulled at his bridle and twitched his glove. He was
not accustomed to be alone when he entered foreign
capitals.

"But other thoughts had Moscow mine," as Púshkin
wrote, and she set fire to herself.

The cholera appeared, and once again the people's
capital showed itself full of feeling and power!

§21

IN August of 1830 we went to stay at Vasílevskoë, and
broke our journey as usual at Perkhushkov, where our
house looked like a castle in a novel of Mrs. Radcliffe's.
After taking a meal and feeding the horses, we were preparing to resume our journey, and Bakai, with a towel
round his waist, was just calling out to the coachman,
"All right!" when a mounted messenger signed to us to
stop. This was a groom belonging to my uncle, the Senator. Covered with dust and sweat, he jumped off his horse
and delivered a packet to my father. The packet contained the *Revolution of July*! Two pages of the *Journal
des Débats,* which he brought with him as well as a letter,

I read over a hundred times till I knew them by heart; and for the first time I found the country tiresome.

It was a glorious time and events moved quickly. The spare figure of Charles X had hardly disappeared into the fogs of Holyrood, when Belgium burst into flame and the throne of the citizen-king began to totter. The revolutionary spirit began to work in men's mouths and in literature: novels, plays, and poetry entered the arena and preached the good cause.

We knew nothing then of the theatrical element which is part of all revolutionary movements in France, and we believed sincerely in all we heard.

If anyone wishes to know how powerfully the news of the July revolution worked on the rising generation, let him read what Heine wrote, when he heard in Heligoland that "the great Pan, the pagan god, was dead." There is no sham enthusiasm there: Heine at thirty was just as much carried away, just as childishly excited, as we were at eighteen.

We followed every word and every incident with close attention—bold questions and sharp replies, General Lafayette and General Lamarque. Not only did we know all about the chief actors—on the radical side, of course —but we were warmly attached to them, and cherished their portraits, from Manuel and Benjamin Constant to Dupont de l'Eure and Armand Carrel.

§22

OUR special group consisted of five to begin with, and then we fell in with a sixth, Vadim Passek.

There was much that was new to us in Vadim. We five had all been brought up in very much the same way:

we knew no places but Moscow and the surrounding country; we had read the same books and taken lessons from the same teachers; we had been educated either at home or in the boarding-school connected with the University. But Vadim was born in Siberia, during his father's exile, and had suffered poverty and privation. His father was his teacher, and he was one of a large family, who grew up familiar with want but free from all other restraints. Siberia has a stamp of its own, quite unlike the stamp of provincial Russia; those who bear it have more health and more elasticity. Compared to Vadim we were tame. His courage was of a different kind, heroic and at times overbearing; the high distinction of suffering had developed in him a special kind of pride, but he had also a generous warmth of heart. He was bold, and even imprudent to excess; but a man born in Siberia and belonging to a family of exiles has this advantage over others, that Siberia has for him no terrors.

As soon as we met, Vadim rushed into our arms. Very soon we became intimate. It should be said that there was nothing of the nature of ceremony or prudent precaution in our little coterie of those days.

"Would you like to know Ketcher, of whom you have heard so much?" Vadim once asked me.

"Of course I should."

"Well, come at seven to-morrow evening, and don't be late; he will be at our house."

When I arrived, Vadim was out. A tall man with an expressive face was waiting for him and shot a glance, half good-natured and half formidable, at me from under his spectacles. I took up a book, and he followed my example.

"I say," he began, as he opened the book, "are you Herzen?"

And so conversation began and soon grew fast and furious. Ketcher soon interrupted me with no ceremony: "Excuse me! I should be obliged if you would address me as 'thou.'"

"By all means!" said I. And from that minute—perhaps it was the beginning of 1831—we were inseparable friends; and from that minute Ketcher's friendly laugh or fierce shout became a part of my life at all its stages.

The acquaintance with Vadim brought a new and gentler element into our camp.

As before, our chief meeting-place was Ogaryóv's house. His invalid father had gone to live in the country, and he lived alone on the ground-floor of their Moscow house, which was near the University and had a great attraction for us all. Ogaryóv had that magnetic power which forms the first point of crystallisation in any medley of disordered atoms, provided the necessary affinity exists. Though scattered in all directions, they become imperceptibly the heart of an organism. In his bright cheerful room with its red and gold wall-paper, amid the perpetual smell of tobacco and punch and other—I was going to say, eatables and drinkables, but now I remember that there was seldom anything to eat but cheese—we often spent the time from dark till dawn in heated argument and sometimes in noisy merriment. But, side by side with that hospitable students' room, there grew more and more dear to us another house, in which we learned—I might say, for the first time—respect for family life.

Vadim often deserted our discussions and went off home: when he had not seen his mother and sisters for some time, he became restless. To us our little club was the centre of the world, and we thought it strange that he should prefer the society of his family; were not we a family too?

Then he introduced us to his family. They had lately returned from Siberia; they were ruined, yet they bore that stamp of dignity which calamity engraves, not on every sufferer, but on those who have borne misfortune with courage.

§23

THEIR father was arrested in Paul's reign, having been informed against for revolutionary designs. He was thrown into prison at Schlüsselburg and then banished to Siberia. When Alexander restored thousands of his father's exiles, Passek was *forgotten*. He was a nephew of the Passek who became Governor of Poland, and might have claimed a share of the fortune which had now passed into other hands.

While detained at Schlüsselburg, Passek had married the daughter of an officer of the garrison. The young girl knew that exile would be his fate, but she was not deterred by that prospect. In Siberia they made a shift at first to get on, by selling their last belongings, but the pressure of poverty grew steadily worse and worse, and the process was hastened by their increasing family. Yet neither destitution nor manual toil, nor the absence of warm clothing and sometimes of daily food—nothing prevented them from rearing a whole family of lion-cubs, who inherited from their father his dauntless pride and self-confidence. He educated them by his example, and they were taught by their mother's self-sacrifice and bitter tears. The girls

were not inferior to the boys in heroic constancy. Why
shrink from using the right word?—they were a family
of heroes. No one would believe what they endured and
did for one another; and they held their heads high
through it all.

When they were in Siberia, the three sisters had at one
time a single pair of shoes between them; and they kept
it to walk out in, in order to hide their need from the
public eye.

At the beginning of the year 1826 Passek was permitted to return to Russia. It was winter weather, and
it was a terrible business for so large a family to travel
from Tobolsk without furs and without money; but exile
becomes most unbearable when it is over, and they were
longing to be gone. They contrived it somehow. The
foster-mother of one of the children, a peasant woman,
brought them her poor savings as a contribution, and
only asked that they would take her too; the post-boys
brought them as far as the Russian frontier for little payment or none at all; the children took turns in driving
or walking; and so they completed the long winter journey
from the Ural ridge to Moscow. Moscow was their dream
and their hope; and at Moscow they found starvation
waiting for them.

When the authorities pardoned Passek, they never
thought of restoring to him any part of his property. On
his arrival, worn out by exertions and privations, he fell
ill; and the family did not know where they were to get
to-morrow's dinner.

The father could bear no more; he died. The widow
and children got on as best they could from day to day.
The greater the need, the harder the sons worked; three

of them took their degree at the University with brilliant success. The two eldest, both excellent mathematicians, went to Petersburg; one served in the Navy and the other in the Engineers, and both contrived to give lessons in mathematics as well. They practised strict self-denial and sent home all the money they earned.

I have a vivid recollection of their old mother in her dark jacket and white cap. Her thin pale face was covered with wrinkles, and she looked much older than she was; the eyes alone still lived and revealed such a fund of gentleness and love, and such a past of anxiety and tears. She was in love with her children; they were wealth and distinction and youth to her; she used to read us their letters, and spoke of them with a sacred depth of feeling, while her feeble voice sometimes broke and trembled with unshed tears.

Sometimes there was a family gathering of them all at Moscow, and then the mother's joy was beyond description. When they sat down to their modest meal, she would move round the table and arrange things, looking with such joy and pride at her young ones, and sometimes mutely appealing to me for sympathy and admiration. They were really, in point of good looks also, an exceptional family. At such times I longed to kiss her hand and fall upon her neck.

She was happy then; it would have been well if she had died at one of those meetings.

In the space of two years she lost her three eldest sons. Diomid died gloriously, honoured by the foe, in the arms of victory, though he laid down his life in a quarrel that was not his. As a young general, he was killed in action against Circassians. But laurels cannot mend a mother's broken heart. The other two were less fortunate: the weight of Russian life lay heavy upon them and crushed them at last.

Alas! poor mother!

§24

VADIM died in February of 1843. I was present at his death; it was the first time I had witnessed the death of one dear to me, and I realised the unrelieved horror, the senseless irrationality, and the stupid injustice of the tragedy.

Ten years earlier Vadim had married my cousin Tatyana, and I was best man at the wedding. Family life and change of conditions parted us to some extent. He was happy in his quiet life, but outward circumstances were unfavourable and his enterprises were unsuccessful. Shortly before I and my friends were arrested, he went to Khárkov, where he had been promised a professor's chair in the University. This trip saved him from prison; but his name had come to the ears of the police, and the University refused to appoint him. An official admitted to him that a document had been received forbidding his appointment, because the Government knew that he was connected with *disaffected persons*.

So Vadim remained without employment, *i.e.* without bread to eat. That was his form of punishment.

We were banished. Relations with us were dangerous. Black years of want began for him; for seven years he struggled to earn a bare living, suffering from contact with rough manners and hard hearts, and unable to exchange messages with his friends in their distant place of exile; and the struggle proved too hard even for his powerful frame.

"One day we had spent all our money to the last penny;"—his wife told me this story later—"I had tried to borrow ten *roubles* the day before, but I failed, because I had borrowed already in every possible quarter. The shops refused to give us any further credit, and our one thought was—what will the children get to eat to-morrow? Vadim sat in sorrow near the window; then he got up, took his hat, and said he meant to take a walk. I saw that he was very low, and I felt frightened; and yet I was glad that he should have something to divert his thoughts. When he went out, I threw myself upon the bed and wept bitter tears, and then I began to think what was to be done. Everything of any value, rings and spoons, had been pawned long ago. I could see no re-source but one—to go to our relations and beg their cold charity, their bitter alms. Meanwhile Vadim was walking aimlessly about the streets till he came to the Petrovsky Boulevard. As he passed a bookseller's shop there, it occurred to him to ask whether a single copy of his book had been sold. Five days earlier he had enquired, with no result; and he was full of apprehension when he en-tered the shop. 'Very glad to see you,' said the man; 'I have heard from my Petersburg agent that he has sold 300 *roubles*' worth of your books. Would you like pay-ment now?' And the man there and then counted out fifteen gold pieces. Vadim's joy was so great that he was bewildered. He hurried to the nearest eating-house, bought food, fruit, and a bottle of wine, hired a cab, and drove home in triumph. I was adding water to some remnants of soup, to feed the children, and I meant to give him a little, pretending that I had eaten something already; and then suddenly he came in, carrying his parcel and the bottle of wine, and looking as happy and cheerful as in times past."

Then she burst out sobbing and could not utter another word.

After my return from banishment I saw him occasionally in Petersburg and found him much changed. He kept his old convictions, but he kept them as a warrior, feeling that he is mortally wounded, still grasps his sword. He was exhausted and depressed, and looked forward without hope. And such I found him in Moscow in 1842; his circumstances were improved to some extent, and his works were appreciated, but all this came too late.

Then consumption—that terrible disease which I was fated to watch once again*—declared itself in the autumn of 1842, and Vadim wasted away.

A month before he died, I noticed with horror that his powers of mind were failing and growing dim like a flickering candle; the atmosphere of the sick-room grew darker steadily. Soon it cost him a laborious effort to find words for incoherent speech, and he confused words of similar sound; at last, he hardly spoke except to express anxiety about his medicines and the hours for taking them.

At three o'clock one February morning, his wife sent for me. The sick man was in distress and asking for me. I went up to his bed and touched his hand; his wife named me, and he looked long and wearily at me but failed to recognise me and shut his eyes again. Then the children were brought, and he looked at them, but I do not think he recognised them either. His breathing became more difficult; there were intervals of quiet fol-

* Herzen's wife died of consumption at Nice in 1852.

lowed by long gasps. Just then the bells of a neighbouring church rang out; Vadim listened and then said,
"That's for early Mass," and those were his last words.
His wife sobbed on her knees beside the body; a young
college friend, who had shown them much kindness during the last illness, moved about the room, pushing away
the table with the medicine-bottles and drawing up the
blinds. I left the house; it was frosty and bright out of
doors, and the rising sun glittered on the snow, just as
if all was right with the world. My errand was to order
a coffin.

When I returned, the silence of death reigned in the
little house. In accordance with Russian custom, the dead
man was lying on the table in the drawing-room, and an
artist-friend, seated at a little distance, was drawing,
through his tears, a portrait of the lifeless features. Near
the body stood a tall female figure, with folded arms and
an expression of infinite sorrow; she stood silent, and no
sculptor could have carved a nobler or more impressive
embodiment of grief. She was not young, but still retained
the traces of a severe and stately beauty; wrapped up in a
long mantle of black velvet trimmed with ermine, she
stood there like a statue.

I remained standing at the door.

The silence went on for several minutes; but suddenly
she bent forward, pressed a kiss on the cold forehead,
and said, "Good-bye, good-bye, dear Vadim"; then she
walked with a steady step into an inner room. The painter
went on with his work; he nodded to me, and I sat down
by the window in silence; we felt no wish to talk.

The lady was Mme. Chertkóv, the sister of Count
Zachar Chernyshev, one of the exiled Decembrists.

Melchizedek, the Abbot of St. Peter's Monastery, himself offered that Vadim should be buried within the convent walls. He knew Vadim and respected him for his
researches into the history of Moscow. He had once been
a simple carpenter and a furious dissenter; but he was
converted to Orthodoxy, became a monk, and rose to be
Prior and finally Abbot. Yet he always kept the broad
shoulders, fine ruddy face, and simple heart of the carpenter.

When the body appeared before the monastery gates,
Melchizedek and all his monks came out to meet the
martyr's poor coffin, and escorted it to the grave, singing
the funeral music. Not far from his grave rests the dust
of another who was dear to us, Venevitínov, and his epi-
taph runs—

"He knew life well but left it soon"—

and Vadim knew it as well.

But Fortune was not content even with his death. Why
indeed did his mother live to be so old? When the period
of exile came to an end, and when she had seen her children in their youth and beauty and fine promise for the
future, life had nothing more to give her. Any man who
values happiness should seek to die young. Permanent
happiness is no more possible than ice that will not melt.

Vadim's eldest brother died a few months after Diomid,
the soldier, fell in Circassia: a neglected cold proved fatal
to his enfeebled constitution. He was the oldest of the
family, and he was hardly forty.

Long and black are the shadows thrown back by these
three coffins of three dear friends; the last months of my

youth are veiled from me by funeral crape and the incense of thuribles.

.   .   .   .

§25

AFTER dragging on for a year, the affair of Sungurov and our other friends who had been arrested came to an end. The charge, as in our case and in that of Petrashev's group, was that they *intended* to form a secret society and had held treasonable conversations. Their punishment was to be sent to Orenburg, to join the colours.

And now our turn came. Our names were already entered on the black list of the secret police. The cat dealt her first playful blow at the mouse in the following way.

When our friends, after their sentence, were starting on their long march to Orenburg without warm enough clothing, Ogaryóv and Kiréevski each started a subscription for them, as none of them had money. Kiréevski took the proceeds to Staal, the commandant, a very kind-hearted old soldier, of whom more will be said hereafter. Staal promised to transmit the money, and then said:

"What papers are those you have?"

"The subscribers' names," said Kiréevski, "and a list of subscriptions."

"Do you trust me to pay over the money?" the old man asked.

"Of course I do."

"And I fancy the subscribers will trust you. Well, then, what's the use of our keeping these names?" and Staal threw the list into the fire; and I need hardly say that was a very kind action.

Ogaryóv took the money he had collected to the prison

himself, and no difficulty was raised. But the prisoners
took it into their heads to send a message of thanks from
Orenburg, and asked some functionary who was travelling to Moscow to take a letter which they dared not
trust to the post. The functionary did not fail to profit
by such an excellent opportunity of proving his loyalty
to his country: he laid the letter before the head of the
police at Moscow.

Volkov, who had held this office, had gone mad, his
delusion being that the Poles wished to elect him as their
king, and Lisovski had succeeded to the position. Lisovski
was a Pole himself; he was not a cruel man or a bad man;
but he had spent his fortune, thanks to gambling and a
French actress, and, like a true philosopher, he preferred
the situation of chief of the police at Moscow to a situation in the slums of that city.

He summoned Ogaryóv, Ketcher, Satin, Vadim, Obolenski, and others, and charged them with having relations
with political prisoners. Ogaryóv replied that he had written to none of them and had received no letter; if one of
them had written to him, he could not be responsible for
that. Lisovski then said:

"You raised a subscription for them, which is even
worse. The Tsar is merciful enough to pardon you for
once; but I warn you, gentlemen, that you will be strictly
watched, and you had better be careful."

He looked meaningly at all the party and his eye fell on
Ketcher, who was older and taller than the rest, and was
lifting his eyebrows and looking rather fierce. He added,
"I wonder that you, Sir, considering your position in
society, are not ashamed to behave so." Ketcher was only
a country doctor; but, from Lisovski's words, he might

have been Chancellor of the imperial Orders of Knight-hood.

I was not summoned; it is probable that the letter did not contain my name.

This threat we regarded as a promotion, a consecra-tion, a powerful incentive. Lisovski's warning was oil on the flames; and, as if to make it easier for the police, we all took to velvet caps of the Karl Sand* fashion and tri-color neckties.

Colonel Shubinski now climbed up with the velvet tread of a cat into Lisovski's place, and soon marked his predecessor's weakness in dealing with us: our business was to serve as one of the steps in his official career, and we did what was wanted.

§26

BUT first I shall add a few words about the fate of Sun-gurov and his companions.

Kolreif returned to Moscow, where he died in the arms of his grief-stricken father.

Kostenetski and Antonovitch both distinguished them-selves as private soldiers in the Caucasus and received commissions.

The fate of the unhappy Sungurov was far more tragic. On reaching the first stage of their journey from Moscow, he asked permission of the officer, a young man of twenty, to leave the stifling cottage crammed with con-victs for the fresh air. The officer walked out with him. Sungurov watched for an opportunity, sprang off the road, and disappeared. He must have known the district well, for he eluded the officer; but the police got upon

*The German student who shot Kotzebue.

his tracks next day. When he saw that escape was impossible, he cut his throat. He was carried back to Moscow, unconscious and bleeding profusely. The unlucky officer was deprived of his commission.

Sungurov did not die. He was tried again, not for a political offence but for trying to escape. Half his head was shaved; and to this outward ignominy the court added a *single stroke* of the whip to be inflicted inside the prison. Whether this was actually carried out, I do not know. He was then sent off to work in the mines at Nerchinsk.

His name came to my ears just once again and then vanished for ever.

When I was at Vyatka, I happened to meet in the street a young doctor, a college friend; and we spoke about old times and common acquaintances.

"Good God!" said the doctor, "do you know whom I saw on my way here? I was waiting at a post-house for fresh horses. The weather was abominable. An officer in command of a party of convicts came in to warm himself. We began to talk; and hearing that I was a doctor, he asked me to take a look at one of the prisoners on march; I could tell him whether the man was shamming or really very bad. I consented: of course, I intended in any case to back up the convict. There were eighteen convicts, as well as women and children, in one smallish barrack-room; some of the men had their heads shaved, and some had not; but they were all fettered. They opened out to let the officer pass; and we saw a figure wrapped in a convict's overcoat and lying on some straw in a corner of the dirty room.

" 'There's your patient,' said the officer. No fibs on my

part were necessary: the man was in a high fever. He was a horrible sight: he was thin and worn out by prison and marching; half his head was shaved, and his beard was growing; he was rolling his eyes in delirium and constantly calling for water.

" 'Are you feeling bad, my man?' I said to the patient, and then I told the officer that he was quite unable to march.

"The man fixed his eyes on me and then muttered, 'Is that you?' He addressed me by name and added, in a voice that went through me like a knife, 'You won't know me again.'

" 'Excuse me,' I said; 'I have forgotten your name,' and I took his hot dry hand in my own.

" 'I am Sungurov,' he answered. Poor fellow!" repeated the doctor, shaking his head.

"Well, did they leave him there?" I asked.

"No: a cart was got for him."

After writing the preceding narrative, I learned that Sungurov died at Nerchinsk.

CHAPTER VII

End of College Life—The "Schiller" Stage—Youth—The Artistic Life—Saint-Simonianism and N. Polevói—Polezháev.

§1

THE storm had not yet burst over our heads when my college course came to an end. My experience of the final stage of education was exactly like that of everyone else—constant worry and sleepless nights for the sake of a painful and useless test of the memory, superficial cramming, and all real interest in learning crowded out by the nightmare of examination. I wrote an astronomical dissertation for the gold medal, and the silver medal was awarded me. I am sure that I should not be able now to understand what I wrote then, and that it was worth its weight—*in silver*.

I have sometimes dreamt since that I was a student preparing for examination; I thought with horror how much I had forgotten and how certain I was to fail, and then I woke up, to rejoice with all my heart that the sea and much else lay between me and my University, and that no one would ever examine me again or venture to place me at the bottom of the list. My professors would really be astonished, if they could discover how much I have gone backward in the interval.

When the examinations were over, the professors shut themselves up to count the marks, and we walked up and down the passage and the vestibule, the prey of hopes and fears. Whenever anyone left the meeting, we rushed to him, eager to learn our fate; but the decision took a long time. At last Heiman came out and said to me, "I congratulate you; you have passed." "Who else? who else?" I asked; and some names were mentioned. I felt both sad and pleased. As I walked out of the college gates, I felt that I was leaving the place otherwise than yesterday or ever before, and becoming a stranger to that great family party in which I had spent four years of youth and happiness. On the other hand, I was pleased by the feeling that I was now admittedly grown up, and also—I may as well confess it—by the fact that I had got my degree at the first time of asking.

I owe so much to my *Alma Mater* and I continued so long after my degree to live her life and near her, that I cannot recall the place without love and reverence. She will not accuse me of ingratitude. In this case at least it is easy to be grateful; for gratitude is inseparable from love and bright memories of youthful development. Writing in a distant foreign land, I send her my blessing!

§2

THE year which we spent after leaving College formed a triumphant conclusion to the first period of our youth. It was one long festival of friendship, of high spirits, of inspiration and exchange of ideas.

We were a small group of college friends who kept together after our course was over, and continued to share the same views and the same ideals. Not one of us thought of his future career or financial position. I should not praise this attitude in grown-up people, but I value it highly in a young man. Except where it is dried up by the corrupting influence of vulgar respectability, youth is everywhere unpractical, and is especially bound to be so in a young country which has many ideals and has realised few of them. Besides, the unpractical sphere is not always a fool's paradise: every aspiration for the future involves some degree of imagination; and, but for unpractical people, practical life would never get beyond a tiresome repetition of the old routine.

Enthusiasm of some kind is a better safeguard against real degradation than any sermon. I can remember youthful follies, when high spirits carried us sometimes into excesses; but I do not remember a single disgraceful incident among our set, nothing that a man need be really ashamed of or seek to forget and cover up. Bad things are done in secret; and there was nothing secret in our way of life. Half our thoughts—more than half—were not directed towards that region where idle sensuality and morbid selfishness are concentrated on impure designs and make vice thrice as vicious.

§3

I HAVE a sincere pity for any nation where old heads grow on young shoulders; youth is a matter, not only of years, but of temperament. The German student, in the height of his eccentricity, is a hundred times better than the young Frenchman or Englishman with his dull grown-up airs; as to American boys who are men at fifteen—I find them simply repulsive.

In old France the young nobles were really young and fine; and later, such men as Saint Just and Hoche, Marceau and Desmoulins, heroic children reared on Rousseau's dark gospel, were young too, in the true sense of the word. The Revolution was the work of young men: neither Danton nor Robespierre, nor Louis XVI himself survived his thirty-fifth year. Under Napoleon, the young men all became subalterns; the Restoration, the "resurrection of old age," had no use for young men; and everybody became grown-up, business-like, and dull.

The last really young Frenchmen were the followers of Saint Simon.* A few exceptions only prove the fact that their young men have no liveliness or poetry in their disposition. Escousse and Lebras blew their brains out, just because they were young men in a society where all were old. Others struggled like fish jerked out of the water upon a muddy bank, till some of them got caught on the barricades and others on the Jesuits' hook.

Still youth must assert itself somehow, and therefore most young Frenchmen go through an "artistic" period: that is, those who have no money spend their time in humble cafés of the Latin quarter with humble grisettes, and those who have money resort to large cafés and more expensive ladies. They have no "Schiller" stage; but they have what may be called a "Paul de Kock" stage, which soon consumes in poor enough fashion all the strength and vigour of youth, and turns out a man quite fit to be a commercial traveller. The "artistic" stage leaves at the

*Claude Henri, Comte de Saint Simon (1760-1825), founded at Paris a society which was called by his name. His views were socialistic.

bottom of the soul one passion only—the thirst for money, which excludes all other interests and determines all the rest of life; these practical men laugh at abstract questions and despise women—this is the result of repeated conquests over those whose profession it is to be defeated. Most young men, when going through this stage, find a guide and philosopher in some hoary sinner, an extinct celebrity who lives by sponging on his young friends— an actor who has lost his voice, or an artist whose hand has begun to shake. Telemachus imitates his Mentor's pronunciation and his drinks, and especially his contempt for social problems and profound knowledge of gastronomy.

In England this stage takes a different form. There young men go through a stormy period of amiable eccentricity, which consists in silly practical jokes, absurd extravagance, heavy pleasantries, systematic but carefully concealed profligacy, and useless expeditions to the ends of the earth. Then there are horses, dogs, races, dull dinners; next comes the wife with an incredible number of fat, red-cheeked babies, business in the City, the *Times*, parliament, and old port which finally clips the Englishman's wings.

We too did foolish things and were riotous at times, but the prevailing tone was different and the atmosphere purer. Folly and noise were never an object in themselves. We believed in our mission; and though we may have made mistakes, yet we respected ourselves and one another as the instruments of a common purpose.

§4

BUT what were these revels of ours like? It would suddenly occur to one of us that this was the fourth of December and that the sixth was St. Nicholas' Day. Many of us were named after the Saint, Ogaryóv himself and at least three more. "Well, who shall give a dinner on the day?" "I will—I will." "I'll give one on the seventh." "Pooh! what's the seventh? We must contribute and all give it together; and that will be a grand feed."

"All right. Where shall we meet?"

"So-and-so is ill. Clearly we must go to him."

Then followed plans and calculations which gave a surprising amount of occupation to both hosts and guests at the coming banquet. One Nikolai went off to a restaurant to order the supper, another elsewhere to order cheese and savouries; our wine invariably came from the famous shop of Deprez. We were no connoisseurs and never soared above champagne; indeed, our youthful palates deserted even champagne in favour of a brand called *Rivesaltes Mousseux*. I once noticed this name on the card of a Paris restaurant, and called for a bottle of it, in memory of 1833. But alas! not even sentiment could induce me to swallow more than one glass.

The wine had to be tasted before the feast, and as the samples evidently gave great satisfaction, it was necessary to send more than one mission for this purpose.

§5

In this connexion I cannot refrain from recording something that happened to our friend Sokolovski. He could never keep money and spent at once whatever he got. A year before his arrest, he paid a visit to Moscow. As he had been successful in selling the manuscript of a poem, he determined to give a dinner and to ask not only us but such bigwigs as Polevói, Maximovitch, and others. On the day before, he went out with Polezháev, who was in Moscow with his regiment, to make his purchases; he bought all kinds of needless things, cups and even a *samovár*, and finally wine and eatables, such as stuffed turkeys, patties, and so on. Five of us went that evening to his rooms, and he proposed to open a single bottle for our benefit. A second followed, and at the end of the evening, or rather, at dawn of the next day, it appeared that the wine was all drunk and that Sokolovski had no more money. After paying some small debts, he had spent all his money on the dinner. He was much distressed, but, after long reflexion, plucked up courage and wrote to all the bigwigs that he was seriously ill and must put off his party.

§6

FOR our "feast of the four birthdays" I wrote out a regular programme, which was honoured by the special attention of Golitsyn, one of the Commissioners at our trial, who asked me if the programme had been carried out exactly.

"*À la lettre!*" I replied. He shrugged his shoulders, as if his own life had been a succession of Good Fridays spent in a monastery.

Our suppers were generally followed by a lively discussion over a question of the first importance, which was this—how ought the punch to be made? Up to this point, the eating and drinking went on usually in perfect harmony, like a bill in parliament which is carried *nem. con.* But over the punch everyone had his own view; and the previous meal enlivened the discussion. Was the punch to be set on fire now, or to be set on fire later? How was it to be set on fire? Was champagne or sauterne to be used to put it out? Was the pineapple to be put in while it was still alight, or not?

"While it's burning, of course! Then all the flavour will pass into the punch."

"Nonsense! The pineapple floats and will get burnt. That will simply spoil it."

"That is all rubbish," cries Ketcher, high above the rest; "but I'll tell you what does matter—we must put out the candles."

When the candles were out, all faces looked blue in the flickering light of the punch. The room was not large, and the burning rum soon raised the temperature to a tropical height. All were thirsty, but the punch was not ready. But Joseph, a French waiter sent from the restaurant, rose to the occasion: he brewed a kind of antithesis to the punch—an iced drink compounded of various wines with a foundation of brandy; and as he poured in the French wine, he explained, like a true son of the *grande nation,* that the wine owed its excellence to having twice crossed the equator—*"Oui, oui, messieurs, deux fois l'équateur, messieurs!"*

Joseph's cup was as cold as the North Pole. When it was finished, there was no need of any further liquid; but Ketcher now called out, "Time to put out the punch!" He was stirring a fiery lake in a soup-tureen, while the last lumps of sugar hissed and bubbled as they melted.

In goes the champagne, and the flame turns red and careers over the surface of the punch, looking somehow angry and menacing.

Then a desperate shout: "My good man, are you mad?

The wax is dropping straight off the bottle into the punch!"

"Well, just you try yourself, in this heat, to hold the bottle so that the wax won't melt!"

"You should knock it off first, of course," continues the critic.

"The cups, the cups—have we enough to go round? How many are we—ten, twelve, fourteen? That's right."

"We've not got fourteen cups."

"Then the rest must take glasses."

"The glasses will crack."

"Not a bit of it, if you put the spoon in."

The candles are re-lit, the last little tongue of flame darts to the centre of the bowl, twirls round, and disappears.

And all admit that the punch is a success, a splendid success.

§7

NEXT day I awake with a headache, clearly due to the punch. That comes of mixing liquors. Punch is poison; I vow never to touch it in future.

My servant, Peter, comes in. "You came in last night, Sir, wearing someone else's hat, not so good a hat as your own."

"The deuce take my hat!"

"Perhaps I had better go where you dined last night and enquire?"

"Do you suppose, my good man, that one of the party went home bare-headed?"

"It can do no harm—just in case."

Now it dawns upon me that the hat is a pretext, and

that Peter has been invited to the scene of last night's revelry.

"All right, you can go. But first tell the cook to send me up some pickled cabbage."

"I suppose, Sir, the birthday party went off well last night?"

"I should rather think so! There never was such a party in all my time at College."

"I suppose you won't want me to go to the University with you to-day?"

I feel remorse and make no reply.

"Your papa asked me why you were not up yet. But I was a match for him. 'He has a headache,' I said, 'and complained when I called him; so I left the blinds down.' And your papa said I was right."

"For goodness sake, let me go to sleep! You wanted to go, so be off with you!"

"In a minute, Sir; I'll just order the cabbage first."

Heavy sleep again seals my eyelids, and I wake in two hours' time, feeling a good deal fresher. I wonder what my friends are doing. Ketcher and Ogaryóv were to spend the night where we dined. I must admit that the punch was very good; but its effect on the head is annoying. To drink it out of a tumbler is a mistake; I am quite determined in future to drink it always out of a *liqueur*-glass.

Meanwhile my father has read the papers and interviewed the cook as usual.

"Have you a headache to-day?" he asks.

"Yes, a bad one."

"Perhaps you've been working too hard."

But the way he asked the question showed he did not believe that.

"Oh, I forgot: you were dining with your friends last night, eh?"

"Yes, I was."

"A birthday party? And they treated you handsomely, I've no doubt. Did you have soup made with Madeira? That sort of thing is not to my taste. I know one of your young friends is too often at the bottle; but I can't imagine where he gets the taste from. His poor father used to give a dinner on his birthday, the twenty-ninth of June, and ask all his relations; but it was always a very modest, decent affair. But this modern fashion of champagne and sardines à l'huile—I don't like to see it. Your other friend, that unfortunate young Ogaryóv, is even worse. Here he is, left to himself in Moscow, with his pockets full of money. He is constantly sending his coachman, Jeremy, for wine; and the coachman has no objection, because the dealer gives him a present."

"Well, I did have lunch with Ogaryóv. But I don't think my headache can be due to that. I think I will take a turn in the open air; that always does me good."

"By all means, but I hope you will dine at home."

"Certainly; I shan't be long."

§8

BUT I must explain the allusion to Madeira in the soup. A year or more before the grand birthday party, I went out for a walk with Ogaryóv one day in Easter week, and, in order to escape dinner at home, I said that I had been invited to dine at their house by Ogaryóv's father.

My father did not care for my friends in general and

used to call them by wrong names, though he always made
the same mistake in addressing any of them; and Ogaryóv
was less of a favourite than any, both because he wore
his hair long and because he smoked without being asked
to do so. But on the other hand, my father could hardly
mutilate his own grandnephew's surname; and also
Ogaryóv's father, both by birth and fortune, belonged to
the select circle of people whom my father recognised.
Hence he was pleased to see me going often to their house,
but he would have been still better pleased if the house
had contained no son.

He thought it proper therefore for me to accept the
invitation. But Ogaryóv and I did not repair to his father's
respectable dining-room. We went first to Price's place
of entertainment. Price was an acrobat, whom I was delighted to meet later with his accomplished family in both
Geneva and London. He had a little daughter, whom we
admired greatly and had christened Mignon.* When we
had seen Mignon perform and decided to come back for
the evening performance, we went to dine at the best
restaurant in Moscow. I had one gold piece in my pocket,
and Ogaryóv had about the same sum. At that time we
had no experience in ordering dinners. After long con-
sultation we ordered fish-soup made with champagne, a
bottle of Rhine wine, and a tiny portion of game. The
result was that we paid a terrific bill and left the restaurant feeling exceedingly hungry. Then we went back to
see Mignon a second time.

When I was saying good-night to my father, he said,
"Surely you smell of wine."

*After the character in Goethe's *Wilhelm Meister*. The Prices were
evidently English.

"That is probably because there was Madeira in the soup at dinner," I replied.

"Madeira? That must be a notion of M. Ogaryóv's son-in-law; no one but a guardsman would think of such a thing."

And from that time until my banishment, whenever my father thought that I had been drinking wine and that my face was flushed, he invariably attributed it to Madeira in the soup I had taken.

§9

On the present occasion, I hurried off to the scene of our revelry and found Ogaryóv and Ketcher still there. The latter looked rather the worse for wear; he was finding fault with some of last night's arrangements and was severely critical. Ogaryóv was trying a hair of the dog that bit him, though there was little left to drink after the party, and that little was now diminished by the descent of my man Peter, who was by this time in full glory, singing a song and drumming on the kitchen table downstairs.

§10

When I recall those days, I cannot remember a single incident among our set such as might weigh upon a man's conscience and cause shame in recollection; and this is true of every one of the group without a single exception.

Of course, there were Platonic lovers among us, and disenchanted youths of sixteen. Vadim even wrote a play, in order to set forth the "terrible experience of a broken heart." The play began thus—*A garden, with a house in the distance; there are lights in the windows. The stage is empty. A storm is blowing. The garden gate clinks and bangs in the wind.*

"Are the garden and the gate your only *dramatis per-sonae*?" I asked him. He was rather offended. "What nonsense you talk!" he said; "it is no joking matter but an actual experience. But if you take it so, I won't read any more." But he did, none the less.

There were also love affairs which were by no means Platonic, but there were none of those low intrigues which ruin the woman concerned and debase the man; there were no "kept mistresses"; that disgusting phrase did not even exist. Cool, safe, prosaic profligacy of the bourgeois fashion, profligacy by contract, was unknown to our group.

If it is said that I approve of the worst form of profligacy, in which a woman sells herself for the occasion, I say that it is you, not I, who approve of it—not you in particular but people in general. That custom rests so securely on the present constitution of society that it needs no patronage of mine.

Our interest in general questions and our social ideals saved us; and a keen interest in scientific and artistic matters helped us too. These preoccupations had a purifying effect, just as lighted paper makes grease-spots vanish. I have kept some of Ogaryóv's letters written at that time; and they give a good idea of what was mostly in our minds. For example, he writes to me on June 7, 1833:

"I think we know one another well enough to speak frankly. You won't show my letter to anyone. Well, for some time past I have been so filled—crushed, I might say—with feelings and ideas, that I think—but 'think' is too weak: I have an indelible impression—that I was born to be a poet, whether writer of verse or composer of music, never mind which. I feel it impossible to part from this belief; I have a kind of intuition that I am a poet. Granting that I still write badly, still this inward fire and this abundance of feeling make me hope that some day I shall write decently—please excuse the triviality of the phrase. Tell me, my dear friend, whether I can believe in my vocation. Perhaps you know better than I do myself, and you will not be misled."

He writes again on August 18:

"So you answer that I am a poet, a true poet. Is it possible that you understand the full significance of your words? If you are right, my feelings do not deceive me, and the object and aspiration of my whole life is not a mere dream. Are you right, I wonder? I feel sure that I am not merely raving. No one knows me better than you do—of that I am sure. Yes! that high vocation is not mere raving, no mere illusion; it is too high for deception, it is real, I live by virtue of it and cannot imagine a different life for myself. If only I could compose, what a symphony would take wing from my brain just now! First a majestic *adagio*; but it has not power to express all; I need a *presto,* a wild stormy *presto. Adagio* and *presto* are the two extremes. A fig for your *andante* and *allegro moderato*! They are mere mediocrities who can only lisp, incapable alike of strong speech or strong feeling."

To us this strain of youthful enthusiasm sounds strange, from long disuse; but these few lines of a youth under twenty show clearly enough that the writer is insured against commonplace vice and commonplace virtue, and that, though he may stumble into the mire, he will come out of it undefiled.

There is no want of self-confidence in the letter; but

the believer has doubts and a passionate desire for confirmation and a word of sympathy, though that hardly needed to be spoken. It is the restlessness of creative activity, the uneasy looking about of a pregnant soul.

"As yet," he writes in the same letter, "I can't catch the sounds that my brain hears; a physical incapacity limits my fancy. But never mind! A poet I am, and poetry whispers to me truth which I could never have discovered by cold logic. Such is my theory of revelation."

Thus ends the first part of our youth, and the second begins with prison. But before starting on that episode, I must record the ideas towards which we were tending when the prison-doors closed on us.

§11

THE period that followed the suppression of the Polish revolt in 1830 was a period of rapid enlightenment. We soon perceived with inward horror that things were going badly in Europe and especially in France—France to which we looked for a political creed and a banner; and we began to distrust our own theories.

The simple liberalism of 1826, which by degrees took, in France, the form sung by Béranger and preached by men like La Fayette and Benjamin Constant, lost its magic power over us after the destruction of Poland.

It was then that some young Russians, including Vadim, took refuge in the profound study of Russian history, while others took to German philosophy.

But Ogaryóv and I did not join either of these groups. Certain ideals had become so much a part of us that we could not lightly give them up. Our belief in the sort of dinner-table revolution dear to Béranger was shaken; but we sought something different, which we could not find either in Nestor's *Chronicle** or in the transcendentalism of Schelling.

§12

DURING this period of ferment and surmise and endeavour to understand the doubts that frightened us, there came into our hands the pamphlets and sermons of the Saint-Simonians, and the report of their trial. We were much impressed by them.

Superficial and unsuperficial critics alike have had their laugh at *Le Père Enfantin*† and his apostles; but a time is coming when a different reception will be given to those forerunners of socialism.

Though these young enthusiasts wore long beards and high waistcoats, yet their appearance in a prosaic world was both romantic and serious. They proclaimed a new belief, they had something to say—a principle by virtue of which they summoned before their judgement-seat the old order of things, which wished to try them by the *code Napoléon* and the religion of the House of Orleans.

First, they proclaimed the emancipation of women—summoning them to a common task, giving them control of their own destiny, and making an alliance with them on terms of equality.

Their second dogma was the restoration of the body to credit—*la réhabilitation de la chair*.

These mighty watchwords comprise a whole world of new relations between human beings—a world of health and spirit and beauty, a world of natural and therefore

*The earliest piece of literature in Russian.
†Barthèlemy Enfantin (1796-1864) carried on the work of Saint-Simon in Paris.

pure morality. Many mocked at the "freedom of women" and the "recognition of the rights of the flesh," attributing a low and unclean meaning to these phrases; for our minds, corrupted by monasticism, fear the flesh and fear women. A religion of life had come to replace the religion of death, a religion of beauty to replace the religion of penance and emaciation, of fasting and prayer. The crucified body had risen in its turn and was no longer abashed. Man had reached a harmonious unity: he had discovered that he is a single being, not made, like a pendulum, of two different metals that check each other; he realised that the foe in his members had ceased to exist.

It required no little courage to preach such a message to all France, and to attack those beliefs which are so strongly held by all Frenchmen and so entirely powerless to influence their conduct.

To the old world, mocked by Voltaire and shattered by the Revolution, and then patched and cobbled for their own use by the middle classes, this was an entirely new experience. It tried to judge these dissenters, but its own hypocritical pretences were brought to light by them in open court. When the Saint-Simonians were charged with religious apostasy, they pointed to the crucifix in the court which had been veiled since the revolution of 1830; and when they were accused of justifying sensuality, they asked their judge if he himself led a chaste life.

A new world was knocking at the door, and our hearts and minds flew open to welcome it. The socialism of Saint Simon became the foundation of our beliefs and has remained an essential part of them.

With the impressibility and frankness of youth, we were easily caught up by the mighty stream and early passed across that Jordan, before which whole armies of mankind stop short, fold their arms, and either march backwards or hunt about for a ford; but there is no ford over Jordan!

We did not all cross. Socialism and rationalism are to this day the touchstones of humanity, the rocks which lie in the course of revolution and science. Groups of swimmers, driven by reflexion or the waves of circumstance against these rocks, break up at once into two camps, which, under different disguises, remain the same throughout all history, and may be distinguished either in a great political party or in a group of a dozen young men. One represents logic; the other, history: one stands for dialectics; the other for evolution. Truth is the main object of the former, and feasibility of the latter. There is no question of choice between them: thought is harder to tame than any passion and pulls with irresistible force. Some may be able to put on the drag and stop themselves by means of feeling or dreams or fear of consequences; but not all can do this. If thought once masters a man, he ceases to discuss whether the thing is practicable, and whether the enterprise is hard or easy: he seeks truth alone and carries out his principles with inexorable impartiality, as the Saint-Simonians did in their day and as Proudhon* does still.

Our group grew smaller and smaller. As early as 1833, the "liberals" looked askance at us as backsliders. Just before we were imprisoned, Saint-Simonianism raised a barrier between me and Polevói. He had an extraordinarily active and adroit mind, which could rapidly assimilate any food; he was a born journalist, the very man to

*Pierre Joseph Proudhon (1809-1863), a French publicist and socialist.

chronicle successes and discoveries and the battles of politicians or men of science. I made his acquaintance towards the end of my college course and saw a good deal of him and his brother, Xenophon. He was then at the height of his reputation; it was shortly before the suppression of his newspaper, the *Telegraph*.

To Polevói the latest discovery, the freshest novelty either of incident or theory, was the breath of his nostrils, and he was changeable as a chameleon. Yet, for all his lively intelligence, he could never understand the Saint-Simonian doctrine. What was to us a revelation was to him insanity, a mere Utopia and a hindrance to social progress. I might declaim and expound and argue as much as I pleased—Polevói was deaf, grew angry and even bitter. He especially resented opposition on the part of a student; for he valued his influence over the young, and these disputes showed him that it was slipping out of his grasp.

One day I was hurt by the absurdity of his criticisms and told him that he was just as benighted as the foes against whom he had been fighting all his life. Stung to the quick by my taunt he said, "Your time will come too, when, in recompense for a lifetime of labour and effort, some young man with a smile on his face will call you a back number and bid you get out of his way." I felt sorry for him and ashamed of having hurt his feelings; and yet I felt also that this complaint, more suitable to a worn-out gladiator than a tough fighter, contained his own condemnation. I was sure then that he would never go forward, and also that his active mind would prevent him from remaining where he was, in a position of unstable equilibrium.

His subsequent history is well known: he wrote *Parasha, the Siberian Girl.*

If a man cannot pass off the stage when his hour has struck and cannot adopt a new rôle, he had better die. That is what I felt when I looked at Polevói, and at Pius the Ninth, and at how many others!

§13

To complete my chronicle of that sad time, I should record here some details about Polezháev.

Even at College he became known for his remarkable powers as a poet. One of his productions was a humorous poem called *Sashka,* a parody of Púshkin's *Onégin;* he trod on many corns in the pretty and playful verse, and the poem, never intended for print, allowed itself the fullest liberty of expression.

When the Tsar Nicholas came to Moscow for his coronation in the autumn of 1826, the secret police furnished him with a copy of the poem.

So, at three one morning, Polezháev was wakened by the Vice-Chancellor and told to put on his uniform and appear at the office. The Visitor of the University was waiting for him there: he looked to see that Polezháev's uniform had no button missing and no button too many, and then carried him off in his own carriage, without offering any explanation.

They drove to the house of the Minister of Education. The Minister of Education also gave Polezháev a seat in his carriage, and this time they drove to the Palace itself.

Prince Liven proceeded to an inner room, leaving Polezháev in a reception room, where, in spite of the early hour—it was 6 a.m.—several courtiers and other high functionaries were waiting. They supposed that the young man had distinguished himself in some way and began a conversation with him at once; one of them proposed to engage him as tutor to his son.

He was soon sent for. The Tsar was standing, leaning on a desk and talking to Liven. He held a manuscript in his hand and darted an enquiring glance at Polezháev as he entered the room. "Did you write these verses?" he asked.

"Yes," said Polezháev.

"Well, Prince," the Tsar went on, "I shall give you a specimen of University education; I shall show you what the young men learn there." Then he turned to Polezháev and added, "Read this manuscript aloud."

Polezháev's agitation was such that he could not read it; and he said so.

"Read it at once!"

The loud voice restored his strength to Polezháev, and he opened the manuscript. He said afterwards that he had never seen *Sashka* so well copied or on such fine paper.

At first he read with difficulty, but by degrees he took courage and read the poem to the end in a loud lively tone. At the most risky passages the Tsar waved his hand to the Minister and the Minister closed his eyes in horror.

"What do you say, Prince?" asked Nicholas, when the reading was over. "I mean to put a stop to this profligacy. These are surviving relics of the old mischief,* but I shall root them out. What character does he bear?"

Of course the Minister knew nothing about his char-

*I.e., the Decembrist conspiracy.

acter; but some humane instinct awoke in him, and he said, "He bears an excellent character, Your Majesty."

"You may be grateful for that testimony. But you must be punished as an example to others. Do you wish to enter the Army?"

Polezháev was silent.

"I offer you this means of purification. Will you take it?"

"I must obey when you command," said Polezháev. The Tsar came close up to him and laid a hand on his shoulder. He said: "Your fate depends upon yourself. If I forget about you, you may write to me." Then he kissed Polezháev on the forehead.

This last detail seemed to me so improbable that I made Polezháev repeat it a dozen times; he swore that it was true.

From the presence of the Tsar, Polezháev was taken to Count Diebitch, who had rooms in the Palace. Diebitch was roused out of his sleep and came in yawning. He read through the document and asked the *aide-de-camp,* "Is this the man?" "Yes," was the reply.

"Well, good luck to you in the service! I was in it myself and worked my way up, as you see; perhaps you will be a field-marshal yourself some day." That was Diebitch's kiss—a stupid, ill-timed, German joke. Polezháev was taken to camp and made to serve with the colours.

When three years had passed, Polezháev recalled what the Tsar had said and wrote him a letter. No answer came. After a few months he wrote again with the same result. Feeling sure that his letters were not delivered, he deserted, his object being to present a petition in person. But he behaved foolishly: he hunted up some college friends in Moscow and was entertained by them, and of course further secrecy was impossible. He was arrested at Tver and sent back to his regiment as a deserter; he had to march all the way in fetters. A court-martial sentenced him to run the gauntlet, and the sentence was forwarded to the Tsar for confirmation.

Polezháev determined to commit suicide before the time of his punishment. For long he searched in the prison for some sharp instrument, and at last he confided in an old soldier who was attached to him. The soldier understood and sympathised with his wish; and when he heard that the reply had come, he brought a bayonet and said with tears in his eyes as he gave it to Polezháev, "I sharpened it with my own hands."

But the Tsar ordered that Polezháev should not be flogged.

It was at this time that he wrote that excellent poem which begins—

> "No consolation
> Came when I fell;
> In jubilation
> Laughed fiends of Hell."

He was sent to the Caucasus, where he distinguished himself and was promoted corporal. Years passed, and the tedium and hopelessness of his position were too much for him. For him it was impossible to become a poet at the service of the police, and that was the only way to get rid of the knapsack.

There was, indeed, one other way, and he preferred it: he drank, in order to forget. There is one terrible poem of his—*To Whiskey*.

He got himself transferred to a regiment of carabineers quartered at Moscow. This was a material improvement in his circumstances, but cruel consumption had already fastened on his lungs. It was at this time I made his acquaintance, about 1833. He dragged on for four years more and died in the military hospital.

When one of his friends went to ask for the body, to bury it, no one knew where it was. The military hospital carries on a trade in dead bodies, selling them to the University and medical schools, manufacturing skeletons, and so on. Polezháev's body was found at last in a cellar; there were other corpses on the top of it, and the rats had gnawed one of the feet.

His poems were published after his death, and it was intended to add a portrait of him in his private's uniform. But the censor objected to this, and the unhappy victim appears with the epaulettes of an officer—he was promoted while in the hospital.

PART II

PRISON AND EXILE

(1834-1838)

CHAPTER I

A Prophecy—Ogaryóv's Arrest—The Fires—A Moscow Liberal
—Mihail Orlóv—The Churchyard.

§1

ONE morning in the spring of 1834 I went to
Vadim's house. Though neither he nor any of
his brothers or sisters were at home, I went upstairs to his little room, sat down, and began to write.

The door opened softly, and Vadim's mother came in.
Her tread was scarcely audible; looking tired and ill, she
went to an armchair and sat down. "Go on writing," she
said; "I just looked in to see if Vadya had come home.
The children have gone out for a walk, and the downstairs
rooms are so empty and depressing that I felt sad and
frightened. I shall sit here for a little, but don't let me
interfere with what you are doing."

She looked thoughtful, and her face showed more clearly
than usual the shadow of past suffering, and that suspicious fear of the future and distrust of life which is the
invariable result of great calamities when they last long
and are often repeated.

We began to talk. She told me something of their life
in Siberia. "I have come through much already," she said,

shaking her head, "and there is more to come: my heart forebodes evil."

I remembered how, sometimes, when listening to our free talk on political subjects, she would turn pale and heave a gentle sigh; and then she would go away to another room and remain silent for a long time.

"You and your friends," she went on, "are on the road that leads to certain ruin—ruin to Vadya and yourself and all of you. You know I love you like a son"—and a tear rolled down her worn face.

I said nothing. She took my hand, tried to smile, and went on: "Don't be vexed with me; my nerves are upset. I quite understand. You must go your own way; for you there is no other; if there were, you would be different people. I know this, but I cannot conquer my fears; I have borne so much misfortune that I have no strength for more. Please don't say a word of this to Vadya, or he will be vexed and argue with me. But here he is!"—and she hastily wiped away her tears and once more begged me by a look to keep her secret.

Unhappy mother! Saint and heroine! Corneille's *qu'il mourût** was not a nobler utterance than yours.

Her prophecy was soon fulfilled. Though the storm passed harmless this time over the heads of her sons, yet the poor lady had much grief and fear to suffer.

§2

"Arrested him?" I called out, springing out of bed, and pinching myself, to find out if I was asleep or awake.

"Two hours after you left our house, the police and a

---

* Said of his son by the father in Corneille's play, *Horace.*

party of Cossacks came and arrested my master and seized his papers."

The speaker was Ogaryóv's valet. Of late all had been quiet, and I could not imagine what pretext the police had invented. Ogaryóv had only come to Moscow the day before. And why had they arrested him, and not me?

To do nothing was impossible. I dressed and went out without any definite purpose. It was my first experience of misfortune. I felt wretched and furious at my own impotence.

I wandered about the streets till at last I thought of a friend whose social position made it possible for him to learn the state of the case, and, perhaps, to mend matters. But he was then living terribly far off, at a house in a distant suburb. I called the first cab I saw and hurried off at top speed. It was then seven o'clock in the morning.

§3

EIGHTEEN months before this time we had made the acquaintance of this man, who was a kind of a celebrity in Moscow. Educated in Paris, he was rich, intelligent, well-informed, witty, and independent in his ideas. For complicity in the Decembrist plot he had been imprisoned in a fortress till he and some others were released; and though he had not been exiled, he wore a halo. He was in the public service and had great influence with Prince Dmitri Golitsyn, the Governor of Moscow, who liked people with independent views, especially if they could express them in good French; for the Governor was not strong in Russian.

V.—as I shall call him—was ten years our senior and surprised us by his sensible comments on current events, his knowledge of political affairs, his eloquent French, and the ardour of his liberalism. He knew so much and so thoroughly; he was so pleasant and easy in conversation; his views were so clearly defined; he had a reply to every question and a solution of every problem. He read everything—new novels, pamphlets, newspapers, poetry, and was working seriously at zoology as well; he drew up reports for the Governor and was organising a series of school-books.

His liberalism was of the purest tricolour hue, the liberalism of the Left, midway between Mauguin and General Lamarque.*

The walls of his study in Moscow were covered with portraits of famous revolutionaries, from John Hampden and Bailly to Fieschi and Armand Carrel,† and a whole library of prohibited books was ranged beneath these patron saints. A skeleton, with a few stuffed birds and scientific preparations, gave an air of study and concentration to the room and toned down its revolutionary appearance.

We envied his experience and knowledge of the world; his subtle irony in argument impressed us greatly. We thought of him as a practical reformer and rising statesman.

§4

V. was not at home. He had gone to Moscow the evening before, for an interview with the Governor; his valet

---

*French politicians prominent about 1830.

†Bailly, Mayor of Paris, was guillotined in 1793. Fieschi was executed in 1836 for an attempt on the life of Louis Philippe. Armand Carrel was a French publicist and journalist who fell in a duel in 1836.

said that he would certainly return within two hours. I waited for him.

The country-house which he occupied was charming. The study where I waited was a high spacious room on the ground-floor, with a large door leading to a terrace and garden. It was a hot day; the scent of trees and flowers came from the garden; and some children were playing in front of the house and laughing loudly. Wealth, ease, space, sun and shade, flowers and verdure—what a contrast to the confinement and close air and darkness of a prison! I don't know how long I sat there, absorbed in bitter thoughts; but suddenly the valet who was on the terrace called out to me with an odd kind of excitement.

"What is it?" I asked.

"Please come here and look."

Not wishing to annoy the man, I walked out to the terrace, and stood still in horror. All round a number of houses were burning; it seemed as if they had all caught fire at once. The fire was spreading with incredible speed.

I stayed on the terrace. The man watched the fire with a kind of uneasy satisfaction, and he said, "It's spreading grandly; that house on the right is certain to be burnt."

There is something revolutionary about a fire: fire mocks at property and equalises fortunes. The valet felt this instinctively.

Within half an hour, a whole quarter of the sky was covered with smoke, red below and greyish black above. It was the beginning of those fires which went on for five months, and of which we shall hear more in the sequel.

At last V. arrived. He was in good spirits, very cordial

and friendly, talking of the fires past which he had come and of the common report that they were due to arson. Then he added, half in jest: "It's Pugatchóv* over again. Just look out, or you and I will be caught by the rebels and impaled."

"I am more afraid that the authorities will lay us by the heels," I answered. "Do you know that Ogaryóv was arrested last night by the police?"

"The police! Good heavens!"

"That is why I came. Something must be done. You must go to the Governor and find out what the charge is; and you must ask leave for me to see him."

No answer came, and I looked at V. I saw a face that might have belonged to his elder brother—the pleasant colour and features were changed; he groaned aloud and was obviously disturbed.

"What's the matter?" I asked.

"You know I told you, I always told you, how it would end. Yes, yes, it was bound to happen. It's likely enough they will shut me up too, though I am perfectly innocent. I know what the inside of a fortress is like, and it's no joke, I can tell you."

"Will you go to the Governor?"

"My dear fellow, what good would it do? Let me give you a piece of friendly advice: don't say a word about Ogaryóv; keep as quiet as you can, or harm will come of it. You don't know how dangerous affairs like this are. I frankly advise you to keep out of it. Make what stir you like, you will do Ogaryóv no good and you will get

---

*The leader of a famous rebellion in Catherine's reign. Many nobles were murdered with brutal cruelty.

caught yourself. That is what autocracy means—Russian subjects have no rights and no means of defence, no advocates and no judges."

But his brave words and trenchant criticisms had no attractions for me on this occasion: I took my hat and departed.

§5

I FOUND a general commotion going on at home. My father was angry with me because Ogaryóv had been arrested; my uncle, the Senator, was already on the scene, rummaging among my books and picking out those which he thought dangerous; he was very uneasy.

On my table I found an invitation to dine that day with Count Orlóv. Possibly he might be able to do something? Though I had learned a lesson by my first experiment, it could do no harm to try.

Mihail Orlóv was one of the founders of the famous Society of Welfare;* and if he missed Siberia, he was less to blame for that than his brother, who was the first to gallop up with his squadron of the Guards to the defence of the Winter Palace, on December 14, 1825. Orlóv was confined at first to his own estates, and allowed to settle in Moscow a few years later. During his solitary life in the country he studied political economy and chemistry. The first time I met him he spoke of a new method of naming chemical compounds. Able men who take up some science late in life often show a tendency to rearrange the furniture, so to speak, to suit their own ideas. Orlóv's system was more complicated than the French

*An imitation of the *Tugenbund* formed by German students in 1808. In Russia the society became identified with the Decembrists.

system, which is generally accepted. As I wished to attract his attention, I argued in a friendly way that, though his system was good, it was not as good as the old one.

He contested the point, but ended by agreeing with me.

My little trick was successful, and we became intimate. He saw in me a rising possibility, and I saw in him a man who had fought for our ideals, an intimate friend of our heroes, and a shining light amid surrounding darkness.

Poor Orlóv was like a caged lion. He beat against the bars of his cage at every turn; nowhere could he find elbow-room or occupation, and he was devoured by a passion for activity.

More than once since the collapse of France* I have met men of this type, men to whom political activity was an absolute necessity, who never could find rest within the four walls of their study or in family life. To them solitude is intolerable: it makes them fanciful and un-reasonable; they quarrel with their few remaining friends, and are constantly discovering plots against themselves, or else they make plots of their own, in order to unmask the imaginary schemes of their enemies.

A theatre of action and spectators are as vital to these men as the air they breathe, and they are capable of real heroism under such conditions. Noise and publicity are essential to them; they must be making speeches and hearing the objections of their opponents; they love the excitement of contest and the fever of danger, and, if deprived of these stimulants, they grow depressed and spiritless, run to seed, lose their heads, and make mis-

*I.e., after December 2, 1851.

takes. Ledru-Rollin* is a man of this type; and he, by the way, especially since he has grown a beard, has a personal resemblance to Orlóv.

Orlóv was a very fine-looking man. His tall figure, dignified bearing, handsome manly features, and entirely bald scalp seemed to suit one another perfectly, and lent an irresistible attraction to his outward appearance. His head would make a good contrast with the head of General Yermólov, that tough old warrior, whose square frowning forehead, penthouse of grey hair, and penetrating glance gave him the kind of beauty which fascinated Marya Kochubéi in the poem.†

Orlóv was at his wits' end for occupation. He started a factory for stained-glass windows of medieval patterns and spent more in producing them than he got by selling them. Then he tried to write a book on "Credit," but that proved uncongenial, though it was his only outlet. The lion was condemned to saunter about Moscow with nothing to do, and not daring even to use his tongue freely.

Orlóv's struggles to turn himself into a philosopher and man of science were most painful to watch. His intellect, though clear and showy, was not at all suited to abstract thought, and he confused himself over the application of newly devised methods to familiar subjects, as in the case of chemistry. Though speculation was decidedly not his forte, he studied metaphysics with immense perseverance.

Being imprudent and careless in his talk, he was con-

*Alexandre Ledru-Rollin (1807-1874), a French liberal politician and advocate of universal suffrage.

†See Púshkin's *Poltáva*. Marya, who was young and beautiful, fell in love with Mazeppa, who was old and war-worn and her father's enemy.

stantly making slips; he was carried away by his instincts, which were always chivalrous and generous, and then he suddenly remembered his position and checked himself in mid-course. In these diplomatic withdrawals he was even less successful than in metaphysics or scientific terminology: in trying to clear himself of one indiscretion, he often slipped into two or three more. He got blamed for this; people are so superficial and unobservant that they think more of words than actions, and attach more importance to particular mistakes than to a man's general character. It was unfair to expect of him a high standard of consistency; he was less to blame than the sphere in which he lived, where every honourable feeling had to be hidden, like smuggled goods, up your sleeve, and uttered behind closed doors. If you spoke above your breath, you would spend the whole day in wondering whether the police would soon be down upon you.

§6

It was a large dinner. I happened to sit next General Raevski, Orlóv's brother-in-law. Raevski also had been in disgrace since the famous fourteenth of December. As a boy of fourteen he had served under his distinguished father at the battle of Borodino; and he died eventually of wounds received in the Caucasus. I told him about Ogaryóv and asked whether Orlóv would be able and willing to take any steps.

Raevski's face clouded over, but it did not express that querulous anxiety for personal safety which I had seen earlier in the day; he evidently felt disgust mixed with bitter memories.

"Of willingness there can be no question in such a

case," he said; "but I doubt if Orlóv has the power to do much. Pass through to the study after dinner, and I will bring him to you there." He was silent for a moment and then added, "So your turn has come too; those depths will drown you all."

Orlóv questioned me and then wrote to the Governor, asking for an interview. "The Prince is a gentleman," he said; "if he does nothing, at least he will tell us the truth."

I went next day to hear the answer. Prince Dmitri Golitsyn had replied that Ogaryóv had been arrested by order of the Tsar, that a commission of enquiry had been appointed, and that the charge turned chiefly on a dinner given on June 24, at which seditious songs had been sung. I was utterly puzzled. That day was my father's birthday; I had spent the whole day at home, and Ogaryóv was there too.

My heart was heavy when I left Orlóv. He too was unhappy: when I held out my hand at parting, he got up and embraced me, pressed me tight to his broad chest and kissed me. It was just as if he felt that we should not soon meet again.

§7

I ONLY saw him once more, just six years later. He was then near death; I was struck by the signs of illness and depression on his face, and the marked angularity of his features was a shock to me. He felt that he was breaking up, and knew that his affairs were in hopeless disorder. Two months later he died, of a clot of blood in the arteries.

At Lucerne there is a wonderful monument carved by Thorwaldsen in the natural rock—a niche containing the figure of a dying lion. The great beast is mortally

wounded; blood is pouring from the wound, and a broken
arrow sticks up out of it. The grand head rests on the
paw; the animal moans and his look expresses agony.
That is all; the place is shut off by hills and trees and
bushes; passers-by would never guess that the king of
beasts lies there dying.

I sat there one day for a long time and looked at this
image of suffering, and all at once I remembered my last
visit to Orlóv.

§8

As I drove home from Orlóv's house, I passed the office
of General Tsinski, chief of the police; and it occurred to
me to make a direct application to him for leave to see
Ogaryóv.

Never in my life had I paid a visit to any person connected with the police. I had to wait a long time; but at
last the Chief Commissioner appeared. My request surprised him.

"What reason have you for asking this permission?"

"Ogaryóv and I are cousins."

"Cousins?" he asked, looking me straight in the face.

I said nothing, but returned His Excellency's look
exactly.

"I can't give you leave," he said; "your kinsman is in
solitary confinement. I am very sorry."

My ignorance and helplessness were torture to me.
Hardly any of my intimate friends were in Moscow; it
was quite impossible to find out anything. The police
seemed to have forgotten me or to ignore me. I was utterly
weary and wretched. But when all the sky was covered
with gloomy clouds and the long night of exile and prison

was coming close, just then a radiant sunbeam fell upon me.

§9

A FEW words of deep sympathy, spoken by a girl* of sixteen, whom I regarded as a child, put new life in me.

This is the first time that a woman figures in my narrative; and it is practically true that only one woman figures in my life.

My young heart had been set beating before by fleeting fancies of youth; but these vanished like the shapes of cloudland before this figure, and no new fancies ever came.

Our meeting was in a churchyard. She leant on a gravestone and spoke of Ogaryóv, till my sorrow grew calm.

"We shall meet to-morrow," she said, and gave me her hand, smiling through her tears.

"To-morrow," I repeated, and looked long after her retreating figure.

The date was July 19, 1834.

*This was Natálya Zakhárin, Herzen's cousin, who afterwards became his wife.

CHAPTER II

Arrest—The Independent Witness—A Police-Station—Patri-archal Justice.

§1

W E shall meet to-morrow," I repeated to myself as I was falling asleep, and my heart
felt unusually light and happy.

At two in the morning I was wakened by my father's valet; he was only half-dressed and looked frightened.

"An officer is asking for you."

"What officer?"

"I don't know."

"Well, I do," I said, as I threw on my dressing-gown. A figure wrapped in a military cloak was standing at the drawing-room door; I could see a white plume from my window, and there were some people behind it—I could make out a Cossack helmet.

Our visitor was Miller, an officer of police. He told me that he bore a warrant from the military Governor of Moscow to examine my papers. Candles were brought. Miller took my keys, and while his subordinates rum-maged among my books and shirts, attended to the papers himself. He put them all aside as suspicious; then he turned suddenly to me and said:

"I beg you will dress meanwhile; you will have to go with me."

"Where to?" I asked.

"To the police-station of the district," he said, in a reassuring voice.

"And then?"

"There are no further orders in the Governor's warrant."

I began to dress.

Meanwhile my mother had been awakened by the terrified servants, and came in haste from her bedroom to see me. When she was stopped half-way by a Cossack, she screamed; I started at the sound and ran to her. The officer came with us, leaving the papers behind him. He apologised to my mother and let her pass; then he scolded the Cossack, who was not really to blame, and went back to the papers.

My father now appeared on the scene. He was pale but tried to keep up his air of indifference. The scene became trying: while my mother wept in a corner, my father talked to the officer on ordinary topics, but his voice shook. I feared that if this went on it would prove too much for me, and I did not wish that the understrappers of the police should have the satisfaction of seeing me shed tears.

I twitched the officer's sleeve and said we had better be off.

He welcomed the suggestion. My father then left the room, but returned immediately; he was carrying a little sacred picture, which he placed round my neck, saying

that his father on his deathbed had blessed him with it.
I was touched: the nature of this gift proved to me how
great was the fear and anxiety that filled the old man's
heart. I knelt down for him to put it on; he raised me
to my feet, embraced me, and gave me his blessing.

It was a representation on enamel of the head of John
the Baptist on the charger. Whether it was meant for an
example, a warning, or a prophecy, I don't know, but it
struck me as somehow significant.

My mother was almost fainting.

I was escorted down the stairs by all the household
servants, weeping and struggling to kiss my face and
hands; it might have been my own funeral with me to
watch it. The officer frowned and hurried on the proceedings.

Once outside the gate, he collected his forces—four
Cossacks and four policemen.

There was a bearded man sitting outside the gate, who
asked the officer if he might now go home.

"Be off!" said Miller.

"Who is that?" I asked, as I took my seat in the cab.

"He is a witness: you know that the police must take
a witness with them when they make an entrance into a
private house."

"Is that why you left him outside?"

"A mere formality," said Miller; "it's only keeping the
man out of his bed for nothing."

Our cab started, escorted by two mounted Cossacks.

§2

THERE was no private room for me at the police-station,
and the officer directed that I should spend the rest of

the night in the office. He took me there himself; dropping into an armchair and yawning wearily, he said: "It's a dog's life. I've been up since three, and now your business has kept me till near four in the morning, and at nine I have to present my report."

"Good-bye," he said a moment later and left the room. A corporal locked me in, and said that I might knock at the door if I needed anything.

I opened the window: day was beginning and the morning breeze was stirring. I asked the corporal for water and drank a whole jugful. Of sleep I never even thought. For one thing, there was no place to lie down; the room contained no furniture except some dirty leather-covered chairs, one armchair, and two tables of different sizes, both covered with a litter of papers. There was a night-light, too feeble to light up the room, which threw a flickering white patch on the ceiling; and I watched the patch grow paler and paler as the dawn came on.

I sat down in the magistrate's seat and took up the paper nearest me on the table—a permit to bury a servant of Prince Gagárin's and a medical certificate to prove that the man had died according to all the rules of the medical art. I picked up another—some police regulations. I ran through it and found an article to this effect: "Every prisoner has a right to learn the cause of his arrest or to be discharged within three days." I made a mental note of this item.

An hour later I saw from the window the arrival of our butler with a cushion, coverlet, and cloak for me. He made some request to the corporal, probably for leave to visit me; he was a grey-haired old man, to several of

whose children I had stood godfather while a child myself; the corporal gave a rough and sharp refusal. One of
our coachmen was there too, and I hailed them from the
window. The soldier, in a fuss, ordered them to be off.
The old man bowed low to me and shed tears; and the
coachman, as he whipped up his horse, took off his hat
and rubbed his eyes. When the carriage started, I could
bear it no more: the tears came in a flood, and they were
the first and last tears I shed during my imprisonment.

§3

TOWARDS morning the office began to fill up. The first
to appear was a clerk, who had evidently been drunk the
night before and was not sober yet. He had red hair and
a pimpled face, a consumptive look, and an expression of
brutish sensuality; he wore a long, brick-coloured coat,
ill-made, ill-brushed, and shiny with age. The next comer
was a free-and-easy gentleman, wearing the cloak of a non-
commissioned officer. He turned to me at once and asked:
"They got you at the theatre, I suppose?"
"No; I was arrested at home."
"By Fyodor Ivanovitch?"
"Who is Fyodor Ivanovitch?"
"Why, Colonel Miller."
"Yes, it was he."
"Ah, I understand, Sir"—and he winked to the red-
haired man, who showed not the slightest interest. The
other did not continue the conversation; seeing that I
was not charged as drunk and disorderly, he thought me
unworthy of further attention; or perhaps he was afraid
to converse with a political prisoner.

A little later, several policemen appeared, rubbing their eyes and only half awake; and finally the petitioners and suitors.

A woman who kept a disorderly house made a complaint against a publican. He had abused her publicly in his shop, using language which she, as a woman, could not venture to repeat before a magistrate. The publican swore he had never used such language; the woman swore that he had used it repeatedly and very loudly, and she added that he had raised his hand against her and would have laid her face open, had she not ducked her head. The shopman said, first, that she owed him money, and, secondly, that she had insulted him in his own shop, nay more, had threatened to kill him by the hands of her bullies.

She was a tall, slatternly woman with swollen eyes; her voice was piercingly loud and high, and she had an extraordinary flow of language. The shopman relied more on gesture and pantomime than on his eloquence.

In the absence of the judge, one of the policemen proved to be a second Solomon. He abused both parties in fine style. "You're too well off," he said; "that's what's the matter with you; why can't you stop at home and keep the peace, and be thankful to us for letting you alone? What fools you are! Because you have had a few words you must run at once before His Worship and trouble him! How dare you give yourself airs, my good woman, as if you had never been abused before? Why your very trade can't be named in decent language!" Here the shopman showed the heartiest approval by his gestures; but his turn came next. "And you, how dare you stand there in your shop and bark like an angry dog? Do you want to be locked up? You use foul language, and raise your fist as well; it's a sound thrashing you want."

This scene had the charm of novelty for me; it was the first specimen I had seen of patriarchal justice as administered in Russia, and I have never forgotten it.

The pair went on shouting till the magistrate came in. Without even asking their business, he shouted them down at once. "Get out of this! Do you take this place for a bad house or a gin-shop?" When he had driven out the offenders, he turned on the policeman: "I wonder you are not ashamed to permit such disorder. I have told you again and again. People lose all respect for the place; it will soon be a regular bear-garden for the mob; you are too easy with them." Then he looked at me and said:

"Who is that?"

"A prisoner whom Fyodor Ivanovitch brought in," answered the policeman; "there is a paper about him somewhere, Sir."

The magistrate ran through the paper and then glanced at me. As I kept my eyes fixed on him, ready to retort the instant he spoke, he was put out and said, "I beg your pardon."

But now the business began again between the publican and his enemy. The woman wished to take an oath, and a priest was summoned; I believe both parties were sworn, and there was no prospect of a conclusion. At this point I was taken in a carriage to the Chief Commissioner's office—I am sure I don't know why, for no one spoke a word to me there—and then brought back to the police-station, where a room right under the belfry was prepared for my occupation. The corporal observed that if I wanted food I must send out for it: the prison ration would not be issued for a day or two; and besides, as it only amounted to three or four *kopecks* a day, a gentleman "under a cloud" did not usually take it.

Along the wall of my room there was a sofa with a dirty cover. It was past midday and I was terribly weary. I threw myself on the sofa and fell fast asleep. When I woke, I felt quite easy and cheerful. Of late I had been tormented by my ignorance of Ogaryóv's fate; now, my own turn had come, the black cloud was right overhead, I was in the thick of the danger, instead of watching it in the distance. I felt that this first prosecution would serve us as a consecration for our mission.

CHAPTER III

Under the Belfry—A Travelled Policeman—The Incendiaries.

§1

A MAN soon gets used to prison, if he has any interior life at all. One quickly gets accustomed to the silence and complete freedom of one's cage —there are no cares and no distractions.

They refused me books at first, and the police-magistrate declared that it was against the rules for me to get books from home. I then proposed to buy some. "I suppose you mean some serious book—a grammar of some kind, I dare say? Well, I should not object to that; for other books, higher authority must be obtained." Though the suggestion that I should study grammar to relieve boredom was exceedingly comic, yet I caught at it eagerly and asked him to buy me an Italian grammar and dictionary. I had two ten-*rouble* notes on me, and I gave him one. He sent at once to buy the books, and despatched by the same messenger a letter to the Chief Commissioner, in which, taking my stand on the article I had read, I asked him to explain the cause of my arrest or to release me.

The magistrate, in whose presence I wrote the letter, urged me not to send it. "It's no good, I swear it's no good your bothering His Excellency. They don't like people who give them trouble. It can't result in anything, and it may hurt you."

A policeman turned up in the evening with a reply: His Excellency sent me a verbal message, to the effect that I should learn in good time why I was arrested. The messenger then produced a greasy Italian grammar from his pocket, and added with a smile, "By good luck it happens that there is a vocabulary here; so you need not buy one." The question of change out of my note was not alluded to. I was inclined to write again to His Excellency; but to play the part of a little Hampden seemed to me rather too absurd in my present quarters.

§2

I HAD been in prison ten days, when a short policeman with a swarthy, pock-marked face came to my room at ten in the evening, bringing an order that I was to dress and present myself before the Commission of Enquiry.

While I was dressing, a serio-comic incident occurred. My dinner was sent me every day from home; our servant delivered it to the corporal on duty, and he sent a private upstairs with it. A bottle of wine from outside was allowed daily, and a friend had taken advantage of this permission to send me a bottle of excellent hock. The private and I contrived to uncork the bottle with a couple of nails; the bouquet of the wine was perceptible at a distance, and I looked forward to the pleasure of drinking it for some days to come.

There is nothing like prison life for revealing the childishness in a grown man and the consolation he finds in trifles, from a bottle of wine to a trick played on a turnkey.

Well, the pock-marked policeman found out my bottle, and, turning to me, asked if he might have a taste. Though I was vexed, I said I should be very glad. I had no glass. The wretch took a cup, filled it to the very brim, and emptied it into himself without drawing breath. No one but a Russian or a Pole can pour down strong drink in this fashion: I have never in any part of Europe seen a glass or cup of spirits disposed of with equal rapidity. To add to my sorrow at the loss of this cupful, my friend wiped his lips with a blue tobacco-stained handkerchief, and said as he thanked me, "Something like Madeira, *that* is!" I hated the sight of him and felt a cruel joy that his parents had not vaccinated him and nature had not spared him the small-pox.

§3

THIS judge of wine went with me to the Chief Commissioner's house on the Tver Boulevard, where he took me to a side room and left me alone. Half an hour later, a fat man with a lazy, good-natured expression came in, carrying papers in a wallet; he threw the wallet on a chair and sent the policeman who was standing at the door off on some errand.

"I suppose," he said to me, "you are mixed up in the affair of Ogaryóv and the other young men who were lately arrested." I admitted it.

"I've heard about it casually," he went on; "a queer business! I can't understand it at all."

"Well, I've been in prison a fortnight because of it, and not only do I not understand it, but I know nothing about it."

"That's right!" said the man, looking at me attentively. "Continue to know nothing about it! Excuse me, if I give you a piece of advice. You are young, and your blood is still hot, and you want to be talking; but it's a mistake. Just you remember that you know nothing about it. Nothing else can save you."

I looked at him in surprise; but his expression did not suggest anything base. He guessed my thoughts and said with a smile:

"I was a student at Moscow University myself twelve years ago."

A clerk of some kind now came in. The fat man, who was evidently his superior, gave him some directions and then left the room, after pressing a finger to his lips with a friendly nod to me. I never met him again and don't know now who he was; but experience proved to me that his advice was well meant.

§4

My next visitor was a police-officer, not Colonel Miller this time. He summoned me to a large, rather fine room where five men were sitting at a table, all wearing military uniform except one who was old and decrepit. They were smoking cigars and carrying on a lively conversation, lying back in their chairs with their jackets unbuttoned. The Chief Commissioner, Tsinski, was in the chair.

When I came in, he turned to a figure sitting modestly in a corner of the room and said, "May I trouble Your Reverence?" Then I made out that the figure in the corner was an old priest with a white beard and a mottled face. The old man was drowsy and wanted to go home; he was thinking of something else and yawning with his hand before his face. In a slow and rather sing-song voice he began to admonish me: he said it was sinful to conceal the truth from persons appointed by the Tsar, and useless, because the ear of God hears the unspoken word; he did not fail to quote the inevitable texts—that all power is from God, and that we must render to Caesar the things that are Caesar's. Finally, he bade me kiss the Holy Gospel and the True Cross in confirmation of a vow (which however I did not take and he did not ask) to reveal the whole truth frankly and openly.

When he had done, he began hastily to wrap up the Gospel and the Cross; and the President, barely rising in his seat, told him he might go. Then he turned to me and translated the priest's address into the language of this world. "One thing I shall add to what the priest has said —it is impossible for you to conceal the truth even if you wish to." He pointed to piles of papers, letters, and portraits, scattered on purpose over the table: "Frank confession alone can improve your position; it depends on yourself, whether you go free or are sent to the Caucasus."

Questions were then submitted in writing, some of them amusingly simple—"Do you know of the existence of any secret society? Do you belong to any society, learned or otherwise? Who are its members? Where do they meet?"

To all this it was perfectly simple to answer "No" and nothing else.

"I see you know nothing," said the President, reading

over the answers; "I warned you beforehand that you will complicate your situation."

And that was the end of the first examination.

§5

EIGHT years later a lady, who had once been beautiful, and her beautiful daughter, were living in a different part of this very house where the Commission sat; she was the sister of a later Chief Commissioner.

I used to visit there and always had to pass through the room where Tsinski and Company used to sit on us. There was a portrait of the Emperor Paul on the wall, and I used to stop in front of it every time I passed, either as a prisoner or as a visitor. Near it was a little drawing-room where all breathed of beauty and femininity; and it seemed somehow out of place beside frowning Justice and criminal trials. I felt uneasy there, and sorry that so fair a bud had found such an uncongenial spot to open in as the dismal brick walls of a police-office. Our talk, and that of a small number of friends who met there, sounded ironical and strange to the ear within those walls, so familiar with examinations, informations, and reports of domiciliary visits—within those walls which parted us from the mutter of policemen, the sighs of prisoners, the jingling spurs of officers, and the clanking swords of Cossacks.

§6

WITHIN a week or a fortnight the pock-marked police-man came again and went with me again to Tsinski's house. Inside the door some men in chains were sitting or lying, surrounded by soldiers with rifles; and in the front room there were others, of various ranks in society, not chained but strictly guarded. My policeman told me that these were incendiaries. As Tsinski himself had gone to the scene of the fires, we had to wait for his return. We arrived at nine in the evening; and at one in the morning no one had asked for me, and I was still sitting very peacefully in the front hall with the incendiaries. One or other of them was summoned from time to time; the police ran backward and forward, the chains clinked, and the soldiers, for want of occupation, rattled their rifles and went through the manual exercise. Tsinski arrived about one, black with smoke and grime, and hurried on to his study without stopping. Half an hour later my policeman was summoned; when he came back, he looked pale and upset and his face twitched convulsively. Tsinski followed him, put his head in at the door, and said: "Why, the members of the Commission were waiting for you, M. Herzen, the whole evening. This fool brought you here at the hour when you were summoned to Prince Golitsyn's house instead. I am very sorry you have had to wait so long, but I am not to blame. What can one do, with such subordinates? I suppose he has been fifty years in the service, and is as great a blockhead as ever. Well," he added, turning to the policeman and addressing him in a much less polite style, "be off now and go back."

All the way home the man kept repeating: "Lord! what bad luck! A man never knows what's going to happen to him. He will do for me now. He wouldn't matter so much; but the Prince will be angry, and the Commissioner will catch it for your not being there. Oh, what a misfortune!"

I forgave him the hock, especially when he declared that, though he was once nearly drowned at Lisbon, he was less scared then than now. This adventure surprised me so much that I roared with laughter. "How utterly absurd! What on earth took you to Lisbon?" I asked. It turned out that he had served in the Fleet twenty-five years before. The statesman in Gógol's novel, who declares that every servant of the State in Russia meets with his reward sooner or later,* certainly spoke the truth. For death spared my friend at Lisbon, in order that he might be scolded like a naughty boy by Tsinski, after forty years' service.

Besides, he was hardly at all to blame in the matter. The Tsar was dissatisfied with the original Commission of Enquiry, and had appointed another, with Prince Serghéi Golitsyn as chairman; the other members were Staal, the Commandant of Moscow, another Prince Golitsyn, Shubenski, a colonel of police, and Oranski, formerly paymaster-general. As my Lisbon friend had received no notice that the new Commission would sit at a different place, it was very natural that he should take me to Tsinski's house.

§7

WHEN we got back, we found great excitement there too: three fires had broken out during the evening, and the Commissioners had sent twice to ask what had become of me and whether I had run away. If Tsinski had not abused my escort sufficiently, the police-magistrate fully made up for any deficiencies; and this was natural, because he himself was partly to blame for not asking where exactly I was to be sent.

*Gógol, *Dead Souls*, Part I, chap. 10.

In a corner of the office there was a man lying on two chairs and groaning, who attracted my attention. He was young, handsome, and well-dressed. The police-surgeon advised that he should be sent to the hospital early next morning, as he was spitting blood and in great suffering. I got the details of this affair from the corporal who took me to my room. The man was a retired officer of the Guards, who was carrying on a love affair with a maid-servant and was with her when a fire broke out in the house. The panic caused by incendiarism was then at its height; and, in fact, never a day passed without my hearing the tocsin ring repeatedly, while at night I could always see the glow of several fires from my window. As soon as the excitement began, the officer, wishing to save the girl's reputation, climbed over a fence and hid himself in an outbuilding of the next house, intending to come out when the coast was clear. But a little girl had seen him in the court-yard, and told the first policeman who came on the scene that an incendiary was hiding in the shed. The police made for the place, accompanied by a mob, dragged the officer out in triumph, and dealt with him so vigorously that he died next morning.

The police now began to sift the men arrested for arson. Half of them were let go, but the rest were detained on suspicion. A magistrate came every morning and spent three or four hours in examining the charges. Some were flogged during this process; and then their yells and cries and entreaties, the shrieks of women, the harsh voice of the magistrate, and the drone of the clerk's reading— all this came to my ears. It was horrible beyond endurance. I dreamed of these sounds at night, and woke up in horror at the thought of these poor wretches, lying on straw a few feet away, in chains, with flayed and bleeding backs, and, in all probability, quite innocent.

§8

In order to know what Russian prisons and Russian police and justice really are, one must be a peasant, a servant or workman or shopkeeper. The political prisoners, who are mostly of noble birth, are strictly guarded and vindictively punished; but they suffer infinitely less than the unfortunate "men with beards." With them the police stand on no ceremony. In what quarter can a peasant or workman seek redress? Where will he find justice?

The Russian system of justice and police is so haphazard, so inhuman, so arbitrary and corrupt, that a poor malefactor has more reason to fear his trial than his sentence. He is impatient for the time when he will be sent to Siberia; for his martyrdom comes to an end when his punishment begins. Well, then, let it be remembered that three-fourths of those arrested on suspicion by the police are acquitted by the court, and that all these have gone through the same ordeal as the guilty.

Peter the Third abolished the torture-chamber, and the Russian star-chamber.

Catherine the Second abolished torture.

Alexander the First abolished it over again.

Evidence given under torture is legally inadmissible, and any magistrate applying torture is himself liable to prosecution and severe punishment.

That is so: and all over Russia, from Behring Straits to the Crimea, men suffer torture. Where flogging is unsafe, other means are used—intolerable heat, thirst, salt food; in Moscow the police made a prisoner stand bare-

footed on an iron floor, at a time of intense frost; the man
died in a hospital, of which Prince Meshcherski was president, and he told the story afterwards with horror. All
this is known to the authorities; but they all agree with
Selifan* in Gógol's novel—"Why not flog the peasants?
The peasants need a flogging from time to time."

§9

THE board appointed to investigate the fires sat, or, in
other words, flogged, for six months continuously, but
they were no wiser at the end of the flogging. The Tsar
grew angry: he ordered that the business should be completed in three days. And so it was: guilty persons were
discovered and sentenced to flogging, branding, and penal
servitude. All the hall-porters in Moscow were brought
together to witness the infliction of the punishment. It
was winter by then, and I had been moved to the Krutitski Barracks; but a captain of police, a kind-hearted old
man, who was present at the scene, told me the details I
here record. The man who was brought out first for
flogging addressed the spectators in a loud voice: he swore
that he was innocent, and that he did not know what
evidence he had given under torture; then he pulled off
his shirt and turned his back to the people, asking them
to look at it.

A groan of horror ran through the crowd: his whole
back was raw and bleeding, and that livid surface was
now to be flogged over again. The protesting cries and
sullen looks of the crowd made the police hurry on with
the business: the executioners dealt out the legal number

*Gógol, *Dead Souls,* Part I, chap. 3. Selifan, a coachman, is a peasant
himself.

of lashes, the branding and fettering took place, and the affair seemed at an end. But the scene had made an impression and was the subject of conversation all through the city. The Governor reported this to the Tsar, and the Tsar appointed a new board, which was to give special attention to the case of the man who had addressed the crowd.

Some months later I read in the newspapers that the Tsar, wishing to compensate two men who had been flogged for crimes of which they were innocent, ordered that they should receive 200 *roubles* for each lash, and also a special passport, to prove that though branded they were not guilty. These two were the man who had addressed the crowd, and one of his companions.

§10

THE cause of these incendiary fires which alarmed Moscow in 1834 and were repeated ten years later in different parts of the country, still remains a mystery. That it was not all accidental is certain: fire as a means of revenge —"The red cock," as it is called—is characteristic of the nation. One is constantly hearing of a gentleman's house or corn-kiln or granary being set on fire by his enemies. But what was the motive for the fires at Moscow in 1834, nobody knows, and the members of the Board of Enquiry least of all.

The twenty-second of August was the Coronation Day; and some practical jokers dropped papers in different parts of the city, informing the inhabitants they need not trouble about illuminating, because there would be plenty of light otherwise provided.

The authorities of the city were in great alarm. From

early morning my police-station was full of troops, and a squadron of dragoons was stationed in the court-yard. In the evening bodies of cavalry and infantry patrolled the streets; cannon were ready in the arsenal. Police-officers, with constables and Cossacks, galloped to and fro; the Governor himself rode through the city with his *aides-de-camp*. It was strange and disquieting to see peaceful Moscow turned into a military camp. I watched the court-yard from my lofty window till late at night. Dismounted dragoons were sitting in groups near their horses, while others remained in the saddle; their officers walked about, looking with some contempt at their comrades of the police; staff-officers, with anxious faces and yellow collars on their jackets, rode up, did nothing, and rode away again.

There were no fires.

Immediately afterwards the Tsar himself came to Moscow. He was dissatisfied with the investigation of our affair, which was just beginning, dissatisfied because we had not been handed over to the secret police, dissatisfied because the incendiaries had not been discovered—in short, he was dissatisfied with everything and everybody.

CHAPTER IV

The Krutitski Barracks—A Policeman's Story—The Officers.

§1

THREE days after the Tsar came to Moscow, a police-officer called on me late in the evening—all these things are done in the dark, to spare the nerves of the public—bringing an order for me to pack up and start off with him.

"Where to?" I asked.

"You will see shortly," he answered with equal wit and politeness. That was enough: I asked no more questions, but packed up my things and started.

We drove on and on for an hour and a half, passed St. Peter's Monastery, and stopped at a massive stone gateway, before which two constables were pacing, armed with carbines. This building was the Krutitski Monastery, which had been converted into a police-barracks.

I was taken to a smallish office, where everyone was dressed in blue, officers and clerks alike. The orderly officer, wearing full uniform and a helmet, asked me to wait and even proposed that I should light my pipe which I was holding. Having written out an acknowledgement that a fresh prisoner had been received, and handed it to my escort, he left the room and returned with another officer, who told me that my quarters were ready and asked me to go there. A constable carried a light, and we descended a staircase, passed through a small yard, and entered by a low door a long passage lighted by a single lantern. On both sides of the passage there were low doors; and the orderly officer opened one of these, which led into a tiny guard-room and thence into a room of moderate size, damp, cold, and smelling like a cellar. The officer who was escorting me now addressed me in French: he said that he was *désolé d'être dans la nécessité* of rummaging my pockets, but that discipline and his duty required it. After this noble exordium he turned without more ado to the gaoler and winked in my direction; and the man instantly inserted into my pocket an incredibly large and hairy paw. I pointed out to the polite officer that this was quite unnecessary: I would empty out all my pockets myself, without any forcible measures being used. And I asked what I could possibly have on me after six weeks in prison.

"Oh, we know what they are capable of at police-stations," said the polite officer, with an inimitable smile of superiority, and the orderly officer also smiled sarcastically; but they told the turnkey merely to look on while I emptied my pockets.

"Shake out any tobacco you have on the table," said the polite officer.

I had in my tobacco-pouch a pencil and a penknife wrapped up in paper. I remembered about them at once, and, while talking to the officer, I fiddled with the pouch till the knife came out in my hand; then I gripped it behind the pouch, while boldly pouring out the tobacco on the table. The turnkey gathered it together again. I had saved my knife and my pencil, and I had also paid out my polite friend for his contempt of my former gaolers.

This little incident put me in excellent humour, and I began cheerfully to survey my new possessions.

§2

THE monks' cells, built 300 years ago, had sunk deep into the ground, and were now put to a secular use for political prisoners.

My room contained a bedstead without a mattress, a small table with a jug of water on it, and a chair; a thin tallow candle was burning in a large copper candlestick. The damp and cold struck into the marrow of my bones; the officer ordered the stove to be lighted, and then I was left alone. A turnkey promised to bring some straw; meanwhile I used my overcoat as a pillow, lay down on the bare bedstead, and lit a pipe. I very soon noticed that the ceiling was covered with black beetles. Not having seen a light for a long time, the black beetles hurried to the lighted patch in great excitement, jostling one another, dropping on the table, and then running wildly about along the edge of it.

I don't like black beetles, nor uninvited guests in general. My neighbours seemed to me horribly repulsive, but there was nothing to be done: I could not begin by complaining of black beetles, and I suppressed my dislike of them. Besides, after a few days all the insects migrated to the next room, where the turnkey kept up a higher temperature; only an occasional specimen would look in on me, twitch his whiskers, and then hurry back to the warmth.

§3

IN spite of my entreaties, the turnkey insisted on closing the stove after he had lighted it. I soon felt uncomfortable and giddy, and I decided to get up and knock on the wall. I did get up, but I remember no more.

When I came to myself I was lying on the floor and my head was aching fiercely. A tall, grey-haired turnkey was standing over me with his arms folded, and watching me with a steady, expressionless stare, such as may be seen in the eyes of the dog watching the tortoise, in a well-known bronze group.

Seeing that I was conscious, he began: "Your Honour had a near shave of suffocation. But I put some pickled horse-radish to your nose, and now you can drink some *kvass*."* When I had drunk, he lifted me up and laid me on my bed. I felt very faint, and the window, which was double, could not be opened. The turnkey went to the office to ask that I might go out into the court; but the orderly officer sent a message that he could not undertake the responsibility in the absence of the colonel and adjutant. I had to put up with the foul atmosphere.

§4

BUT I became accustomed even to these quarters, and conjugated Italian verbs and read any books I could get. At first, the rules were fairly strict: when the bugle sounded for the last time at nine in the evening, a turnkey came in, blew out my candle, and locked me up for the

*A sort of beer.

night. I had to sit in darkness till eight next morning. I was never a great sleeper, and the want of exercise made four hours' sleep ample for me in prison; hence the want of a light was a serious deprivation. Besides this, a sentry at each end of the passage gave a loud prolonged cry of "All's well-l-l-l!" every quarter of an hour.

After a few weeks, however, the colonel allowed me to have a light. My window was beneath the level of the court, so that the sentry could watch all my movements; and no blind or curtain to the window was allowed. He also stopped the sentries from calling out in the passage. Later, we were permitted to have ink and a fixed number of sheets of paper, on condition that none were torn up; and we were allowed to walk in the yard once in twenty-four hours, accompanied by a sentry and the officer of the day, while outside the yard there was a fence and a chain of sentries.

The life was monotonous and peaceful; military precision gave it a kind of mechanical regularity like the caesura in verse. In the morning I made coffee over the stove with the help of the turnkey; at ten the officer of the day made his appearance, bringing in with him several cubic feet of frost, and clattering with his sword; he wore cloak and helmet and gloves up to his elbows; at one the turnkey brought me a dirty napkin and a bowl of soup, which he held by the rim in such a way that his two thumbs were noticeably cleaner than the other fingers. The food was tolerable; but it must be remembered that we were charged two *roubles* a day for it, which mounts up to a considerable sum for a poor man in the course of nine months. The father of one prisoner said frankly that he could not pay, whereupon he was told it would be stopped out of his salary; had he not been drawing Government pay, he would probably have been put in prison himself. There was also a Government allowance for our keep; but the quarter-masters put this in their pockets and stopped the mouths of the officers with orders for the theatres on first nights and benefits.

After sunset complete silence set in, only interrupted by the distant calls of the sentries, or the steps of a soldier crunching over the snow right in front of my window. I generally read till one, before I put out my candle. In my dreams I was free once more. Sometimes I woke up thinking: "What a horrid nightmare of prison and gaolers! How glad I am it's not true!"—and suddenly a sword rattled in the passage, or the officer of the day came in with his lantern-bearer, or a sentry called out "Who goes there?" in his mechanical voice, or a bugle, close to the window, split the morning air with reveille.

§5

WHEN I was bored and not inclined to read, I talked to my gaolers, especially to the old fellow who had treated me for my fainting fit. The colonel, as a mark of favour, excused some of the old soldiers from parade and gave them the light work of guarding a prisoner; they were in charge of a corporal—a spy and a scoundrel. Five or six of these veterans did all the work of the prison.

The old soldier I am speaking of was a simple creature, kind-hearted himself and grateful for any kindness that was shown him, and it is likely that not much had been shown him in the course of his life. He had served through the campaign of 1812 and his breast was covered with medals. His term of service had expired, but he stayed on as a volunteer, having no place to go to. "I wrote twice," he used to say, "to my relations in the Government of Mogilev, but I got no answer; so I suppose that all my people are dead. I don't care to go home, only to beg my bread in old age." How barbarous is the system of military service in Russia, which detains a man for twenty years with the colours! But in every sphere of life we sacrifice the individual without mercy and without reward.

Old Philimonov professed to know German; he had learned it in winter quarters after the taking of Paris. In fact, he knew some German words, to which he attached Russian terminations with much ingenuity.

§6

IN his stories of the past there was a kind of artlessness which made me sad. I shall record one of them.

He served in Moldavia, in the Turkish campaign of 1805; and the commander of his company was the kindest of men, caring like a father for each soldier and always foremost in battle. "Our captain was in love with a Moldavian woman, and we saw that he was in bad spirits; the reason was that she was often visiting another officer. One day he sent for me and a friend of mine—a fine soldier he was and lost both legs in battle afterwards—and said to us that the woman had jilted him; and he asked if we were willing to help him and teach her a lesson. 'Surely, Your Honour,' said we; 'we are at your service at any time.' He thanked us and pointed out the house where the officer lived. Then he said, 'Take your stand to-night on the bridge which she must cross to get to his house; catch hold of her quietly, and into the river with her!' 'Very good, Your Honour,' said we. So I and my chum got hold of a sack and went to the bridge; there we sat, and near midnight the girl came running past. 'What are you hurrying for?' we asked. Then we gave her one over the head; not a sound did she make, bless her; we put her in the sack and threw it into the river. Next day our captain went to the other officer and said: 'You must not be angry with the girl: we detained her; in fact, she is now at the bottom of the river. But I am quite prepared to take a little walk with you, with swords or pistols, as you prefer.' Well, they fought, and our captain was badly wounded in the chest; he wasted away, poor fellow, and after three months gave back his soul to God."

"But was the woman really drowned?" I asked.

"Oh, yes, Sir," said the soldier.

I was horrified by the childlike indifference with which the old man told me this story. He appeared to guess my feelings or to give a thought for the first time to his victim; for he added, to reassure me and make it up with his own conscience:

"You know, Sir, she was only a benighted heathen, not like a Christian at all."

§7

IT is the custom to serve out a glass of brandy to the gaolers on saints' days and royal birthdays; and Philimonov was allowed to decline this ration till five or six were due to him, and then to draw it all at once. He marked on a tally the number of glasses he did not drink, and applied for the lot on one of the great festivals. He poured all the brandy into a soup-tureen, crumbled bread into it, and then supped it with a spoon. When this repast was over, he smoked a large pipe with a tiny mouthpiece;

his tobacco, which he cut up himself, was strong beyond belief. As there was no seat in his room, he curled himself up on the narrow space of the window-sill; and there he smoked and sang a song about grass and flowers, pronouncing the words worse and worse as the liquor gained power over him. But what a constitution the man had! He was over sixty and had been twice wounded, and yet he could stand such a meal as I have described.

§8

BEFORE I end these Wouverman-Callot* sketches of barrack-life and this prison-gossip which only repeats the recollections of all captives like myself, I shall say something also of the officers.

Most of them were not spies at all, but good enough people, who had drifted by chance into the constabulary. Young nobles, with little or no education, without fortune or any settled prospects, they had taken to this life, because they had nothing else to do. They performed their duties with military precision, but without a scrap of enthusiasm, as far as I could see; I must except the adjutant, indeed; but then that was just why he *was* adjutant. When I got to know the officers, they granted me all the small indulgences that were in their power, and it would be a sin for me to complain of them.

One of the young officers told me a story of the year 1831, when he was sent to hunt down and arrest a Polish gentleman who was in hiding somewhere near his own estate. He was accused of having relations with agitators. The officer started on his mission, made enquiries, and

*Wouverman (1619-1668), a Dutch painter; Callot (1592-1635), a French painter; both painted outdoor life, soldiers, beggars, etc.

discovered the Pole's hiding place. He led his men there, surrounded the house, and entered it with two constables. The house was empty: they went through all the rooms and hunted about, but no one was to be seen; and yet some trifling signs proved that the house had been occupied not long before. Leaving his men below, the young officer went up to the attics a second time; after a careful search, he found a small door leading to a garret or secret chamber of some kind; the door was locked on the inside, but flew open at a kick. Behind it stood a tall and beautiful woman; she pointed without a word to a man who held in his arms a fainting girl of twelve. It was the Pole and his family. The officer was taken aback. The tall woman perceived this and said, "Can you be barbarous enough to destroy them?" The officer apologised: he urged the stock excuse, that a soldier is bound to implicit obedience; but at last, in despair, as he saw that his words had not the slightest effect, he ended by asking what he was to do. The woman looked haughtily at him, pointed to the door, and said, "Go down at once and say that there is no one here." "I swear I cannot explain it," the officer said, "but down I went and ordered the sergeant to collect the party. Two hours later we were beating every bush on another estate, while our man was slipping across the frontier. Strange, what things women make one do!"

§9

NOTHING in the world can be more stupid and more unfair than to judge a whole class of men in the lump, merely by the name they bear and the predominating characteristics of their profession. A label is a terrible thing. Jean

Paul Richter* says with perfect truth: "If a child tells a lie, make him afraid of doing wrong and tell him that he has told a lie, but don't call him a liar. If you define him as a liar, you break down his confidence in his own character." We are told that a man is a murderer, and we instantly imagine a hidden dagger, a savage expression, and dark designs, as if murder were the regular occupation, the trade, of anyone who has once in his life without design killed a man. A spy, or a man who makes money by the profligacy of others, cannot be honest; but it is possible to be an officer of police and yet to retain some manly worth, just as a tender and womanly heart and even delicacy of feeling may constantly be found in the victims of what is called "social incontinence."

I have an aversion for people who, because they are too stupid or will not take the trouble, never get beyond a mere label, who are brought up short by a single bad action or a false position, either chastely shutting their eyes to it or pushing it roughly from them. People who act thus are generally either bloodless and self-satisfied theorists, repulsive in their purity, or mean, low natures who have not yet had the chance or the necessity to display themselves in their true colours; they are by nature at home in the mire, into which others have fallen by misfortune.

*The German humorist (1763-1825).

CHAPTER V

The Enquiry—Golitsyn Senior—Golitsyn Junior—General Staal
—The Sentence—Sokolovski.

§1

BUT meanwhile what about the charge against us?
and what about the Commission of Enquiry?
The new Commission made just as great a mess
of it as its predecessor. The police had been on our track
for a long time, but their zeal and impatience prevented
them from waiting for a decent pretext, and they did a
silly thing. They employed a retired officer called Skaryatka to draw us on till we were committed; and he made
acquaintance with nearly all of our set. But we very soon
made out what he was and kept him at a distance. Some
other young men, chiefly students, were less cautious, but
these others had no relations of any importance with us.

One of the latter, on taking his degree, entertained his
friends on June 24, 1834. Not one of us was present at
the entertainment; not one of us was even invited. The
students drank toasts, and danced and played the fool;
and one thing they did was to sing in chorus Sokolovski's
well-known song abusing the Tsar.

Skaryatka was present and suddenly remembered that

the day was his birthday. He told a story of selling a horse at a profit and invited the whole party to supper at his rooms, promising a dozen of champagne. They all accepted. The champagne duly appeared, and their host, who had begun to stagger, proposed that Sokolovski's song should be sung over again. In the middle of the song the door opened, and Tsinski appeared with his myrmidons. It was a stupid and clumsy proceeding, and a failure as well.

The police wanted to catch *us* and were looking out for some tangible pretext, in order to trap the five or six victims whom they had marked down; what they actually did was to arrest a score of innocent persons.

§2

BUT the police are not easily abashed, and they arrested us a fortnight later, as concerned in the affair of the students' party. They found a number of letters—letters of Satin's at Sokolovski's rooms, of Ogaryóv's at Satin's, and of mine at Ogaryóv's; but nothing of importance was discovered. The first Commission of Enquiry was a failure; and in order that the second might succeed better, the Tsar sent from Petersburg the Grand Inquisitor, Prince A. F. Golitsyn.

The breed to which he belonged is rare with us; it included Mordvínov, the notorious chief of the Third Section, Pelikan, the Rector of Vilna University, with a few officials from the Baltic provinces and renegade Poles.

§3

BUT it was unfortunate for the Inquisition that Staal, the Commandant of Moscow, was the first member appointed to it. Staal was a brave old soldier and an honest man; he looked into the matter, and found that two quite distinct incidents were involved: the first was the students' party, which the police were bound to punish; the second was the mysterious arrest of some men, whose whole visible fault was limited to some half-expressed opinions, and whom it would be difficult and absurd to try on that charge alone.

Prince A. F. Golitsyn disapproved of Staal's view, and their dispute took a heated turn. The old soldier grew furiously angry; he dashed his sword on the floor and said: "Instead of destroying these young men, you would do better to have all the schools and universities closed, and that would be a warning to other unfortunates. Do as you please, only I shall take no part in it: I shall not set foot again in this place." Having spoken thus, the old man left the room at once.

This was reported to the Tsar that very day; and when the Commandant presented his report next morning, the Tsar asked why he refused to attend the Commission, and Staal told him the reason.

"What nonsense!" said Nicholas; "I wonder you are not ashamed to quarrel with Golitsyn, and I hope you will continue to attend."

"Sir," replied Staal, "spare my grey hairs! I have lived till now without the smallest stain on my honour. My loyalty is known to Your Majesty; my life, what remains of it, is at your service. But this matter touches my honour, and my conscience protests against the proceedings of that Commission."

The Tsar frowned; Staal bowed himself out and never afterwards attended a single meeting.

§4

THE Commission now consisted of foes only. The President was Prince S. M. Golitsyn, a simple old gentleman, who, after sitting for nine months, knew just as little about the business as he did nine months before he took the chair. He preserved a dignified silence and seldom spoke; whenever an examination was finished, he asked, "May he be dismissed?" "Yes," said Golitsyn junior, and then Golitsyn senior signified in a stately manner to the accused, "You may go."

§5

MY first examination lasted four hours. The questions asked were of two kinds. The object of the first was to discover a trend of thought "opposed to the spirit of the Russian government, and ideas that were either revolutionary or impregnated with the pestilent doctrine of Saint-Simonianism"—this is a quotation from Golitsyn junior and Oranski, the paymaster.

Such questions were simple, but they were not really questions at all. The confiscated papers and letters were clear enough evidence of opinions; the questions could only turn on the essential fact, whether the letters were or were not written by the accused; but the Commissioners thought it necessary to add to each expression they had copied out, "In what sense do you explain the following passage in your letter?"

Of course there was nothing to explain, and I wrote meaningless and evasive answers to all the questions. Oranski discovered the following statement in one of my letters: "No written constitution leads to anything: they are all mere contracts between a master and his slaves;

the problem is not to improve the condition of the slaves but to eliminate them altogether." When called upon to explain this statement, I remarked that I saw no necessity to defend constitutional government, and that, if I had done so, I might have been prosecuted.

"There are two sides from which constitutional government can be attacked," said Golitsyn junior, in his excitable, sibilant voice, "and you don't attack it from the point of view of autocracy, or else you would not have spoken of 'slaves.' "

"In that respect I am as guilty as the Empress Catherine, who forbade her subjects to call themselves slaves."

Golitsyn junior was furious at my sarcasm.

"Do you suppose," he said, "that we meet here to carry on academic discussion, and that you are defending a thesis in the lecture-room?"

"Why then do you ask for explanations?"

"Do you pretend not to understand what is wanted of you?"

"I don't understand," I said.

"How obstinate they are, every one of them!" said the chairman, Golitsyn senior, as he shrugged his shoulders and looked at Colonel Shubenski, of the police. I smiled. "Ogaryóv over again," sighed the worthy old gentleman, letting the cat quite out of the bag.

A pause followed this indiscretion. The meetings were all held in the Prince's library, and I turned towards the shelves and examined the books; they included an edition in many volumes of the *Memoirs* of the Duc de Saint-Simon.*

*The author of the famous *Memoirs* (1675-1755) was an ancestor of the preacher of socialism (1760-1825).

I turned to the chairman. "There!" I said, "what an injustice! You are trying me for Saint-Simonianism, and you, Prince, have on your shelves twenty volumes of his works."

The worthy man had never read a book in his life, and was at loss for a reply. But Golitsyn junior darted a furious glance at me and asked, "Don't you see that these are the works of the Duc de Saint-Simon who lived in the reign of Louis XIV?"

The chairman smiled and conveyed to me by a nod his impression that I had made a slip this time; then he said, "You may go."

When I had reached the door, the chairman asked, "Was it he who wrote the article about Peter the Great which you showed me?"

"Yes," answered Shubenski.

I stopped short.

"He has ability," remarked the chairman.

"So much the worse: poison is more dangerous in skilful hands," added the Inquisitor; "a very dangerous young man and quite incorrigible."

These words contained my condemnation.

Here is a parallel to the Saint-Simon incident. When the police-officer was going through books and papers at Ogaryóv's house, he put aside a volume of Thiers's *History of the French Revolution*; when he found a second volume, a third, an eighth, he lost patience. "What a collection of revolutionary works! And here's another!" he added, handing to his subordinate Cuvier's speech *Sur les révolutions du globe terrestre*!

§6

THERE were other questions of a more complicated kind, in which various traps and tricks, familiar to the police and boards of enquiry, were made use of, in order to confuse me and involve me in contradictions. Hints that others had confessed, and moral torture of various kinds, came into play here. They are not worth repeating; it is enough to say that the tricks all failed to make me or my three friends betray one another.

When the last question had been handed out to me, I was sitting alone in the small room where we wrote our replies. Suddenly the door opened, and Golitsyn junior came in, wearing a pained and anxious expression.

"I have come," he said, "to have a talk with you before the end of your replies to our questions. The long friendship between my late father and yours makes me feel a special interest in you. You are young and may have a distinguished career yet; but you must first clear yourself of this business, and that fortunately depends on yourself alone. Your father has taken your arrest very much to heart; his one hope now is that you will be released. The President and I were discussing it just now, and we are sincerely ready to make large concessions; but you must make it possible for us to help you."

I saw what he was driving at. The blood rushed to my head, and I bit my pen with rage.

He went on: "You are on the road that leads straight to service in the ranks or imprisonment, and on the way you will kill your father: he will not survive the day when he sees you in the grey overcoat of a private soldier."

I tried to speak, but he stopped me. "I know what you want to say. Have patience a moment. That you had designs against the Government is perfectly clear; and we must have proofs of your repentance, if you are to be an object of the Tsar's clemency. You deny everything; you give evasive answers; from a false feeling of honour you protect people of whom we know more than you do, and who are by no means as scrupulous as you are; you won't help them, but they will drag you over the precipice in their fall. Now write a letter to the Board; say simply and frankly that you are conscious of your guilt, and that you were led away by the thoughtlessness of youth; and name the persons whose unhappy errors led you astray. Are you willing to pay this small price, in order to redeem your whole future and to save your father's life?"

"I know nothing, and will add nothing to my previous disclosures," I replied.

Golitsyn got up and said in a dry voice: "Very well! As you refuse, we are not to blame." That was the end of my examination.

§7

I MADE my last appearance before the Commission in January or February of 1835. I was summoned there to read through my answers, make any additions I wished, and sign my name. Shubenski was the only Commissioner present. When I had done reading, I said:

"I should like to know what charge can be based on these questions and these answers. Which article of the code applies to my case?"

"The code of law is intended for crimes of a different kind," answered the colonel in blue.

"That is another matter. But when I read over all these literary exercises, I cannot believe that the charge, on which I have spent six months in prison, is really contained there."

"Do you really imagine," returned Shubenski, "that we accepted your statement that you were not forming a secret society?"

"Where is it, then?" I asked.

"It is lucky for you that we could not find the proofs, and that you were cut short. We stopped you in time; indeed, it may be said that we saved you."

Gógol's story, in fact, over again, of the carpenter Poshlepkin and his wife, in *The Revizor*.*

After I had signed my name, Shubenski rang and ordered the priest to be summoned. The priest appeared and added his signature, testifying that all my admissions had been made voluntarily and without compulsion of any kind. Of course, he had never been present while I was examined; and he had not the assurance to ask my account of the proceedings. I thought of the unprejudiced witness who stopped outside our house while the police arrested me.

§8

WHEN the enquiry was over, the conditions of my imprisonment were relaxed to some extent, and near relations could obtain permission for interviews. In this way two more months passed by.

In the middle of March our sentence was confirmed. What it was nobody knew: some said we should be banished to the Caucasus, while others hoped we should all be released. The latter was Staal's proposal, which he submitted separately to the Tsar; he held that we had been sufficiently punished by our imprisonment.

*Gógol, *The Revizor*, Act IV, Scene ii.

At last, on the twentieth of March, we were all brought to Prince Golitsyn's house, to hear our sentence. It was a very great occasion: for we had never met since we were arrested.

A cordon of police and officers of the garrison stood round us, while we embraced and shook hands with one another. The sight of friends gave life to all of us, and we made plenty of noise; we asked questions and told our adventures indefatigably.

Sokolovski was present, rather pale and thin, but as humorous as ever.

§9

SOKOLOVSKI, the author of *Creation* and other meritorious poems, had a strong natural gift for poetry; but this gift was neither improved by cultivation nor original enough to dispense with it. He was not a politician at all, he lived the life of a poet. He was very amusing and amiable, a cheerful companion in cheerful hours, a *bon vivant*, who enjoyed a gay party as well as the rest of us, and perhaps a little better. He was now over thirty.

When suddenly torn from this life and thrown into prison, he bore himself nobly: imprisonment strengthened his character.

He was arrested in Petersburg and then conveyed to Moscow, without being told where he was going. Useless tricks of this kind are constantly played by the Russian police; in fact, it is the poetry of their lives; there is no calling in the world, however prosaic and repulsive, that does not possess its own artistic refinements and mere superfluous adornments. Sokolovski was taken straight to prison and lodged in a kind of dark store-room. Why should he be confined in prison and we in barracks?

He took nothing there with him but a couple of shirts. In England, every convict is forced to take a bath as soon as he enters prison; in Russia, precautionary measures are taken against cleanliness.

Sokolovski would have been in a horrible state had not Dr. Haas sent him a parcel of his own linen.

§10

THIS Dr. Haas, who was often called a fool and a lunatic, was a very remarkable man. His memory ought not to be buried in the jungle of official obituaries—that record of virtues that never showed themselves until their possessors were mouldering in the grave.

He was a little old man with a face like wax; in his black tail-coat, knee-breeches, black silk stockings, and shoes with buckles, he looked as if he had just stepped out of some play of the eighteenth century. In this costume, suitable for a wedding or a funeral, and in the agreeable climate of the 59th degree of north latitude, he used to drive once a week to the Sparrow Hills when the convicts were starting for the first stage of their long march. He had access to them in his capacity of a prison-doctor, and went there to pass them in review; and he always took with him a basketful of odds and ends—eatables and dainties of different kinds for the women, such as walnuts, gingerbread, apples, and oranges. This generosity excited the wrath and displeasure of the 'charitable' ladies, who were afraid of giving pleasure by their charity, and afraid of being more charitable than was absolutely necessary to save the convicts from being starved or frozen.

But Haas was obstinate. When reproached for the fool-

ish indulgence he showed to the women, he would listen
meekly, rub his hands, and reply: "Please observe, my
dear lady; they can get a crust of bread from anyone, but
they won't see sweets or oranges again for a long time,
because no one gives them such things—your own words
prove that. And therefore I give them this little pleasure,
because they won't get it soon again."

Haas lived in a hospital. One morning a patient came
to consult him. Haas examined him and went to his study
to write a prescription. When he returned, the invalid had
disappeared, and so had the silver off the dinner-table.
Haas called a porter and asked whether anyone else had
entered the building. The porter realised the situation:
he rushed out and returned immediately with the spoons
and the patient, whom he had detained with the help of a
sentry. The thief fell on his knees and begged for mercy.
Haas was perplexed.

"Fetch a policeman," he said to one of the porters.
"And you summon a clerk here at once."

The two porters, pleased with their part in detecting
the criminal, rushed from the room; and Haas took advantage of their absence to address the thief. "You are
a dishonest man; you deceived me and tried to rob me;
God will judge you for it. But now run out at the back
gate as fast as you can, before the sentries come back.
And wait a moment—very likely you haven't a penny;
here is half a *rouble* for you. But you must try to mend
your ways: you can't escape God as easily as the policeman."

His family told Haas he had gone too far this time. But
the incorrigible doctor stated his view thus: "Theft is a
serious vice; but I know the police, and how they flog

people; it is a much worse vice to deliver up your neigh-bour to their tender mercies. And besides, who knows? My treatment may soften his heart."

His family shook their heads and protested: and the charitable ladies said, "An excellent man but not quite all right *there*," pointing to their foreheads; but Haas only rubbed his hands and went his own way.

§11

SOKOLOVSKI had hardly got to an end of his narrative be-fore others began to tell their story, several speaking at the same time. It was as if we had returned from a long journey—there was a running fire of questions and friendly chaff.

Satin had suffered more in body that the rest of us: he looked thin and had lost some of his hair. He was on his mother's estate in the Government of Tambóv when he heard of our arrest, and started at once for Moscow, that his mother might not be terrified by a visit from the police. But he caught cold on the journey and was seriously ill when he reached Moscow. The police found him there in his bed. It being impossible to remove him, he was put under arrest in his own house: a sentry was posted inside his bedroom, and a male sister of mercy, in the shape of a policeman, sat by his pillow; hence, when he recovered from delirium, his eyes rested on the scrutinising looks of one attendant or the sodden face of the other.

When winter began he was transferred to a hospital. It turned out that there was no unoccupied room suitable for a prisoner; but that was a trifle which caused no difficulty. A secluded corner *without a stove* was dis-covered in the building, and here he was placed with a sentry to guard him. Nothing like a balcony on the Riviera for an invalid! What the temperature in that stone box was like in winter, may be guessed: the sentry suffered so much that he used at night to go into the passage and warm himself at the stove, begging his prisoner not to tell the officer of the day.

But even the authorities of the hospital could not continue this open-air treatment in such close proximity to the North Pole, and they moved Satin to a room next to that in which people who were brought in frozen were rubbed till they regained consciousness.

§12

BEFORE we had nearly done telling our own experiences and listening to those of our friends, the adjutants began to bustle about, the garrison officers stood up straight, and the policemen came to attention; then the door opened solemnly, and little Prince Golitsyn entered *en grande tenue* with his ribbon across his shoulder; Tsinski was in Household uniform; and even Oranski had put on something special for the joyful occasion—a light green costume, between uniform and mufti. Staal, of course, was not there.

The officers now divided us into three groups. Sokolovski, an artist called Ootkin, and Ibayev formed the first group; I and my friends came next, and then a miscellaneous assortment.

The first three, who were charged with treason, were sentenced to confinement at Schlüsselburg* for an unlimited term.

*A prison-fortress on an island in the Neva, forty miles from Petersburg.

In order to show his easy, pleasant manners, Tsinski asked Sokolovski, after the sentence was read, "I think you have been at Schlüsselburg before?" "Yes, last year," was the immediate answer; "I suppose I knew what was coming, for I drank a bottle of Madeira there."

§13

Two years later Ootkin died in the fortress. Sokolovski was released more dead than alive and sent to the Caucasus, where he died at Pyatigorsk. Of Ibayev it may be said in one sense that he died too; for he became a mystic.

Ootkin, "a free artist confined in prison," as he signed himself in replying to the questions put to him, was a man of forty; he never took part in political intrigue of any kind, but his nature was proud and vehement, and he was uncontrolled in his language and disrespectful to the members of the Commission. For this they did him to death in a damp dungeon where the water trickled down the walls.

But for his officer's uniform, Ibayev would never have been punished so severely. He happened to be present at a party where he probably drank too much and sang, but he certainly drank no more and sang no louder than the rest.

§14

AND now our turn came. Oranski rubbed his spectacles, cleared his throat, and gave utterance to the imperial edict. It was here set forth that the Tsar, having considered the report of the Commission and taking special account of the youth of the criminals, ordered that they should not be brought before a court of justice. On the contrary, the Tsar in his infinite clemency pardoned the majority of the offenders and allowed them to live at home under police supervision. But the ringleaders were to undergo corrective discipline, in the shape of banishment to distant Governments for an unlimited term; they were to serve in the administration, under the supervision of the local authorities.

This last class contained six names—Ogaryóv, Satin, Lakhtin, Sorokin, Obolenski, and myself. My destination was Perm. Lakhtin had never been arrested at all; when he was summoned to the Commission to hear the sentence, he supposed it was intended merely to give him a fright, that he might take thought when he saw the punishment of others. It was said that this little surprise was managed by a relation of Prince Golitsyn's who was angry with Lakhtin's wife. He had weak health and died after three years in exile.

When Oranski had done reading, Colonel Shubenski stepped forward. He explained to us in picked phrases and the style of Lomonossov,* that for the Tsar's clemency we were obliged to the good offices of the distinguished nobleman who presided at the Commission. He expected that we should all express at once our gratitude to the great man, but he was disappointed.

Some of those who had been pardoned made a sign with their heads, but even they stole a glance at us as they did so.

Shubenski then turned to Ogaryóv and said: "You are going to Penza. Do you suppose that is a mere accident? Your father is lying paralysed at Penza; and the Prince asked the Emperor that you might be sent there, that

*I.e., an old-fashioned pompous style. Lomonossov (1711-1765) was the originator of Russian literature and Russian science.

your presence might to some extent lighten the blow he must suffer in your banishment. Do you too think you have no cause for gratitude?"

Ogaryóv bowed; and that was all they got for their pains.

But that good old gentleman, the President, was pleased, and for some reason called me up next. I stepped forward: whatever he or Shubenski might say, I vowed by all the gods that I would not thank them. Besides, my place of exile was the most distant and most disgusting of all.

"So you are going to Perm," said the Prince.

I said nothing. The Prince was taken aback, but, in order to say something, he added, "I have an estate there."

"Can I take any message to your bailiff?" I asked, smiling.

"I send no messages by people like you—mere *carbonari*," said the Prince, by a sudden inspiration.

"What do you want of me then?" I asked.

"Nothing."

"Well, I thought you called me forward."

"You may go," interrupted Shubenski.

"Permit me," I said, "as I am here, to remind you that you, Colonel, said to me on my last appearance before the Commission, that no one charged me with complicity in the students' party; but now the sentence says that I am one of those punished on that account. There is some mistake here."

"Do you mean to protest against the imperial decision?" cried out Shubenski. "If you are not careful, young man, something worse may be substituted for Perm. I shall order your words to be taken down."

"Just what I meant to ask. The sentence says 'according to the report of the Commission': well, my protest is not against the imperial edict but against your report. I call the Prince to witness, that I was never even questioned about the party or the songs sung there."

Shubenski turned pale with rage. "You pretend not to know," he said, "that your guilt is ten times greater than that of those who attended the party." He pointed to one of the pardoned men: "There is a man who sang an objectionable song under the influence of drink; but he afterwards begged forgiveness on his knees with tears. You are still far enough from any repentance."

"Excuse me," I went on; "the depth of my guilt is not the question. But if I am a murderer, I don't want to pass for a thief. I don't want people to say, even by way of defence, that I did so-and-so under the influence of drink."

"If my son, my own son, were as brazen as you, I should myself ask the Tsar to banish him to Siberia."

At this point the Commissioner of Police struck in with some incoherent nonsense. It is a pity that Golitsyn junior was not present; he would have had a chance to air his rhetoric.

All this, as a matter of course, led to nothing.

We stayed in the room for another quarter of an hour, and spent the time, undeterred by the earnest representations of the police-officers, in warm embraces and a long farewell. I never saw any of them again, except Obolenski, before my return from Vyatka.

§15

WE had to face our departure. Prison was in a sense a continuation of our former life; but with our departure for the wilds, it broke off short. Our little band of youthful friends was parting asunder. Our exile was sure to last for several years. Where and how, if ever, should we meet again? One felt regret for that past life—one had been forced to leave it so suddenly, without saying goodbye. Of a meeting with Ogaryóv I had no hope. Two of my intimate friends secured an interview with me towards the end, but I wanted something more.

§16

I WISHED to see once more the girl who had cheered me before and to press her hand as I had pressed it in the churchyard nine months earlier. At that interview I intended to part with the past and greet the future.

We did meet for a few minutes on April 9, 1835, the day before my departure into exile.

Long did I keep that day sacred in memory; it is one of the red-letter days of my life.

But why does the recollection of that day and all the bright and happy days of my past life recall so much that is terrible? I see a grave, a wreath of dark-red roses, two children whom I am leading by the hand, torch-light, a band of exiles, the moon, a warm sea beneath a mountain; I hear words spoken which I cannot understand, and yet they tear my heart.*

All, all, has passed away!

*Herzen's wife, Natalie, died at Nice in 1852 and was buried there under the circumstances here described.

CHAPTER VI

Exile—A Chief Constable—The Volga—Perm.

§1

ON the morning of April 10, 1835, a police-officer conducted me to the Governor's palace, where my parents were allowed to take leave of me in the private part of the office.

This was bound to be an uncomfortable and painful scene. Spies and clerks swarmed round us; we listened while his instructions were read aloud to the police-agent who was to go with me; it was impossible to exchange a word unwatched—in short, more painful and galling surroundings cannot be imagined. It was a relief when the carriage started at last along the Vladimirka River.

> *Per me si va nella città dolente,*
> *Per me si va nell' eterno dolore—**

I wrote this couplet on the wall of one of the post-houses; it suits the vestibule of Hell and the road to Siberia equally well.

One of my intimate friends had promised to meet me at an inn seven *versts* from Moscow.

*Dante, *Inferno*, Canto III.

I proposed to the police-agent that he should have a glass of brandy there; we were at a safe distance from Moscow, and he accepted. We went in, but my friend was not there. I put off our start by every means in my power; but at last my companion was unwilling to wait longer, and the driver was touching up the horses, when suddenly a *troika** came galloping straight up to the door. I rushed out—and met two strangers; they were merchants' sons out for a spree and made some noise as they got off their vehicle. All along the road to Moscow I could not see a single moving spot, nor a single human being. I felt it bitter to get into the carriage and start. But I gave the driver a quarter-*rouble,* and off we flew like an arrow from the bow.

We put up nowhere: the orders were that not less than 200 *versts* were to be covered every twenty-four hours. That would have been tolerable, at any other season; but it was the beginning of April, and the road was covered with ice in some places, and with water and mud in others; and it got worse and worse with each stage of our advance towards Siberia.

§2

My first adventure happened at Pokróv.

We had lost some hours owing to the ice on the river, which cut off all communication with the other side. My guardian was eager to get on, when the post-master at Pokróv suddenly declared that there were no fresh horses. My keeper produced his passport, which stated that horses must be forthcoming all along the road; he was told that the horses were engaged for the Under-Secretary of the Home Office. He began, of course, to wrangle and make

*Three horses harnessed abreast form a *troika.*

a noise; and then they both went off together to get horses from the local peasants.

Getting tired of waiting for their return in the post-master's dirty room, I went out at the gate and began to walk about in front of the house. It was nine months since I had taken a walk without the presence of a sentry.

I had been walking half an hour when a man came up to me; he was wearing uniform without epaulettes and a blue medal-ribbon. He stared very hard at me, walked past, turned round at once, and asked me in an insolent manner:

"Is it you who are going to Perm with a police-officer?"

"Yes," I answered, still walking.

"Excuse me! excuse me! How does the man dare . . . ?"

"Whom have I the honour of speaking to?"

"I am the chief constable of this town," replied the stranger, and his voice showed how deeply he felt his own social importance. "The Under-Secretary may arrive at any moment, and here, if you please, there are political prisoners walking about the streets! What an idiot that policeman is!"

"May I trouble you to address your observations to the man himself?"

"Address him? I shall arrest him and order him a hundred lashes, and send you on in charge of someone else."

Without waiting for the end of his speech, I nodded and walked back quickly to the post-house. Sitting by the window, I could hear his loud angry voice as he threatened my keeper, who excused himself but did not seem seriously alarmed. Presently they came into the room together; I did not turn round but went on looking out of the window.

From their conversation I saw at once that the chief constable was dying to know all about the circumstances of my banishment. As I kept up a stubborn silence, the official began an impersonal address, intended equally for me and my keeper.

"We get no sympathy. What pleasure is it to me, pray, to quarrel with a policeman or to inconvenience a gentleman whom I never set eyes on before in my life? But I have a great responsibility, in my position here. Whatever happens, I get the blame. If public funds are stolen, they attack me; if the church catches fire, they attack me; if there are too many drunk men in the streets, I suffer for it; if too little whisky is drunk,* I suffer for that too." He was pleased with his last remark and went on more cheerfully: "It is lucky you met me, but you might have met the Secretary; and if you had walked past him, he would have said 'A political prisoner walking about! Arrest the chief constable!'"

I got weary at last of his eloquence. I turned to him and said:

"Do your duty by all means, but please spare me your sermons. From what you say I see that you expected me to bow to you; but I am not in the habit of bowing to strangers."

My friend was flabbergasted.

That is the rule all over Russia, as a friend of mine used to say: whoever gets rude and angry first, always wins. If you ever allow a Jack in office to raise his voice, you are lost: when he hears himself shouting, he turns into a wild beast. But if *you* begin shouting at his first rude word, he is certain to be cowed; for he thinks that

*A great revenue was derived by Government from the sale of spirits.

you mean business and are the sort of person whom it is unsafe to irritate.

The chief constable sent my keeper to enquire about the horses; then he turned to me and remarked by way of apology:

"I acted in that way chiefly because of the man. You don't know what our underlings are like—it is impossible to pass over the smallest breach of discipline. But I assure you I know a gentleman when I see him. Might I ask you what unfortunate incident it was that brings you . . ."

"We were bound to secrecy at the end of the trial."

"Oh, in that case . . . of course . . . I should not venture . . . "—and his eyes expressed the torments of curiosity. He held his tongue, but not for long.

"I had a distant cousin, who was imprisoned for about a year in the fortress of Peter and Paul; he was mixed up with . . . you understand. Excuse me, but I think you are still angry, and I take it to heart. I am used to army discipline; I began serving when I was seventeen. I have a hot temper, but it all passes in a moment. I won't trouble your man any further, deuce take him!"

My keeper now came in and reported that it would take an hour to drive in the horses from the fields.

The chief constable told him that he was pardoned at my intercession; then he turned to me and added:

"To show that you are not angry, I do hope you will come and take pot-luck with me—I live two doors away; please don't refuse."

This turn to our interview seemed to me so amusing that I went to his house, where I ate his pickled sturgeon and caviare and drank his brandy and Madeira.

He grew so friendly that he told me all his private

affairs, including the details of an illness from which his wife had suffered for seven years. After our meal, with pride and satisfaction he took a letter from a jar on the table and let me read a "poem" which his son had written at school and recited on Speech-day. After these flattering proofs of confidence, he neatly changed the conversation and enquired indirectly about my offence; and this time I gratified his curiosity to some extent.

This man reminded me of a justice's clerk whom my friend S. used to speak about. Though his chief had been changed a dozen times, the clerk never lost his place and was the real ruler of the district.

"How do you manage to get on with them all?" my friend asked.

"All right, thank you; one manages to rub on somehow. You do sometimes get a gentleman who is very awkward at first, kicks with fore legs and hind legs, shouts abuse at you, and threatens to complain at head-quarters and get you turned out. Well, you know, the likes of us have to put up with that. One holds one's tongue and thinks—'Oh, he'll wear himself out in time; he's only just getting into harness.' And so it turns out: once started, he goes along first-rate."

§3

On getting near Kazán, we found the Volga in full flood. The river spread fifteen *versts* or more beyond its banks, and we had to travel by water for the whole of the last stage. It was bad weather, and a number of carts and other vehicles were detained on the bank, as the ferries had stopped working.

My keeper went to the man in charge and demanded

a raft for our use. The man gave it unwillingly; he said that it was dangerous and we had better wait. But my keeper was in haste, partly because he was drunk and partly because he wished to show his power.

My carriage was placed upon a moderate-sized raft and we started. The weather appeared to improve; and after half an hour the boatman, who was a Tatar, hoisted a sail. But suddenly the storm came on again with fresh violence, and we were carried rapidly downstream. We caught up some floating timber and struck it so hard that our rickety raft was nearly wrecked and the water came over the decking. It was an awkward situation; but the Tatar managed to steer us into a sandbank.

A barge now hove in sight. We called out to them to send us their boat, but the bargemen, though they heard us, went past and gave us no assistance.

A peasant, who had his wife with him in a small boat, rowed up to us and asked what was the matter. "What of that?" he said. "Stop the leak, say a prayer, and start off. There's nothing to worry about; but you're a Tatar, and that's why you're so helpless." Then he waded over to our raft.

The Tatar was really very much alarmed. In the first place, my keeper, who was asleep when the water came on board and wet him, sprang to his feet and began to beat the Tatar. In the second place, the raft was Government property and the Tatar kept saying, "If it goes to the bottom, I shall catch it!" I tried to comfort him by saying that in that case he would go to the bottom too.

"But, if I'm *not* drowned, *bátyushka,* what then?" was his reply.

The peasant and some labourers stuffed up the leak in

the raft and nailed a board over it with their axe-heads; then, up to the waist in the water, they dragged the raft off the sandbank, and we soon reached the channel of the Volga. The current ran furiously. Wind, rain, and snow lashed our faces, and the cold pierced to our bones; but soon the statue of Ivan the Terrible began to loom out from behind the fog and torrents of rain. It seemed that the danger was past; but suddenly the Tatar called out in a piteous voice, "It's leaking, it's leaking!"—and the water did in fact come rushing in at the old leak. We were right in the centre of the stream, but the raft began to move slower and slower, and the time seemed at hand when it would sink altogether. The Tatar took off his cap and began to pray; my servant shed tears and said a final good-bye to his mother at home; but my keeper used bad language and vowed he would beat them both when we landed.

I too felt uneasy at first, partly owing to the wind and rain, which added an element of confusion and disorder to the danger. But then it seemed to me absurd that I should meet my death before I had done anything; the spirit of the conqueror's question—*quid timeas? Caesarem vehis!*—asserted itself;* and I waited calmly for the end, convinced that I should not end my life there, between Uslon and Kazán. Later life saps such proud confidence and makes a man suffer for it; and that is why youth is bold and heroic, while a man in years is cautious and seldom carried away.

A quarter of an hour later we landed, drenched and frozen, near the walls of the Kremlin of Kazán. At the

*The story of Caesar's rebuke to the boatman is told by Plutarch in his *Life of Caesar*, chap. 38.

nearest public-house I got a glass of spirits and a hard-boiled egg, and then went off to the post-house.

§4

IN villages and small towns, the post-master keeps a room for the accommodation of travellers; but in the large towns, where everybody goes to the hotels, there is no such provision. I was taken into the office, and the post-master showed me his own room. It was occupied by women and children and an old bedridden man; there was positively not a corner where I could change my clothes. I wrote a letter to the officer in command of the Kazán police, asking him to arrange that I should have some place where I could warm myself and dry my clothes.

My messenger returned in an hour's time and reported that Count Apraxin would grant my request. I waited two hours more, but no one came, and I despatched my messenger again. He brought this answer—that the colonel who had received Apraxin's order was playing whist at the club, and that nothing could be done for me till next day.

This was positive cruelty, and I wrote a second letter to Apraxin. I asked him to send me on at once and said I hoped to find better quarters after the next stage of my journey. But my letter was not delivered, because the Count had gone to bed. I could do no more. I took off my wet clothes in the office; then I wrapped myself up in a soldier's overcoat and lay down on the table; a thick book, covered with some of my linen, served me as a pillow. I sent out for some breakfast in the morning. By that time the clerks were arriving, and the door-keeper pointed out to me that a public office was an unsuitable place to breakfast in; it made no difference to him personally, but the post-master might disapprove of my proceedings.

I laughed and said that a captive was secure against eviction and was bound to eat and drink in his place of confinement, wherever it might be.

Next morning Count Apraxin gave me leave to stay three days at Kazán and to put up at a hotel.

For those three days I wandered about the city, attended everywhere by my keeper. The veiled faces of the Tatar women, the high cheekbones of their husbands, the mosques of true believers standing side by side with the churches of the Orthodox faith—it all reminds one of Asia and the East. At Vladímir or Nizhni the neighbourhood of Moscow is felt; but one feels far from Moscow at Kazán.

§5

WHEN I reached Perm, I was taken straight to the Governor's house. There was a great gathering there; for it was his daughter's wedding-day; the bridegroom was an officer in the Army. The Governor insisted that I should come in. So I made my bow to the *beau monde* of Perm, covered with mud and dust, and wearing a shabby, stained coat. The Governor talked a great deal of nonsense; he told me to keep clear of the Polish exiles in the town and to call again in the course of a few days, when he would provide me with some occupation in the public offices.

The Governor of Perm was a Little Russian; he was not hard upon the exiles and behaved reasonably in other respects. Like a mole which adds grain to grain in some underground repository, so he kept putting by a trifle for a rainy day, without anyone being the wiser.

§6

From some dim idea of keeping a check over us, he ordered that all the exiles residing at Perm should report themselves at his house, at ten every Saturday morning. He came in smoking his pipe and ascertained, by means of a list which he carried, whether all were present; if anyone was missing, he sent to enquire the reason; he hardly ever spoke to anyone before dismissing us. Thus I made the acquaintance in his drawing-room of all the Poles whom he had told me I was to avoid.

The day after I reached Perm, my keeper departed, and I was at liberty for the first time since my arrest— at liberty, in a little town on the Siberian frontier, with no experience of life and no comprehension of the sphere in which I was now forced to live.

From the nursery I had passed straight to the lecture-room, and from the lecture-room to a small circle of friends, an intimate world of theories and dreams, without contact with practical life; then came prison, with its opportunities for reflexion; and contact with life was only beginning now and here, by the ridge of the Ural Mountains.

Practical life made itself felt at once: the day after my arrival I went to look for lodgings with the porter at the Governor's office; he took me to a large one-storeyed house; and, though I explained that I wanted a small house, or, better still, part of a house, he insisted that I should go in.

The lady who owned the house made me sit on the sofa. Hearing that I came from Moscow, she asked if I had seen M. Kabrit there. I replied that I had never in my life heard a name like it.

"Come, come!" said the old lady; "I mean M. Kabrit," and she gave his Christian name and patronymic. "You don't say, *bátyushka,* that you don't know him! He is our Vice-Governor!"

"Well, I spent nine months in prison," I said smiling, "and perhaps that accounts for my not hearing of him."

"It may be so. And so you want to hire the little house, *bátyushka?*"

"It's a big house, much too big; I said so to the man who brought me."

"Too much of this world's goods are no burden to the back."

"True; but you will ask a large rent for your large house."

"Who told you, young man, about my prices? I've not opened my mouth yet."

"Yes, but I know you can't ask little for a house like this."

"How much do you offer?"

In order to have done with her, I said that I would not pay more than 350 *roubles.*

"And glad I am to get it, my lad! Just drink a glass of Canary, and go and have your boxes moved in here."

The rent seemed to me fabulously low, and I took the house. I was just going when she stopped me.

"I forgot to ask you one thing—do you mean to keep a cow?"

"Good heavens! No!" I answered, deeply insulted by such a question.

"Very well; then I will supply you with cream."

I went home, thinking with horror that I had reached a place where I was thought capable of keeping a cow!

§7

BEFORE I had time to look about me, the Governor informed me that I was transferred to Vyatka: another exile who was destined for Vyatka had asked to be transferred to Perm, where some of his relations lived. The Governor wished me to start next day. But that was impossible; as I expected to stay some time at Perm, I had bought a quantity of things and must sell them, even at a loss of 50 per cent. After several evasive answers, the Governor allowed me to stay for forty-eight hours longer, but he made me promise not to seek an opportunity of meeting the exile from Vyatka.

I was preparing to sell my horse and a variety of rubbish, when the inspector of police appeared with an order that I was to leave in twenty-four hours. I explained to him that the Governor had granted me an extension, but he actually produced a written order, requiring him to see me off within twenty-four hours; and this order had been signed by the Governor after his conversation with me.

"I can explain it," said the inspector; "the great man wishes to shuffle off the responsibility on me."

"Let us go and confront him with his signature," I said.

"By all means," said the inspector.

The Governor said that he had forgotten his promise to me, and the inspector slyly asked if the order had not better be rewritten. "Is it worth the trouble?" asked the Governor, with an air of indifference.

"We had him there," said the inspector to me, rubbing his hands with satisfaction. "What a mean shabby fellow he is!"

§8

THIS inspector belonged to a distinct class of officials, who are half soldiers and half civilians. They are men who, while serving in the Army, have been lucky enough to run upon a bayonet or stop a bullet, and have therefore been rewarded with positions in the police service. Military life has given them an air of frankness; they have learned some phrases about the point of honour and some terms of ridicule for humble civilians. The youngest of them have read Marlinski and Zagóskin,* and can repeat the beginning of *The Prisoner of the Caucasus,*† and they like to quote the verses they know. For instance, whenever they find a friend smoking, they invariably say:

"The amber smoked between his teeth."‡

They are one and all deeply convinced, and let you know their conviction with emphasis, that their position is far below their merits, and that poverty alone keeps them down; but for their wounds and want of money, they would have been generals-in-waiting or commanders of army-corps. Each of them can point to some comrade-in-arms who has risen to the top of the tree. "You see what Kreutz is now," he says; "well, we two were gazetted together on the same day and lived in barracks like brothers, on the most familiar terms. But I'm not a German, and I had no kind of interest; so here I sit, a mere policeman. But you understand that such a position is distasteful to anyone with the feelings of a gentleman."

Their wives are even more discontented. These poor

---

*Popular novelists of the "patriotic" school, now forgotten.
†A poem by Púshkin.
‡*The Fountain of Bakhchisarai*, l. 2.

sufferers travel to Moscow once a year, where their real business is to deposit their little savings in the bank, though they pretend that a sick mother or aunt wishes to see them for the last time.

And so this life goes on for fifteen years. The husband, railing at fortune, flogs his men and uses his fists to the shopkeepers, curries favour with the Governor, helps thieves to get off, steals State papers, and repeats verses from *The Fountain of Bakhchisarai.** The wife, railing at fortune and provincial life, takes all she can lay her hands on, robs petitioners, cheats tradesmen, and has a sentimental weakness for moonlight nights.

I have described this type at length, because I was taken in by these good people at first, and really thought them superior to others of their class; but I was quite wrong.

§9

I TOOK with me from Perm one personal recollection which I value.

At one of the Governor's Saturday reviews of the exiles, a Roman Catholic priest invited me to his house. I went there and found several Poles. One of them sat there, smoking a short pipe and never speaking; misery, hopeless misery, was visible in every feature. His figure was clumsy and even crooked; his face was of that irregular Polish-Lithuanian type which surprises you at first and becomes attractive later: the greatest of all Poles, Thaddei Kosciusko,† had that kind of face. The man's name was Tsichanovitch, and his dress showed that he was terribly poor.

*Another of Púshkin's early works.
†The famous Polish general and patriot (1746-1817).

Some days later, I was walking along the avenue which bounds Perm in one direction. It was late in May; the young leaves of the trees were opening, and the birches were in flower—there were no trees but birches, I think, on both sides of the avenue—but not a soul was to be seen. People in the provinces have no taste for *Platonic* perambulations. After strolling about for a long time, at last I saw a figure in a field by the side of the avenue: he was botanising, or simply picking flowers, which are not abundant or varied in that part of the world. When he raised his head, I recognised Tsichanovitch and went up to him.

He had originally been banished to Verchoturye, one of the remotest towns in the Government of Perm, hidden away in the Ural Mountains, buried in snow, and so far from all roads that communication with it was almost impossible in winter. Life there is certainly worse than at Omsk or Krasnoyarsk. In his complete solitude there, Tsichanovitch took to botany and collected the meagre flora of the Ural Mountains. He got permission later to move to Perm, and to him this was a change for the better: he could hear once more his own language spoken and meet his companions in misfortune. His wife, who had remained behind in Lithuania, wrote that she intended to join him, *walking from the Government of Vilna*. He was expecting her.

When I was transferred so suddenly to Vyatka, I went to say good-bye to Tsichanovitch. The small room in which he lived was almost bare—there was a table and one chair, and a little old portmanteau standing on end near the meagre bed; and that was all the furniture. My cell in the Krutitski barracks came back to me at once.

He was sorry to hear of my departure, but he was so accustomed to privations that he soon smiled almost brightly as he said, "That's why I love Nature; of her you can never be deprived, wherever you are."

Wishing to leave him some token of remembrance, I took off a small sleeve-link and asked him to accept it.

"Your sleeve-link is too fine for my shirt," he said; "but I shall keep it as long as I live and wear it in my coffin."

After a little thought, he began to rummage hastily in his portmanteau. He took from a small bag a wrought-iron chain with a peculiar pattern, wrenched off some of the links, and gave them to me.

"I have a great value for this chain," he said; "it is connected with the most sacred recollections of my life, and I won't give it all to you; but take these links. I little thought that I should ever give them to a Russian, an exile like myself."

I embraced him and said good-bye.

"When do you start?" he asked.

"To-morrow morning; but don't come: when I go back, I shall find a policeman at my lodgings, who will never leave me for a moment."

"Very well. I wish you a good journey and better fortune than mine."

By nine o'clock next morning the inspector appeared at my house, to hasten my departure. My new keeper, a much tamer creature than his predecessor, and openly rejoicing at the prospect of drinking freely during the 350 *versts* of our journey, was doing something to the carriage. All was ready. I happened to look into the street and saw Tsichanovitch walking past. I ran to the window.

"Thank God!" he said. "This is the fourth time I have walked past, hoping to hail you, if only from a distance; but you never saw me."

My eyes were full of tears as I thanked him: I was deeply touched by this proof of tender womanly attachment. But this was the only reason why I was sorry to leave Perm.

§10

ON the second day of our journey, heavy rain began at dawn and went on all day without stopping, as it often does in wooded country; at two o'clock we came to a miserable village of natives. There was no post-house; the native Votyaks, who could neither read nor write, opened my passport and ascertained whether there were two seals or one, shouted out "All right!" and harnessed the fresh horses. A Russian post-master would have kept us twice as long. On getting near this village, I had proposed to my keeper that we should rest there two hours: I wished to get dry and warm and have something to eat. But when I entered the smoky, stifling hut and found that no food was procurable, and that there was not even a public-house within five *versts*, I repented of my purpose and intended to go on.

While I was still hesitating, a soldier came in and brought me an invitation to drink a cup of tea from an officer on detachment.

"With all my heart. Where is your officer?"

"In a hut close by, Your Honour"—and the soldier made a left turn and disappeared. I followed him.

CHAPTER VII

Vyatka—The Office and Dinner-table of His Excellency—Tufáyev.

§1

WHEN I called on the Governor of Vyatka,
he sent a message that I was to call again
at ten next morning.

When I returned, I found four men in the drawing-
room, the inspectors of the town and country police, and
two office clerks. They were all standing up, talking in
whispers, and looking uneasily at the door. The door
opened, and an elderly man of middle height and broad-
shouldered entered the room. The set of his head was like
that of a bulldog, and the large jaws with a kind of carniv-
orous grin increased the canine resemblance; the senile
and yet animal expression of the features, the small, restless grey eyes, and thin lank hair made an impression
which was repulsive beyond belief.

He began by roughly reproving the country inspector
for the state of a road by which His Excellency had
travelled on the previous day. The inspector stood with
his head bent, in sign of respect and submission, and said
from time to time, like servants in former days, "Very
good, Your Excellency."

Having done with the inspector he turned to me. With an insolent look he said:

"I think you have taken your degree at Moscow University?"

"I have."

"Did you enter the public service afterwards?"

"I was employed in the Kremlin offices."

"Ha! Ha! Much they do there! Not too busy there to attend parties and sing songs, eh?" Then he called out, "Alenitsin!"

A young man of consumptive appearance came in. "Hark ye, my friend. Here is a graduate of Moscow University who probably knows everything except the business of administration, and His Majesty desires that we should teach it to him. Give him occupation in your office, and let me have special reports about him. You, Sir, will come to the office at nine to-morrow morning. You can go now. By the way, I forgot to ask how you write."

I was puzzled at first. "I mean your handwriting," he added.

I said I had none of my own writing on me.

"Bring paper and a pen," and Alenitsin handed me a pen.

"What shall I write?"

"What you please," said the clerk; "write, *Upon investigation it turned out.*"

The Governor looked at the writing and said with a sarcastic smile, "Well, we shan't ask you to correspond with the Tsar."

§2

WHILE I was still at Perm, I had heard much about

Tufáyev, but the reality far surpassed all my expectations.

There is no person or thing too monstrous for the conditions of Russian life to produce.

He was born at Tobolsk. His father was, I believe, an exile and belonged to the lowest and poorest class of free Russians. At thirteen he joined a band of strolling players, who wandered from fair to fair, dancing on the tight rope, turning somersaults, and so on. With them he went all the way from Tobolsk to the Polish provinces, making mirth for the lieges. He was arrested there on some charge unknown to me, and then, because he had no passport, sent back on foot to Tobolsk as a vagabond, together with a gang of convicts. His mother was now a widow and living in extreme poverty; he rebuilt the stove in her house with his own hands, when it came to pieces. He had to seek a trade of some kind; the boy learned to read and write and got employment as a clerk in the town office. Naturally quick-witted, he had profited by the variety of his experience; he had learned much from the troupe of acrobats, and as much from the gang of convicts in whose company he had tramped from one end of Russia to the other. He soon became a sharp man of business.

At the beginning of Alexander's reign a Government Inspector was sent to Tobolsk, and Tufáyev was recommended to him as a competent clerk. He did his work so well that the Inspector offered to take him back to Petersburg. Hitherto, as he said himself, his ambition had not aspired beyond a clerkship in some provincial court; but now he set a different value on himself, and resolved with an iron strength of will to climb to the top of the tree.

And he did it. Ten years later we find him acting as

secretary to the Controller of the Navy, and then chief of a department in the office of Count Arakchéyev,* which governed the whole Empire. When Paris was occupied by the Allied Armies in 1815, the Count took his secretary there with him. During the whole time of the occupation, Tufáyev literally never saw a single street in Paris; he sat all day and all night in the office, drawing up or copying documents.

Arakchéyev's office was like those copper-mines where the workmen are kept only for a few months, because, if they stay longer, they die. In this manufactory of edicts and ordinances, mandates and instructions, even Tufáyev grew tired at last and asked for an easier place. He was of course, a man after Arakchéyev's own heart—a man without pretensions or distractions or opinions of his own, conventionally honest, eaten up by ambition, and ranking obedience as the highest of human virtues. Arakchéyev rewarded him with the place of a Vice-Governor, and a few years later made him Governor of Perm. The province, which Tufáyev had passed through as acrobat and convict, first dancing on a rope and then bound by a rope, now lay at his feet.

A Governor's power increases by arithmetical progression with the distance from Petersburg, but increases by geometrical progression in provinces like Perm or Vyatka or Siberia, where there is no resident nobility. That was just the kind of province that Tufáyev needed.

He was a Persian satrap, with this difference—that he was active, restless, always busy and interfering in everything. He would have been a savage agent of the French

*Arakchéyev (1769-1835) was Minister and favourite of Emperor Alexander I; he has been called "the assassin of the Russian people."

Convention in 1794, something in the way of Carrier.*

Profligate in his life, naturally coarse, impatient of all opposition, his influence was extremely harmful. He did not take bribes; and yet, as appeared after his death, he amassed a considerable fortune. He was strict with his subordinates and punished severely those whom he detected in dishonesty; but they stole more under his rule than ever before or since. He carried the misuse of influence to an extraordinary pitch; for instance, when despatching an official to hold an enquiry, he would say, if he had a personal interest in the matter, "You will probably find out so-and-so to be the case," and woe to the official if he did not find out what the Governor foretold.

Perm, when I was there, was still full of Tufáyev's glory, and his partisans were hostile to his successor, who, as a matter of course, surrounded himself with supporters of his own.

§3

BUT on the other hand, there were people at Perm who hated him. One of these was Chebotarev, a doctor employed at one of the factories and a remarkable product of Russian life. He warned me specially against Tufáyev. He was a clever and very excitable man, who had made an unfortunate marriage soon after taking his degree; then he had drifted to Ekaterinburg† and sank with no experience into the slough of provincial life. Though his position here was fairly independent, his career was wrecked, and his chief employment was to mock at the Government officials. He jeered at them in their presence and

*Infamous for his *noyades* at Nantes; guillotined in 1794.
†A town in the Ural district, now polluted by a horrible crime.

said the most insulting things to their faces. But, as he spared nobody, nobody felt particular resentment at his flouts and jeers. His bitter tongue assured him a certain ascendancy over a society where fixed principles were rare, and he forced them to submit to the lash which he was never weary of applying.

I was told beforehand that, though he was a good doctor, he was crack-brained and excessively rude.

But his way of talking and jesting seemed to me neither offensive nor trivial; on the contrary, it was full of humour and concentrated bile. This was the poetry of his life, his revenge, his cry of resentment and, perhaps, in part, of despair also. Both as a student of human nature and as a physician, he had placed these officials under his microscope; he knew all their petty hidden vices; and, encouraged by their dulness and cowardice, he observed no limits in his way of addressing them.

He constantly repeated the same phrase—"It does not matter twopence," or "It won't cost you twopence." I once laughed at him for this, and he said: "What are you surprised at? The object of all speech is to persuade, and I only add to my statements the strongest proof that exists in the world. Once convince a man that it won't cost him twopence to kill his own father and he'll kill him sure enough."

He was always willing to lend moderate sums, as much as a hundred or two hundred *roubles*. Whenever he was appealed to for a loan, he pulled out his pocket-book and asked for a date by which the money would be repaid.

"Now," he said, "I will bet a *rouble* that you will not pay the money on that day."

"My dear Sir, who do you take me for?" the borrower would say.

"My opinion of you does not matter twopence," was the reply; "but the fact is that I have kept an account for six years, and not a single debtor has ever paid me on the day, and very few after it."

When the time had expired, the doctor asked with a grave face for the payment of his bet.

A rich merchant at Perm had a travelling carriage for sale. The doctor called on him and delivered the following speech all in a breath. "You are selling a carriage, I need one. Because you are rich and a millionaire, everyone respects you, and I have come to testify my respect for the same reason. Owing to your wealth, it does not matter twopence to you whether you sell the carriage or not; but I need it, and I am poor. You will want to squeeze me and take advantage of my necessity; therefore you will ask 1,500 *roubles* for it. I shall offer 700 *roubles*; I shall come every day to haggle over the price, and after a week you will let me have it for 750 or 800. Might we not as well begin at once at that point? I am prepared to pay that sum." The merchant was so astonished that he let the doctor have the carriage at his own figure.

But there was no end to the stories of Chebotarev's eccentricity. I shall add two more.

§4

I WAS present once when a lady, a rather clever and cultivated woman, asked him if he believed in mesmerism. "What do you mean by mesmerism?" he asked. The lady talked the usual nonsense in reply. "It does not matter twopence to you," he said, "to know whether I believe in mesmerism or not; but if you like, I will tell you what I have seen in that way." "Please do." "Yes; but you must listen attentively," and then he began to describe some experiments made by a friend of his, a doctor at Khárkov; his description was very lively, clever, and interesting.

While he was talking, a servant brought in some refreshments on a tray, and was leaving the room when the lady said, "You have forgotten the mustard." Chebotarev stopped dead. "Go on, go on," said the lady, a little frightened already. "I'm listening to you." "Pray, Madam, has he remembered the salt?" "I see you are angry with me," said the lady, blushing. "Not in the least, I assure you. I know that you were listening attentively; but I also know that no woman, however intelligent she may be and whatever may be the subject under discussion, can ever soar higher than the kitchen. How then could I venture to be angry with you in particular?"

Another story about him. Being employed as a doctor at the factories of a Countess Pollier, he took a fancy to a boy he saw there, and wished to have him for a servant. The boy was willing, but the steward said that the consent of the Countess must first be obtained. The doctor wrote to her, and she replied that he might have the boy, on condition of paying down a sum equal to the payments due to her from the boy during the next five years. The doctor wrote at once to express his willingness, but he asked her to answer this question. "As Encke's comet may be expected to pass through the orbit of the earth in three years and a half from now, who will be responsible for repaying the money I have advanced, in case the comet drives the earth out of its orbit?"

§5

ON the day I left for Vyatka, the doctor turned up at my house early in the morning. He began with this witticism. "You are like Horace: he sang once and people have been translating him ever since, and so you are translated* from place to place for that song you sang." Then he pulled out his purse and asked if I needed money for the journey. I thanked him and declined his offer. "Why don't you take it? It won't cost you twopence." "I have money." "A bad sign," he said; "the end of the world is coming." Then he opened his notebook and made this entry. "For the first time in fifteen years' practice I have met a man who refused money, and that man was on the eve of departure."

Having had his jest, he sat down on my bed and said seriously: "That's a terrible man you are going to. Keep out of his way as much as ever you can. If he takes a fancy to you, that says little in your favour; but if he dislikes you, he will certainly ruin you; what weapon he will use, false accusation or not, I don't know, but ruin you he will; he won't care twopence."

Thereupon he told me a strange story, which I was able to verify at a later date by means of papers preserved in the Home Office at Petersburg.

§6

TUFÁYEV had a mistress at Perm, the sister of a humble official named Petrovski. The fact was notorious, and the brother was laughed at. Wishing therefore to break off this connexion, he threatened to write to Petersburg and lay information, and, in short, made such a noise and

*The same Russian verb means 'to translate' and 'to transfer.'

commotion that the police arrested him one day as insane and brought him up to be examined before the administration of the province. The judges and the inspector of public health—he was an old German, much beloved by the poor, and I knew him personally—all agreed that Petrovski was insane.

But Chebotarev knew Petrovski and had been his doctor. He told the inspector that Petrovski was not mad at all, and urged a fresh examination; otherwise, he would feel bound to carry the matter further. The administration raised no difficulties; but unfortunately Petrovski died in the mad-house before the day fixed for the second examination, though he was a young man and enjoyed good health.

News of the affair now reached Petersburg. The sister was arrested (Tufáyev ought to have been) and a secret enquiry began. Tufáyev dictated the replies of the witnesses. He surpassed himself in this business. He devised a means to stifle it for ever and to save himself from a second involuntary journey to Siberia. He actually induced the sister to say that her youth and inexperience had been taken advantage of by the late Tsar Alexander when he passed through Perm, and that the quarrel with her brother dated from that event.

Was her story true? Well, *la regina ne aveva molto,** says the story-teller in Púshkin's *Egyptian Nights*.

§7

SUCH was the man who now undertook to teach me the business of administration, a worthy pupil of Arakchéyev, acrobat, tramp, clerk, secretary, Governor, a tender-

*The reference in Púshkin is to Cleopatra's lovers.

hearted, unselfish being, who shut up sane men in mad-houses and made away with them there.

I was entirely at his mercy. He had only to write some nonsense to the Minister at Petersburg, and I should be packed off to Irkutsk. Indeed, writing was unnecessary; he had the right to transfer me to some savage place like Kai or Tsarevo-Sanchursk, where there were no resources and no means of communication. He sent one young Pole to Glazov, because the ladies had the bad taste to prefer him as a partner in the mazurka to His Excellency. In this way Prince Dolgorúkov was transferred from Perm to Verchoturye, a place in the Government of Perm, buried in mountains and snow-drifts, with as bad a climate as Beryózov and even less society.

§8

PRINCE DOLGORÚKOV belonged to a type which is becoming rarer with us; he was a sprig of nobility, of the wrong sort, whose escapades were notorious at Petersburg, Moscow, and Paris. His whole life was spent in folly; he was a spoilt, insolent, offensive practical joker, a mixture of buffoon and fine gentleman. When his pranks exceeded all bounds, he was banished to Perm.

He arrived there with two carriages; the first was occupied by himself and his dog, a Great Dane, the second by his French cook and his parrots. The arrival of this wealthy visitor gave much pleasure, and before long all the town was rubbing shoulders in his dining-room. He soon took up with a young lady of Perm; and this young lady, suspecting that he was unfaithful, turned up unexpectedly at his house one morning, and found him with a maid-servant. A scene followed, and at last the faithless lover took his riding-whip down from its peg; when the lady perceived his intention, she made off; simply attired in a dressing-gown and nothing else, he made after her, and caught her up on the small parade-ground where the troops were exercised. When he had given the jealous lady a few blows with his whip, he strolled home, quite content with his performance.

But these pleasant little ways brought upon him the persecution of his former friends, and the authorities decided to send this madcap of forty on to Verchoturye. The day before he left, he gave a grand dinner, and all the local officials, in spite of the strained relations, came to the feast; for Dolgorúkov had promised them a new and remarkable pie. The pie was in fact excellent and vanished with extraordinary rapidity. When nothing but the crust was left, Dolgorúkov said to his guests with an air of emotion: "It never can be said that I spared anything to make our last meeting a success. I had my dog killed yesterday, to make this pie."

The officials looked first with horror at one another and then round the room for the Great Dane whom they all knew perfectly; but he was not there. The Prince ordered a servant to bring in the mortal remains of his favourite; the skin was all there was to show; the rest was in the stomachs of the people of Perm. Half the town took to their beds in consequence.

Dolgorúkov meanwhile, pleased by the success of the practical joke he had played on his friends, was travelling in triumph to Verchoturye. To his train he had now added a third vehicle containing a hen-house and its inhabitants. At several of the post-houses on his way he carried off the official registers, mixed them up, and altered the figures; the posting-department, who, even with the registers, found it difficult enough to get the returns right, almost went mad in consequence.

§9

THE oppressive emptiness and dumbness of Russian life, when misallied to a strong and even violent temperament, are apt to produce monstrosities of all kinds.

Not only in Dolgorúkov's pie, but in Suvórov's crowing like a cock, in the savage outbursts of Ismailov, in the semi-voluntary insanity of Mamonov,* and in the wild extravagances of Tolstoi, nicknamed "The American," everywhere I catch a national note which is familiar to us all, though in most of us it is weakened by education or turned in some different direction.

Tolstoi I knew personally, just at the time when he lost his daughter, Sara, a remarkable girl with a high poetic gift. He was old then; but one look at his athletic figure, his flashing eyes, and the grey curls that clustered on his forehead, was enough to show how great was his natural strength and activity. But he had developed only stormy passions and vicious propensities. And this is not surprising: in Russia all that is vicious is allowed to grow for long unchecked, while men are sent to a fortress or to Siberia at the first sign of a humane passion. For twenty years Tolstoi rioted and gambled, used his fists to mutilate his enemies, and reduced whole families to beggary, till at last he was banished to Siberia. He made his

---

*Suvórov, the famous general (1729-1800), was very eccentric in his personal habits. Ismailov, a rich landowner at the beginning of the nineteenth century, was infamous for his cruelties. Mamonov (1758-1803) was one of Catherine's favourites.

way through Kamchatka to America and, while there, obtained permission to return to Russia. The Tsar pardoned him, and he resumed his old life the very day after his return. He married a gipsy woman, a famous singer who belonged to a gipsy tribe at Moscow, and turned his house into a gambling-hell. His nights were spent at the card-table, and all his time in excesses; wild scenes of cupidity and intoxication went on round the cradle of his daughter. It is said that he once ordered his wife to stand on the table, and sent a bullet through the heel of her shoe, in order to prove the accuracy of his aim.

His last exploit very nearly sent him back to Siberia. He contrived to entrap in his house at Moscow a tradesman against whom he had an old grudge, bound him hand and foot, and pulled out one of his teeth. It is hardly credible that this should have happened only ten or twelve years ago. The man lodged a complaint. But Tolstoi bribed the police and the judges, and the victim was lodged in prison for false witness. It happened that a well-known man of letters was then serving on the prison committee and took up the affair, on learning the facts from the tradesman. Tolstoi was seriously alarmed; it was clear that he was likely to be condemned. But anything is possible in Russia. Count Orlóv sent secret instructions that the affair must be hushed up, to deprive the lower classes of a direct triumph over the aristocracy, and he also advised that the man of letters should be removed from the committee. This is almost more incredible than the incident of the tooth. But I was in Moscow then myself and well acquainted with the imprudent man of letters. But I must go back to Vyatka.

§10

THE office there was incomparably worse than my prison. The actual work was not hard; but the mephitic atmosphere—the place was like a second Grotto del Cane*— and the monstrous and absurd waste of time made the life unbearable. Alenitsin did not treat me badly. He was even more polite than I expected; having been educated at the grammar school of Kazán, he had some respect for a graduate of Moscow University.

Twenty clerks were employed in the office. The majority of them were entirely destitute of either intellectual culture or moral sense, sons of clerks, who had learned from their cradles to look upon the public service as a means of livelihood and the cultivators of the land as the source of their income. They sold official papers, pocketed small sums whenever they could get them, broke their word for a glass of spirits, and stuck at nothing, however base and ignominious. My own valet stopped playing billiards at the public rooms, because, as he said, the officials cheated shamefully and he could not give them a lesson because of their rank in society.

With these men, whose position alone made them safe from my servant's fists, I had to sit every day from nine till two and again from five till eight.

Alenitsin was head of the whole office, and the desk at which I sat had a chief also, not a bad-hearted man, but drunken and illiterate. There were four other clerks at my desk; and I had to be on speaking terms with them, and with all the rest as well. Apart from the fact that these people would sooner or later have paid me out for

*The grotto near Naples where dogs were held over the sulphurous vapour till they became insensible.

any airs of exclusiveness, it is simply impossible not to get to know people in whose company you spend several hours every day. It must also be remembered how people in the country hang on to a stranger, especially if he comes from the capital, and still more if he has been mixed up in some exciting scandal.

When I had tugged at the oar all day in this galley, I used sometimes to go home quite stupefied and fall on my sofa, worn out and humiliated, and incapable of any work or occupation. I heartily regretted my prison cell with its foul air and black beetles, its locked door and turnkey behind the lock. There I was free and did what I liked without interference; there I enjoyed dead silence and unbroken leisure; I had exchanged these for trivial talk, dirty companions, low ideas, and coarse feelings. When I remembered that I must go back there in the afternoon, and back again to-morrow, I sometimes fell into such fits of rage and despair that I drank wine and spirits for consolation.

Nor was that all. One of my desk-fellows would perhaps look in, for want of something to do; and there he would sit and chatter till the appointed hour recalled us to the office.

§11

AFTER a few months, however, the office life became somewhat less oppressive.

It is not in the Russian character to keep up a steady system of persecution, unless where personal or avaricious motives are involved; and this fact is due to our Russian carelessness and indifference. Those in authority in Russia are generally unlicked and insolent, and it is very easy,

when dealing with them, to come in for the rough side of
their tongue; but a war of pin-pricks is not in their way—
they have not the patience for it, perhaps because it brings
in no profit.

In the heat of the moment, in order to display their
power or prove their zeal, they are capable of anything,
however absurd and unnecessary; but then by degrees
they cease to trouble you.

I found this to be the case in my office. It so happened
that the Ministry of the Interior had just been seized with
a fit of statistics. Orders were issued that committees
should be appointed all over the country, and information
was required from these committees which could hardly
have been supplied in such countries as Belgium and Switzerland. There were also ingenious tables of all kinds for
figures, to show a maximum and minimum as well as
averages, and conclusions based on a comparison of ten
years (for nine of which, if you please, no statistics at
all had been recorded); the morality of the inhabitants
and even the weather were to be included in the report.
For the committee and for the collection of facts not a
penny was allotted; the work had to be done from pure
love of statistics; the rural police were to collect the facts
and the Governor's office to put them in order. The office
was overburdened with work already, and the rural police
preferred to use their fists rather than their brains; both
looked on the statistics committee as a mere superfluity,
an official joke; nevertheless, a report had to be presented, including tables of figures and conclusions based
thereon.

To all our office the job seemed excessively difficult.
It was, indeed, simply impossible; but to that nobody paid

any attention; their sole object was to escape a reprimand. I promised Alenitsin that I would write the introduction and first part of the report, with specimen tables, introducing plenty of eloquent phrases, foreign words, apt quotations, and impressive conclusions, if he would allow me to perform this difficult task at my house instead of at the office. He talked it over with the Governor and gave permission.

The beginning of the report dealt with the committee's activity; and here, as there was nothing to show at present, I dwelt upon hopes and intentions for the future. This composition moved Alenitsin to the depth of his heart and was considered a masterpiece even by the Governor. That was the end of my labours in the department of statistics, but I was made chairman of the committee. Thus I was delivered from the slavery of copying office papers, and my drunken chief became something like my subordinate. Alenitsin only asked, from some idea of keeping up appearances, that I should just look in every day at the office.

To show how utterly impossible it was to draw up serious tables, I shall quote some information received from the town of Kai. There were many absurdities, and this was one.

Persons drowned, 2
Causes of drown-
ing unknown, 2
—
Total 4

Under the heading "Extraordinary Events" the following tragedy was chronicled: "So-and-so, having injured his

brain with spirituous liquors, hanged himself." Under the
heading "Morality of the Inhabitants" this was entered:
"No Jews were found in the town of Kai." There was a
question whether any funds had been allotted to the building of a church, or exchange, or hospital. The answer was:
"Money allotted to the building of an exchange was not
allotted."

§12

STATISTICS saved me from office work, but they had one
bad result—they brought me into personal relations with
the Governor.

There was a time when I hated this man, but that time
has long passed away, and the man has passed away himself—he died about 1845 near Kazán, where he had an
estate. I think of him now without anger; I regard him
as a strange beast encountered in some primeval forest,
which deserves study, but, just because it is a beast, cannot excite anger. But then it was impossible not to fight
him; any decent man must have done so. He might have
damaged me seriously, but accident preserved me; and to
resent the harm which he failed to do me would be absurd
and pitiable.

The Governor was separated from his wife, and the
wife of his cook occupied her place. The cook was banished from the town, his only guilt being his marriage;
and the cook's wife, by an arrangement whose awkward-
ness seemed intentional, was concealed in the back part
of the Governor's residence. Though she was not formally recognised, yet the cook's wife had a little court,
formed out of those officials who were especially devoted
to the Governor—in other words, those whose conduct
could least stand investigation; and their wives and

daughters, though rather bashful about it, paid her stolen visits after dark. This lady possessed the tact which distinguished one of her most famous male predecessors—Catherine's favourite, Potemkin. Knowing her consort's way and anxious not to lose her place, she herself procured for him rivals from whom she had nothing to fear. Grateful for this indulgence, he repaid her with his affection, and the pair lived together in harmony.

The Governor spent the whole morning working in his office. The poetry of his life began at three o'clock. He loved his dinner, and he liked to have company while eating. Twelve covers were laid every day; if the party was less than six, he was annoyed; if it fell to two, he was distressed; and if he had no guest, he was almost desperate and went off to the apartments of his Dulcinea, to dine there. It is not a difficult business to get people together, in order to feed them to excess; but his official position, and the fear his subordinates felt for him, prevented them from availing themselves freely of his hospitality, and him from turning his house into an inn. He had therefore to content himself with heads of departments—though with half of them he was on bad terms—occasional strangers, rich merchants, spirit-distillers, and "curiosities." These last may be compared with the *capacités,* who were to be introduced into the Chamber of Deputies under Louis Philippe. I need hardly say that I was a "curiosity" of the first water at Vyatka.

§13

PEOPLE banished for their opinions to remote parts of Russia are a little feared but by no means confounded with ordinary mortals. For the provincial mind "dangerous people" have that kind of attraction which notorious Don Juans have for women, and notorious courtesans for men. The officials of Petersburg and grandees of Moscow are much more shy of "dangerous" people than the dwellers in the provinces and especially in Siberia.

The exiled Decembrists were immensely respected. Yushnevski's widow was treated as a lady of the first consequence in Siberia; the official figures of the Siberian census were corrected by means of statistics supplied by the exiles; and Minich, in his prison, managed the affairs of the province of Tobolsk, the Governors themselves resorting to him for advice in matters of importance.

The common people are even more friendly to the exiles; they always take the side of men who have been punished. Near the Siberian frontier, the word "exile" disappears, and the word "unfortunate" is used instead. In the eyes of the Russian people, the sentence of a court leaves no stain. In the Government of Perm, the peasants along the road to Tobolsk often put out *kvass* or milk and bread on the window-sill, for the use of some "unfortunate" who may be trying to escape from Siberia.

§14

IN this place I may say something about the Polish exiles. There are some as far west as Nizhni, and after Kazán the number rapidly increases; there were forty of them at Perm and at least as many at Vyatka; and each of the smaller towns contained a few.

They kept entirely apart and avoided all communication with the Russian inhabitants; among themselves they lived like brothers, and the rich shared their wealth with the poor.

I never noticed any special hatred or any liking for them on the part of the Russians. They were simply considered as outsiders; and hardly any of the Poles knew Russian.

I remember one of the exiles who got permission in 1837 to return to his estates in Lithuania. He was a tough old cavalry officer who had served under Poniatovski in several of Napoleon's campaigns. The day before he left, he invited some Poles to dinner, and me as well. After dinner he came up to me with his glass in his hand, embraced me, and said with a soldier's frankness, "Oh, why are you a Russian?" I made no answer, but his question made a strong impression on me. I realised that it was impossible for the present generation to give freedom to Poland. But, since Konarsky's* time, Poles have begun to think quite differently of Russians.

In general, the exiled Poles are not badly treated; but those of them who have no means of their own are shockingly ill off. Such men receive from Government fifteen *roubles* a month, to pay for lodgings, clothing, food, and fuel. In the larger towns, such as Kazán or Tobolsk, they can eke out a living by giving lessons or concerts, by playing at balls or painting portraits or teaching children to dance; but at Perm and Vyatka even these resources did not exist. In spite of that, they never asked Russians for assistance in any form.

§15

THE Governor's invitations to dine on the luxuries of Siberia were a real infliction to me. His dining-room was merely the office over again, in a different shape, cleaner

*A Polish revolutionary; born in 1808, he was shot in February, 1839.

indeed, but more objectionable, because there was not the same appearance of compulsion about it.

He knew his guests thoroughly and despised them. Sometimes he showed his claws, but he generally treated them as a man treats his dogs, either with excessive familiarity or with a roughness beyond all bounds. But all the same he continued to invite them, and they came in a flutter of joy, prostrating themselves before him, currying favour by tales against others, all smiles and bows and complaisance.

I blushed for them and felt ashamed.

Our intimacy did not last long: the Governor soon perceived that I was unfit to move in the highest circles of Vyatka.

After three months he was dissatisfied with me, and after six months he hated me. I ceased to attend his dinners, and never even called at his house. As we shall see later, it was a visit to Vyatka from the Crown Prince* that saved me from his persecution.

In this connexion it is necessary to add that I did nothing whatever to deserve either his attentions and invitations at first, or his anger and ill-usage afterwards. He could not endure in me an attitude which, though not at all rude, was independent; my behaviour was perfectly correct, but he demanded servility.

He was greedily jealous of the power which he had worked hard to gain, and he sought not merely obedience but the appearance of unquestioning subordination. Unfortunately, in this respect he was a true Russian.

The gentleman says to his servant: "Hold your tongue! I will not allow you to answer me back."

*Afterwards Alexander II.

The head of an office says to any subordinate who
ventures on a protest: "You forget yourself. Do you know
to whom you are speaking?"

Tufáyev cherished a secret but intense hatred for everything aristocratic, and it was the result of bitter experience. For him the penal servitude of Arakchéyev's office
was a harbour of refuge and freedom, such as he had
never enjoyed before. In earlier days his employers, when
they gave him small jobs to do, never offered him a chair;
when he served in the Controller's office, he was treated
with military roughness by the soldiers and once horse-
whipped by a colonel in the streets of Vilna. The clerk
stored all this up in his heart and brooded over it; and
now he was Governor, and it was his turn to play the
tyrant, to keep a man standing, to address people famil-
iarly, to speak unnecessarily loudly, and at times to commit long-descended nobles for trial.

From Perm he was promoted to Tver. But the nobles,
however deferential and subservient, could not stand
Tufáyev. They petitioned for his removal, and he was
sent to Vyatka.

There he was in his element once more. Officials and
distillers, factory-owners and officials,—what more could
the heart of man desire? Everyone trembled before him
and got up when he approached; everyone gave him dinners, offered him wine, and sought to anticipate his wishes;
at every wedding or birthday party the first toast proposed was "His Excellency the Governor!"

CHAPTER VIII

Officials—Siberian Governors—A Bird of Prey—A Gentle
Judge—An Inspector Roasted—The Tatar—A Boy of the
Female Sex—The Potato Revolt—Russian Justice.

§1

ONE of the saddest consequences of the revolution effected by Peter the Great is the development of the official class in Russia. These *chin-
óvniks* are an artificial, ill-educated, and hungry class,
incapable of anything except office-work, and ignorant of
everything except official papers. They form a kind of lay
clergy, officiating in the law-courts and police-offices, and
sucking the blood of the nation with thousands of dirty,
greedy mouths.

Gógol raised one side of the curtain and showed us the
Russian *chinóvnik* in his true colours;* but Gógol, without meaning to, makes us resigned by making us laugh,
and his immense comic power tends to suppress resentment. Besides, fettered as he was by the censorship, he
could barely touch on the sorrowful side of that unclean
subterranean region in which the destinies of the ill-starred
Russian people are hammered and shaped.

There, in those grimy offices which we walk through

*Gógol's play, *The Revizor,* is a satire on the Russian bureaucracy.

as fast as we can, men in shabby coats sit and write; first
they write a rough draft and then copy it out on stamped
paper—and individuals, families, whole villages are injured, terrified, and ruined. The father is banished to a
distance, the mother is sent to prison, the son to the Army;
it all comes upon them as suddenly as a clap of thunder,
and in most cases it is undeserved. The object of it all is
money. Pay up! If you don't, an inquest will be held on
the body of some drunkard who has been frozen in the
snow. A collection is made for the village authorities; the
peasants contribute their last penny. Then there are the
police and law-officers—they must live somehow, and
one has a wife to maintain and another a family to edu-
cate, and they are all model husbands and fathers.

This official class is sovereign in the north-eastern Governments of Russia and in Siberia. It has spread and
flourished there without hindrance and without pause; in
that remote region where all share in the profits, theft is
the order of the day. The Tsar himself is powerless against
these entrenchments, buried under snow and constructed
out of sticky mud. All measures of the central Government are emasculated before they get there, and all its
purposes are distorted: it is deceived and cheated, betrayed and sold, and all the time an appearance of servile
fidelity is kept up, and official procedure is punctually
observed.

Speranski* tried to lighten the burdens of the people
by introducing into all the offices in Siberia the principle
of divided control. But it makes little difference whether
the stealing is done by individuals or gangs of robbers.

*Michail Speranski (1772-1839), minister under Alexander I, was
Governor of Siberia in 1819.

He discharged hundreds of old thieves, and took on hundreds of new ones. The rural police were so terrified at first that they actually paid blackmail to the peasants. But a few years passed, and the officials were making as much money as ever, in spite of the new conditions.

A second eccentric Governor, General Velyaminov, tried again. For two years he struggled hard at Tobolsk to root out the malpractices; and then, conscious of failure, he gave it all up and ceased to attend to business at all.

Others, more prudent than he, never tried the experiment: they made money themselves and let others do the same.

"I shall root out bribery," said Senyavin, the Governor of Moscow, to a grey-bearded old peasant who had entered a complaint against some crying act of injustice. The old man smiled.

"What are you laughing at?" asked the Governor.

"Well, I *was* laughing, *bátyushka*; you must forgive me. I was thinking of one of our people, a great strong fellow, who boasted that he would lift the Great Cannon at Moscow; and he did try, but the cannon would not budge."

Senyavin used to tell this story himself. He was one of those unpractical bureaucrats who believe that well-turned periods in praise of honesty, and rigorous prosecution of the few thieves who get caught, have power to cure the widespread plague of Russian corruption, that noxious weed that spreads at ease under the protecting boughs of the censorship.

Two things are needed to cope with it—publicity, and an entirely different organisation of the whole machine. The old national system of justice must be re-introduced, with oral procedure and sworn witnesses and all that the central Government detests so heartily.

§2

PESTEL, one of the Governors of Western Siberia, was like a Roman proconsul, and was outdone by none of them. He carried on a system of open and systematic robbery throughout the country, which he had entirely detached from Russia by means of his spies. Not a letter crossed the frontier unopened, and woe to the writer who dared to say a word about his rule. He kept the merchants of the First Guild in prison for a whole year, where they were chained and tortured. Officials he punished by sending them to the frontier of Eastern Siberia and keeping them there for two or three years.

The people endured him for long; but at last a tradesman of Tobolsk determined to bring the state of things to the Tsar's knowledge. Avoiding the usual route, he went first to Kyakhta and crossed the Siberian frontier from there with a caravan of tea. At Tsárskoë Seló* he found an opportunity to hand his petition to Alexander, and begged him to read it. Alexander was astonished and impressed by the strange matter he read there. He sent for the petitioner, and they had a long conversation which convinced him of the truth of the terrible story. Horrified and somewhat confused, the Tsar said:

"You can go back to Siberia now, my friend; the matter shall be looked into."

"No, Your Majesty," said the man; "I cannot go home now; I would rather go to prison. My interview with Your Majesty cannot be kept secret, and I shall be murdered."

*I.e., "The Tsar's Village," near Petersburg.

Alexander started. He turned to Milorádovitch, who was then Governor of Petersburg, and said:

"I hold you answerable for this man's life."

"In that case," said Milorádovitch, "Your Majesty must allow me to lodge him in my own house." And there the man actually stayed until the affair was settled.

Pestel resided almost continuously at Petersburg. You will remember that the Roman proconsuls also generally lived in the capital.* By his presence and his connexions and, above all, by sharing his booty, he stopped in advance all unpleasant rumours and gossip. He and Rostopchín were dining one day at the Tsar's table. They were standing by the window, and the Tsar asked, "What is that on the church cross over there—something black?" "I cannot make it out," said Rostopchín; "we must appeal to Pestel; he has wonderful sight and can see from here what is going on in Siberia."

The Imperial Council, taking advantage of the absence of Alexander,—he was at Verona or Aix,—wisely and justly decided that, as the complaint referred to Siberia, Pestel, who was fortunately on the spot, should conduct the investigation. But Milorádovitch, Mordvínov, and two others protested against this decision, and the matter was referred to the Supreme Court.

That body gave an unjust decision, as it always does when trying high officials. Pestel was reprimanded, and Treskin, the Civil Governor of Tobolsk, was deprived of his official rank and title of nobility and banished. Pestel was merely dismissed from the service.

Pestel was succeeded at Tobolsk by Kaptsevitch, a pupil of Arakchéyev. Thin and bilious, a tyrant by nature

*Herzen is mistaken here.

and a restless martinet, he introduced military discipline everywhere; but, though he fixed maximum prices, he left all ordinary business in the hands of the robbers. In 1824 the Tsar intended to visit Tobolsk. Throughout the Government of Perm there is an excellent high road, well worn by traffic; it is probable that the soil was favourable for its construction. Kaptsevitch made a similar road all the way to Tobolsk in a few months. In spring, when the snow was melting and the cold bitter, thousands of men were driven in relays to work at the road. Sickness broke out and half the workmen died; but "zeal overcomes all difficulties," and the road was made.

Eastern Siberia is governed in a still more casual fashion. The distance is so great that all rumours die away before they reach Petersburg. One Governor of Irkutsk used to fire cannon at the town when he was cheerful after dinner; another, in the same state, used to put on priest's robes and celebrate the Mass in his own house, in the presence of the Bishop; but, at least, neither the noise of the former nor the piety of the latter did as much harm as the state of siege kept up by Pestel and the restless activity of Kaptsevitch.

§3

It is a pity that Siberia is so badly governed. The choice of Governors has been peculiarly unfortunate. I do not know how Muravyóv acquits himself there—his intelligence and capacity are well known; but all the rest have been failures. Siberia has a great future before it. It is generally regarded as a kind of cellar, full of gold and furs and other natural wealth, but cold, buried in snow, and ill provided with comforts and roads and population. But this is a false view.

The Russian Government is unable to impart that life-giving impulse which would drive Siberia ahead with American speed. We shall see what will happen when the mouths of the Amoor are opened to navigation, and when America meets Siberia on the borders of China.

I said, long ago, that the Pacific Ocean is the Mediterranean of the future; and I have been pleased to see the remark repeated more than once in the New York newspapers. In that future the part of Siberia, lying as it does between the ocean, South Asia, and Russia, is exceedingly important. Siberia must certainly extend to the Chinese frontier: why should we shiver and freeze at Beryózov and Yakutsk, when there are such places as Krasnoyarsk and Minusinsk?

The Russian settlers in Siberia have traits of character which suggest development and progress. The population in general are healthy and well grown, intelligent and exceedingly practical. The children of the emigrants have never felt the pressure of landlordism. There are no great nobles in Siberia, and there is no aristocracy in the towns; authority is represented by the civil officials and military officers; but they are less like an aristocracy than a hostile garrison established by a conqueror. The cultivators are saved from frequent contact with them by the immense distances, and the merchants are saved by their wealth. This latter class, in Siberia, despise the officials: while professing to give place to them, they take them for what they really are—inferiors who are useful in matters of law.

Arms are indispensable to the settler, and everyone

knows how to use them. Familiarity with danger and the habit of prompt action have made the Siberian peasant more soldierly, more resourceful, and more ready to resist, than his Great Russian brother. The distance of the churches has left him more independence of mind: he is lukewarm about religion and very often a dissenter. There are distant villages which the priest visits only thrice a year, when he christens the children in batches, reads the service for the dead, marries all the couples, and hears confession of accumulated sins.

§4.

On this side of the Ural ridge, the ways of governors are less eccentric. But yet I could fill whole volumes with stories which I heard either in the office or at the Governor's dinner-table—stories which throw light on the malpractices and dishonesty of the officials.

§5

"Yes, Sir, he was indeed a marvel, my predecessor was"—thus the inspector of police at Vyatka used to address me in his confidential moments. "Well, of course, we get along fairly, but men like him are born, not made. He was, in his way, I might say, a Caesar, a Napoleon"—and the eyes of my lame friend, the Major, who had got his place as recompense for a wound, shone as he recalled his glorious predecessor.

"There was a gang of robbers, not far from the town. Complaints came again and again to the authorities; now it was a party of merchants relieved of their goods, now the manager of a distillery was robbed of his money. The Governor was in a fuss and drew up edict after edict. Well, as you know, the country police are not brave: they can deal well enough with a petty thief, if there's only one; but here there was a whole gang, and, likely enough, in possession of firearms. As the country police did nothing, the Governor summoned the town inspector and said:

" 'I know that this is not your business at all, but your well-known activity forces me to appeal to you.'

"The inspector knew all about the scandal already.

" 'General,' said he, 'I shall start in an hour. I know where the robbers are sure to be; I shall take a detachment with me; I shall come upon the scoundrels, bring them back in chains, and lodge them in the town prison, before they are three days older.' Just like Suvórov to the Austrian Emperor! And he did what he said he would do: he surprised them with his detachment; the robbers had no time to hide their money; the inspector took it all and marched them off to the town.

"When the trial began, the inspector asked where the money was.

" 'Why, *bátyushka*, we put it into your own hands,' said two of the men.

" 'Mine!' cried the inspector, with an air of astonishment.

" 'Yes, yours!' shouted the thieves.

" 'There's insolence for you!' said the inspector to the magistrate, turning pale with rage. 'Do you expect to make people believe that I was in league with you? I shall show you what it is to insult my uniform; I was a cavalry officer once, and my honour shall not be insulted with impunity!'

"So the thieves were flogged, that they might confess where they had stowed away the money. At first they were obstinate, but when they heard the order that they were to be flogged 'for two pipes,' then the leader of the gang called out—'We plead guilty! We spent the money ourselves.'

" 'You might have said so sooner,' remarked the inspector, 'instead of talking such nonsense. You won't get round me in a hurry, my friend.' 'No, indeed!' muttered the robber, looking in astonishment at the inspector; 'we could teach nothing to Your Honour, but we might learn from you.'

"Well, over that affair the inspector got the Vladímir Order."

"Excuse me," I said, interrupting his enthusiasm for the great man, "but what is the meaning of that phrase 'for two pipes'?"

"Oh, we often use that in the police. One gets bored, you know, while a flogging is going on; so one lights a pipe; and, as a rule, when the pipe is done, the flogging is over too. But in special cases we order that the flogging shall go on till two pipes are smoked out. The men who flog are accustomed to it and know exactly how many strokes that means."

§6

EVER so many stories about this hero were in circulation at Vyatka. His exploits were miraculous. For some reason or another—perhaps a Staff-general or Minister was expected—he wished to show that he had not worn cavalry uniform for nothing, but could put spurs to a charger in fine style. With this object in view, he requisitioned a horse from a rich merchant of the district; it was a grey stallion, and a very valuable animal. The merchant refused it.

"All right," said the inspector; "if you don't choose to do me such a trifling service voluntarily, then I shall take the horse without your leave."

"We shall see about that," said Gold.

"Yes, you shall," said Steel.

The merchant locked up his stable and set two men to guard it. "Foiled for once, my friend!" he thought.

But that night, by a strange accident, a fire broke out in some empty sheds close to the merchant's house. The inspector and his men worked manfully. In order to save the house, they even pulled down the wall of the stable and led out the object of dispute, with not a hair of his mane or tail singed. Two hours later, the inspector was caracoling on a grey charger, on his way to receive the thanks of the distinguished visitor for his courage and skill in dealing with the fire. This incident proved to everyone that he bore a charmed life.

§7

THE Governor was once leaving a party; and, just as his carriage started, a careless driver, in charge of a small sledge, drove into him, striking the traces between the wheelers and leaders. There was a block for a moment, but the Governor was not prevented from driving home in perfect comfort. Next day he said to the inspector: "Do you know whose coachman ran into me last night? He must be taught better."

"That coachman will not do it again, Your Excellency," answered the inspector with a smile; "I have made him smart properly for it."

"Whose coachman was it?"

"Councillor Kulakov's, Your Excellency."

At that moment the old Councillor, whom I found at Vyatka and left there still holding the same office, came into the room.

"You must excuse us," said the Governor, "for giving a lesson to your coachman yesterday."

The Councillor, quite in the dark, looked puzzled.

"He drove into my carriage yesterday. Well, you understand, if he did it to *me*, then . . ."

"But, Your Excellency, my wife and I spent the evening at home, and the coachman was not out at all."

"What's the meaning of this?" asked the Governor.

But the inspector was not taken aback.

"The fact is, Your Excellency, I had such a press of business yesterday that I quite forgot about the coachman. But I confess I did not venture to mention to Your Excellency that I had forgotten. I meant to attend to his business at once."

"Well, there's no denying that you are the right man in the right place!" said the Governor.

§8

SIDE by side with this bird of prey I shall place the portrait of a very different kind of official—a mild and sympathetic creature, a real sucking dove.

Among my acquaintance at Vyatka was an old gentleman who had been dismissed from the service as inspector of rural police. He now drew up petitions and managed lawsuits for other people—a profession which he had been expressly forbidden to adopt. He had entered the service in the year one, had robbed and squeezed and blackmailed in three provinces, and had twice figured in the dock. This veteran liked to tell surprising stories of what he and his contemporaries had done; and he did not conceal his contempt for the degenerate successors who now filled their places.

"Oh, they're mere bunglers," he used to say. "Of course they take bribes, or they couldn't live; but as for dexterity or knowledge of the law, you needn't expect anything of the kind from them. Just to give you an idea, let me tell you of a friend of mine who was a judge for twenty years and died twelve months ago. He was a genius! The peasants revere his memory, and he left a trifle to his family too. His method was all his own. If a peasant came with a petition, the Judge would admit him at once and be very friendly and cheerful.

" 'Well, my friend, tell me your name and your father's name, too.'

"The peasant bows—'Yermolai is my name, *bátyushka*, and my father's name was Grigóri.'

" 'Well, how are you, Yermolai Grigorevitch, and where do you come from?'

" 'I live at Dubilov.'

" 'I know, I know—those mills on the right hand of the high road are yours, I suppose?'

" 'Just so, *bátyushka*, the mills belong to our village.'

" 'A prosperous village, too—good land—black soil.'

" 'We have no reason to murmur against Heaven, Your Worship.'

" 'Well, that's right. I dare say you have a good large family, Yermolai Grigorevitch?'

" 'Three sons and two daughters, Your Worship, and

my eldest daughter's husband has lived in our house these five years.'

" 'And I dare say there are some grandchildren by this time?'

" 'Indeed there are, Your Worship—a few of them too.'

" 'And thank God for it! He told us to increase and multiply. Well, you've come a long way, Yermolai Grigorevitch; will you drink a glass of brandy with me?'

"The visitor seems doubtful. The Judge fills the glass, saying:

" 'Come, come, friend—the holy fathers have not forbidden us the use of wine and oil on this day.'

" 'It is true that we are allowed it, but strong drink brings a man to all bad fortune.' Thereupon he crosses himself, bows to his host, and drinks the dram.

" 'Now, with a family like that, Grigorevitch, you must find it hard to feed and clothe them all. One horse and one cow would never do for you—you would run short of milk for such a number.'

" 'One horse, *bátyushka*! That wouldn't do at all. I've three, and I had a fourth, a roan, but it died in St. Peter's Fast; it was bewitched; our carpenter Doroféi hates to see others prosper, and he has the evil eye.'

" 'Well, that does happen sometimes. But you have good pasture there, and I dare say you keep sheep.'

" 'Yes, we have some sheep.'

" 'Dear me, we have had quite a long chat, Yermolai Grigorevitch. I must be off to Court now—the Tsar's service, as you know. Have you any little business to ask me about, I wonder?"

" 'Indeed I have, Your Worship.'

" 'Well, what is it? Have you been doing something foolish? Be quick and tell me, because I must be starting.'

" 'This is it, Your Honour. Misfortune has come upon me in my old age, and I trust to you. It was Assumption Day; we were in the public-house, and I had words with a man from another village—a nasty fellow he is, who steals our wood. Well, we had some words, and then he raised his fist and struck me on the breast. "Don't you use your fists off your own dunghill," said I; and I wanted to teach him a lesson, so I gave him a tap. Now, whether it was the drink or the work of the Evil One, my fist went straight into his eye, and the eye was damaged. He went at once to the police—"I'll have the law of him," says he.'

"During this narrative the Judge—a fig for your Petersburg actors!—becomes more and more solemn; the expression of his eyes becomes alarming; he says not a word.

"The peasant sees this and changes colour; he puts his hat down on the ground and takes out a handkerchief to wipe the sweat off his brow. The Judge turns over the leaves of a book and still keeps silence.

" 'That is why I have come to see you, *bátyushka*,' the peasant says in a strained voice.

" 'What can I do in such a case? It's a bad business! What made you hit him in the eye?'

" 'What indeed, *bátyushka*! It was the enemy led me astray.'

" 'Sad, very sad! Such a thing to ruin a whole family! How can they get on without you—all young, and the grandchildren mere infants! A sad thing for your wife, too, in her old age!'

"The man's legs begin to tremble. 'Does Your Honour think it's as bad as all that?'

" 'Take the book and read the act yourself. But perhaps you can't read? Here is the article dealing with injuries to the person—"shall first be flogged and then banished to Siberia." '

" 'Oh, save a man from ruin, save a fellow-Christian from destruction! Is it impossible . . . '

" 'But, my good man, we can't go against the law. So far as it's in our hands, we might perhaps lower the thirty strokes to five or so.'

" 'But about Siberia?'

" 'Oh, there we're powerless, my friend.'

"The peasant at this point produces a purse, takes a paper out of the purse and two or three gold pieces out of the paper; with a low bow he places them on the table.

" 'What's all that, Yermolai Grigorevitch?'

" 'Save me, *bátyushka*!'

" 'No more of that! I have my weak side and I take a present at times; my salary is small and I have to do it. But if I do, I like to give something in return; and what can I do for you? If only it had been a rib or a tooth! But the eye! Take your money back.'

"The peasant is dumbfounded.

" 'There is just one possibility: I might speak to the other judges and write a line to the county town. The matter will probably go to the court there, and I have friends there who will do all they can. But they're men of a different kidney, and three yellow-boys will not go far in that quarter.'

"The peasant recovers a little.

" '*I* don't want anything—I'm sorry for your family; but it's no use offering *them* less than 400 *roubles*.'

" 'Four hundred *roubles*! How on earth can I get such a mint of money as that, in these times? It's quite beyond me, I swear.'

" 'It's not easy, I agree. We can lessen the flogging; the man's sorry, we shall say, and he was not sober at the time. People *do* live in Siberia, after all; and it's not so very far from here. Of course, you might manage it by selling a pair of horses and one of the cows and the sheep. But you would have to work many years to replace all that stock; and if you don't pay up, your horses will be left all right but you'll be off on the long tramp yourself. Think it over, Grigorevitch; no hurry; we'll do nothing till to-morrow; but I must be going now.' And the Judge pockets the coins he had refused, saying, 'It's quite un-necessary—I only take it to spare your feelings.'

"Next day, an old Jew turns up at the Judge's house, lugging a bag that contains 350 *roubles* in coinage of all dates.

"The Judge promises his assistance. The peasant is tried, and tried over again, and well frightened; then he gets off with a light sentence, or a caution to be more prudent in future, or a note against his name as a suspicious character. And the peasant for the rest of his life prays that God will reward the Judge for his kindness.

"Well, that's a specimen of the neat way they used to do it"—so the retired inspector used to wind up his story.

§9

IN Vyatka the Russian tillers of the soil are fairly independent, and get a bad name in consequence from the officials, as unruly and discontented. But the Finnish natives, poor, timid, stupid people, are a regular gold mine to the rural police. The inspectors pay the governors twice the usual sum when they are appointed to districts where the Finns live.

The tricks which the authorities play on these poor wretches are beyond belief.

If the land-surveyor is travelling on business and passes a native village, he never fails to stop there. He takes the theodolite off his cart, drives in a post and pulls out his chain. In an hour the whole village is in a ferment. "The land-measurer! the land-measurer!" they cry, just as they used to cry, "The French! the French!" in the year '12. The elders come to pay their respects: the surveyor goes on measuring and making notes. They ask him not to cheat them out of their land, and he demands twenty or thirty *roubles*. They are glad to give it and collect the money; and he drives on to the next village of natives.

Again, if the police find a dead body, they drag it about for a fortnight—the frost makes this possible—through the Finnish villages. In each village they declare that they have just found the corpse and mean to start an inquest; and the people pay blackmail.

Some years before I went to Vyatka, a rural inspector, a famous blackmailer, brought a dead body in a cart into a large village of Russian settlers, and demanded, I think, 200 *roubles*. The village elder consulted the community; but they would not go beyond one hundred. The inspector would not lower his price. The peasants got angry: they shut him up with his two clerks in the police-office and threatened, in their turn, to burn them alive. The inspector did not take them seriously. The peasants piled straw around the house; then, by way of ultimatum, they held up a hundred-*rouble* note on a pole in front of the window. The hero inside asked for a hundred more. Thereupon the peasants fired the straw at all four corners, and all the three Mucius Scaevolas of the rural police were burnt to death. At a later time this matter came before the Supreme Court.

These native settlements are in general much less thriving than the Russian villages.

"You don't seem well off, friend," I said to the native owner of a hut where I was waiting for fresh horses; it was a wretched, smoky, lop-sided cabin, with windows looking over the yard at the back.

"What can we do, *bátyushka*? We are poor, and keep our money for a rainy day."

"A rainy day? It looks to me as if you'd got it already. But drink that for comfort"—and I filled a glass with rum.

"We don't drink," said the Finn, with a greedy look at the glass and a suspicious look at me.

"Come, come, you'd better take it."

"Well, drink first yourself."

I drank, and then he followed my example. "What are you doing?" he asked. "Have you come on business from Vyatka?"

"No," I answered; "I'm a traveller on my way there." He was considerably relieved to hear this; he looked all round, and added by way of explanation, "The rainy day is when the inspector or the priest comes here."

I should like to say something here about the latter of these personages.

§10

OF the Finnish population some accepted Christianity before Peter's reign, others were baptised in the time of Elizabeth,* and others have remained heathen. Most of those who changed their religion under Elizabeth are still secretly attached to their own dismal and savage faith.

Every two or three years the police-inspector and the priest make a tour of the villages, to find out which of the natives have not fasted in Lent, and to enquire the reasons. The recusants are harried and imprisoned, flogged and fined. But the visitors search especially for some proof that the old heathen rites are still kept up. In that case, there is a real 'rainy day'—the detective and the missionary raise a storm and exact heavy blackmail; then they go away, leaving all as it was before, to repeat their visit in a year or two.

In the year 1835 the Holy Synod thought it necessary to convert the heathen Cheremisses to Orthodoxy. Archbishop Philaret nominated an active priest named Kurbanovski as missionary. Kurbanovski, a man eaten up by the Russian disease of ambition, set to work with fiery zeal. He tried preaching at first, but soon grew tired of it; and, in point of fact, not much is to be done by that ancient method.

The Cheremisses, when they heard of this, sent their own priests to meet the missionary. These fanatics were ingenious savages: after long discussions, they said to him: "The forest contains not only silver birches and tall pines but also the little juniper. God permits them all to grow and does not bid the juniper be a pine tree. We men

*Elizabeth, daughter of Peter the Great, reigned from 1741 to 1762.

are like the trees of the forest. Be you the silver birches, and let us remain the juniper. We don't interfere with you, we pray for the Tsar, pay our dues, and provide recruits for the Army; but we are not willing to be false to our religion."

Kurbanovski saw that they could not agree, and that he was not fated to play the part of Cyril and Methodius.* He had recourse to the secular arm; and the local police-inspector was delighted—he had long wished to show his zeal for the church; he was himself an unbaptised Tatar, a true believer in the Koran, and his name was Devlet Kildéyev.

He took a detachment of his men and proceeded to besiege the Cheremisses. Several villages were baptised. Kurbanovski sang the *Te Deum* in church and went back to Moscow, to receive with humility the velvet cap for good service; and the Government sent the Vladímir Cross to the Tatar.

But there was an unfortunate misunderstanding between the Tatar missionary and the local mullah. The mullah was greatly displeased when this believer in the Koran took to preaching the Gospel and succeeded so well. During Ramadan, the inspector boldly put on his cross and appeared in the mosque wearing it; he took a front place, as a matter of course. The mullah had just begun to chant the Koran through his nose, when he suddenly stopped and said that he dared not go on, in the presence of a true believer who had come to the mosque wearing a Christian emblem.

*In the ninth century Cyril and his brother Methodius, two Greek monks of Salonica, introduced Christianity among the Slavs. They invented the Russian alphabet.

The congregation protested; and the discomfited inspector was forced to put his cross in his pocket.

I read afterwards in the archives of the Home Office an account of this brilliant conversion of the Cheremisses. The writer mentioned the zealous cooperation of Devlet Kildéyev, but unfortunately forgot to add that his zeal for the Church was the more disinterested because of his firm belief in the truth of Islam.

§11

BEFORE I left Vyatka, the Department of Imperial Domains was committing such impudent thefts that a commission of enquiry was appointed; and this commission sent out inspectors into all the provinces. A new system of control over the Crown tenants was introduced after that time. ·

Our Governor at that time was Kornilov; he had to nominate two subordinates to assist the inspectors, and I was one of the two. I had to read a multitude of documents, sometimes with pain, sometimes with amusement, sometimes with disgust. The very headings of the subjects for investigation struck me with astonishment—

(1) *The loss and total disappearance of a police-station, and the destruction of the plan by the gnawing of mice.*

(2) *The loss of twelve miles of arable land.*

(3) *The transference of the peasant's son Vasili to the female sex.*

The last item was so remarkable that I read the details at once from beginning to end.

There was a petition to the Governor from the father of the child. The petitioner stated that fifteen years ago a daughter had been born to him, whom he wished to call Vasilissa; but the priest, not being sober, christened the girl Vasili, and entered the name thus on the register. This fact apparently caused little disturbance to the father; but when he found he would soon be required to provide a recruit for the Army and pay the poll-tax for the child, he informed the police. The police were much puzzled. They began by refusing to act, on the ground that he ought to have applied earlier. The father then went to the Governor, and the Governor ordered that this boy of the female sex should be formally examined by a doctor and a midwife. But at this point, matters were complicated by a correspondence with the ecclesiastical authorities; and the parish priest, whose predecessor, under the influence of drink, had been too prudish to recognise differences of sex, now appeared on the scene; the matter went on for years, and I rather think the girl was never cleared of the suspicion of being a boy.

The reader is not to suppose that this absurd story is a mere humorous invention of mine.

During the Emperor Paul's reign a colonel of the Guards, making his monthly report, returned as dead an officer who had gone to the hospital; and the Tsar struck his name off the lists. But unfortunately the officer did not die; he recovered instead. The colonel induced him to return to his estates for a year or two, hoping to find an opportunity of putting matters straight; and the officer agreed. But his heirs, having read of his death in the Gazette, positively refused to recognise him as still alive; though inconsolable for their loss, they insisted upon their right of succession. The living corpse, whom the Gazette had killed once, found that he was likely to die over again, by starvation this time. So he travelled to Petersburg and handed in a petition to the Tsar.

This beats even my story of the girl who was also a boy.

§12

IT is a miry slough, this account of our provincial administration; yet I shall add a few words more. This publicity is the last paltry compensation to those who suffered unheard and unpitied.

Government is very ready to reward high officials with grants of unoccupied land. There is no great harm in that, though it might be wiser to keep it for the needs of an increasing population. The rules governing such allotments of land are rather detailed; it is illegal to grant the banks of a navigable river, or wood fit for building purposes, or both sides of a river; and finally, land reclaimed by peasants may in no case be taken from them, even though the peasants have no title to the land except prescription.

All this is very well, on paper; but in fact this allotment of land to individuals is a terrible instrument by which the Crown is robbed and the peasants oppressed.

Most of the magnates to whom the leases are granted either sell their rights to merchants, or try, by means of the provincial authorities, to secure some privileges contrary to the rules. Thus it happened, by mere chance, of course, that Count Orlóv himself got possession of the road and pastures used by droves of cattle in the Government of Saratov.

No wonder, then, that the peasants of a certain district in Vyatka were deprived one fine morning of all their

land, right up to their houses and farmyards, the soil
having passed into the possession of some merchants who
had bought the lease from a relation of Count Kankrin.*
The merchants next put a rent on the land. The law was
appealed to. The Crown Court, being bribed by the merchants and fearing a great man's cousin, put a spoke in
the wheel; but the peasants, determined to go on to the
bitter end, chose two shrewd men from among themselves
and sent them off to Petersburg. The matter now came
before the Supreme Court. The judges suspected that the
peasants were in the right; but they were puzzled how
to act, and consulted Kankrin. That nobleman admitted
frankly that the land had been taken away unjustly; but
he thought there would be difficulty in restoring it, because it *might* have been re-sold since, and because the
new owners *might* have made some improvements. He
therefore suggested that advantage should be taken of
the vast extent of the Crown lands, and that the same
quantity of land should be granted to the peasants, but
in another district. This solution pleased everyone except
the peasants: in the first place, it was no trifle to reclaim
fresh land; and, in the second place, the land offered them
turned out to be a bog. As the peasants were more interested in growing corn than in shooting snipe, they sent
in a fresh petition.

The Crown Court and the Treasury then treated this
as a fresh case. They discovered a law which provided
that, in cases where unsuitable land had been allotted, the
grant should not be cancelled but an addition of 50 per
cent should be made; they therefore directed that the

*Count Kankrin (1774-1845) was Minister of Finance from 1823
till his death. He carried through some important reforms in the currency.

peasants should get half a bog in addition to the bog they had been given already.

The peasants sent in a third petition to the Supreme Court. But, before this was discussed, the Board of Agriculture sent them plans of their new land, duly bound and coloured; with a neat diagram of the points of the compass arranged in a star, and suitable explanations of the rhombus R R Z and the rhombus Z Z R, and, above all, with a demand for a fixed payment per acre. When the peasants saw that, far from getting back their good land, they were to be charged money for their bog, they flatly refused to pay.

The rural inspector informed the Governor of this; and the Governor sent troops under the command of the town inspector of Vyatka. The latter went to the spot, arrested several men and beat them, restored order in the district, took money, handed over the 'guilty' to the Criminal Court, and was hoarse for a week after, owing to the strain on his voice. Several of the offenders were sentenced to flogging and banishment.

Two years afterwards, when the Crown Prince was passing through the district, these peasants presented a petition, and he ordered the matter to be examined. It was at this point that I had to draw up a report of all the proceedings. Whether anything sensible was done in consequence of this fresh investigation, I do not know. I have heard that the exiles were restored, but I never heard that the land had been given back.

§13

IN the next place I shall refer to the famous episode of the "potato-rebellion."

In Russia, as formerly throughout Europe, the peasants were unwilling to grow potatoes, from an instinctive feeling that potatoes are poor food and not productive of health and strength. Model landlords, however, and many Crown settlements used to grow these tubers long before the "potato-revolt."

In the Government of Kazán and part of Vyatka, the people had grown a crop of potatoes. When the tubers were taken up, it occurred to the Board of Agriculture to start communal pits for storing them. The pits were authorised, ordered, and constructed; and in the beginning of winter the peasants, with many misgivings, carted their potatoes to the communal pits. But they positively refused, when they were required in the spring to plant these same potatoes in a frozen condition. What, indeed, can be more insulting to labouring men than to bid them do what is obviously absurd? But their protest was represented as a rebellion. The minister despatched an official from Petersburg; and this intelligent and practical man excused the farmers of the first district he visited from planting the frozen potatoes, and charged for this dispensation one *rouble* per head. He repeated this operation in two other districts; but the men of the fourth district flatly refused either to plant the potatoes or to pay the money. "You have excused the others," they said; "you are clearly bound to let us off too." The official then tried to end the business by threats and corporal punishment; but the peasants armed themselves with poles and routed the police. The Governor sent a force of Cossacks to the spot; and the neighbouring districts backed up the rebels.

It is enough to say that cannon roared and rifles cracked before the affair was over. The peasants took to the woods and were routed out of their covert like wild animals by the Cossacks. They were caught, chained, and sent to Kosmodemyansk to be tried by court-martial.

By a strange chance there was a simple, honest man, an old major of militia, serving on the court-martial; and he ventured to say that the official from Petersburg was to blame for all that had happened. But everyone promptly fell on the top of him and squashed him and suppressed him; they tried to frighten him and said he ought to be ashamed of his attempt "to ruin an innocent man."

The enquiry went on just as enquiries do in Russia: the peasants were flogged on examination, flogged as a punishment, flogged as an example, and flogged to get money out of them; and then a number of them were exiled to Siberia.

It is worthy of remark that the Minister passed through Kosmodemyansk during the trial. One thinks he might have looked in at the court-martial himself or summoned the dangerous major to an interview. He did nothing of the kind.

The famous Turgot,* knowing how unpopular the potato was in France, distributed seed-potatoes to a number of dealers and persons in Government employ, with strict orders that the peasants were to have none. But at the same time he let them know privately that the peasants were not to be prevented from helping themselves. The result was that in a few years potatoes were grown all over the country.

All things considered, this seems to me a better method than the cannon-ball plan.

*Turgot (1727-1781) was one of the Ministers of Finance under Louis XVI.

§14

In the year 1836 a strolling tribe of gipsies came to
Vyatka and encamped there. These people wandered at
times as far as Tobolsk and Irbit, carrying on from time
immemorial their roving life of freedom, accompanied of
course by a bear that had been taught to dance and children that had been taught nothing; they lived by doctor-
ing horses, telling fortunes, and petty theft. At Vyatka
they went on singing their songs and stealing chickens,
till the Governor suddenly received instructions, that, if
the gipsies turned out to have no passports—no gipsy
was ever known to possess one—a certain interval should
be allowed them, within which they must register themselves as members of the village communities where they
happened to be at the time.

If they failed to do so by the date mentioned, then all
who were fit for military service were to be sent to the
colours, the rest to be banished from the country, and
all their male children to be taken from them.

Tufáyev himself was taken aback by this decree. He
gave notice of it to the gipsies, but he reported to Petersburg that it could not be complied with. The registration
would cost money; the consent of the communities must
be obtained, and they would want money for admitting
the gipsies. After taking everything into consideration,
Tufáyev proposed to the Minister—and he must get due
credit for the proposal—that the gipsies should be treated
leniently and given an extension of time.

In reply the Minister ordered him to carry out the
original instructions when the time had expired. The Governor hardened his heart and sent a detachment to surround the gipsy encampment; when that was done, the

police brought up a militia battalion, and scenes that beggar description are said to have followed—women, with their hair flying loose, ran frantically to and fro, shrieking and sobbing, while white-haired old women clutched hold of their sons. But order triumphed, and the police-inspector secured all the boys and the recruits, and the rest were marched off by stages to their place of exile.

But a question now arose: where were the kidnapped children to be put, and at whose cost were they to be maintained?

In former days there had been schools for foundlings which cost the Crown nothing; but these had been abolished, as productive of immorality. The Governor advanced the money from his own pocket and consulted the Minister. The Minister replied that, until further orders, the children were to be looked after by the old people in the alms-house.

To make little children live with dying old men and women, and to force them to breathe the atmosphere of death; and on the other hand, to force the aged and worn-out to look after the children for nothing—that was a real inspiration!

§15

WHILE I am on this subject, I shall tell here the story of what happened eighteen months later to a bailiff of my father's. Though a peasant, he was a man of intelligence and experience; he had several teams of his own which he hired out, and he served for twenty years as bailiff of a small detached village.

In the year which I spent at Vladímir, he was asked by the people of a neighbouring village to supply a substitute as a recruit for the Army; and he turned up in the town with the future defender of his country at the end of a rope. He seemed perfectly self-confident and sure of success.

"Yes, *bátyushka*," he said to me, combing with his fingers his thick brown beard with some grey in it, "it all depends on how you manage these things. We put forward a lad two years ago, but he was a very poor miserable specimen, and the men were very much afraid that he would not do. 'Well,' said I, 'you must begin by collecting some money—the wheel won't go round unless you grease it!' So we had a talk together, and the village produced twenty-five gold pieces. I drove into the town, had a talk with the people in the Crown Court, and then went straight to the President's house—a clever man, *bátyushka*, and an old acquaintance of mine. He had me taken into his study, where he was lying on the sofa with a bad leg. I put the facts before him. He laughed and said, 'All right, all right! But you tell me how many of *them* you have brought with you; for I know what an old skin-flint you are.' I put ten gold pieces on the table with a low bow. He took them up and played with them. 'Well,' says he, 'I'm not the only person who expects payment; have you brought any more?' 'Well,' said I, 'we can go as far as ten more.' 'You can count for yourself,' says he, 'where they are to go to: the doctor will want a couple, and the inspector of recruits another couple, and the clerk —I don't think more than three will be needed in that quarter; but you had better give me the lot, and I'll try to arrange it for you.' "

"Well, did you give it?" I asked.

"Certainly I did; and the man was passed for the Army all right."

Enlightened by this method of rounding off accounts, and attracted probably by the five gold pieces to whose ultimate destination he had made no allusion, the bailiff was sure of success this time also. But there is many a slip between the bribe and the palm that closes on it. Count Essen, an Imperial *aide-de-camp*, was sent to Vladímir to inspect the recruits. The bailiff, with his golden arguments in his pocket, found his way into the presence of the Count. But unfortunately the Count was no true Russian, but a son of the Baltic provinces which teach German devotion towards the Russian Tsar. He got angry, raised his voice, and, worse than all, rang his bell; in ran a secretary, and police-officers on the top of him. The bailiff, who had never dreamed of the existence of a man in uniform who would refuse a bribe, lost his head altogether; instead of holding his tongue, he swore by all his gods that he had never offered money, and wished that his eyes might fall out and he might die of thirst, if he had ever thought of such a thing. Helpless as a sheep, he was taken off to the police-station, where he probably repented of his folly in insulting a high officer by offering him so little.

Essen was not content with his own clear conscience nor with having given the man a fright. He probably wished to lay the axe to the tree of Russian corruption, to punish vice, and to make a salutary example. He therefore reported the bailiff's nefarious attempt to the police, the Governor, and the Recruiting Office. The offender was put in prison and ordered to be tried. Thanks to the absurd law, which is equally severe on the honest man who gives a bribe and the official who pockets it, the affair looked bad, and I resolved at all costs to save the bailiff.

I went at once to the Governor, but he refused to interfere. The President and Councillors of the Criminal Court shook their heads: the *aide-de-camp* was interested in the case, and that frightened them. I went to Count Essen himself, and he was very gracious—he had no wish that the bailiff should suffer, but thought he needed a lesson: "Let him be tried and acquitted," he said. When I repeated this to the inspector of police, he remarked: "The fact is, these gentlemen don't understand business. If the Count had simply sent him to me, I should have warmed the fool's back for walking into a river without asking if there was a ford; then I should have sent him about his business, and all parties would have been satisfied. But the court complicates matters."

I have never forgotten what the Count said and what the inspector said: they expressed so neatly and clearly the view of justice entertained in the Russian Empire.

Between these Pillars of Hercules of our national jurisprudence, the bailiff had fallen into the deep water, in other words, into the Criminal Court. A few months later the court came to a decision: the criminal was to be flogged and then banished to Siberia. His son and all his relations came to me, begging me to save the father and head of the family. I felt intense pity myself for the sufferer, who was perfectly innocent. I called again on the President and Councillors; again I tried to prove that they were injuring themselves by punishing this man so severely. "You know very well yourselves," I said, "that no lawsuit is ever settled without bribes; and you will starve yourselves, unless you take the truly Christian view that

every gift is good and perfect."* By begging and bowing
and sending the bailiff's son to bow still lower, I attained
half of my object. The man was condemned to suffer a
certain number of lashes within the prison walls, but he
was not exiled; and he was forbidden to undertake any
business of the kind in future for other peasants.

When I found that the Governor and state-attorney had
confirmed this remission, I went off to beg the police that
the flogging might be lightened; and they, partly flattered
by this personal appeal, and partly pitying a martyr in
a cause so near to their own hearts, and also because they
knew the man was well-to-do, promised me that the punishment should be merely nominal.

A few days later the bailiff came to my house one morning; he looked thin, and there was more grey in his beard.
For all his joy, I soon perceived that he had something
on his mind.

"What's troubling you?" I asked.

"Well, I wish I could get it all over at once."

"I don't understand you."

"What I mean is—when will the flogging be?"

"But haven't you been flogged?"

"No."

"But they've let you out, and I suppose you're going
home."

"Home? Yes, I'm going home, but I keep thinking about
the flogging; the secretary spoke of it, I am sure I heard
him."

I was really quite puzzled. At last I asked him if he
had a written discharge of any kind. He handed it to me.
I read there the original sentence at full length, and then

*There is a reference to the Epistle of James, i. 17.

a postscript, that he was to be flogged within the prison walls by sentence of the court and then to be discharged, in possession of this certificate.

I burst out laughing. "You see, you've been flogged already."

"No, *bátyushka,* I've not."

"Well, if you're not content, go back and ask them to flog you; perhaps the police will take pity upon you."

Seeing me laugh, he too smiled, but he shook his head doubtfully and said, "It's a very queer business."

A very irregular business, many will say; but let them reflect that it is this kind of irregularity alone which makes life possible in Russia.

CHAPTER IX

Alexander Vitberg.

§1

IN the midst of all this ugliness and squalor, these petty and repulsive persons and scenes, in this world of chicanery and red tape, I recall the sad and noble figure of a great artist.

I lived at his side for two years and a half and saw this strong man breaking up under the pressure of persecution and misfortune.

Nor can it be said that he succumbed without a protest; for ten long years he struggled desperately. When he went into exile, he still hoped to conquer his enemies and right himself; in fact, he was still eager for the conflict, still full of projects and expedients. But at Vyatka he saw that all was over.

He might have accepted this discovery but for the wife and children at his side, and the prospect of long years of exile, poverty, and privation; he grew greyer and older, not day by day, but hour by hour. I was two years at Vyatka, and when I left, he was ten years older than when I came.

Let me tell the story of this long martyrdom.

§2

THE Emperor Alexander could not believe in his victory
over Napoleon. Glory was a burden to him, and he quite
sincerely gave it to God's name instead. Always inclined
to mysticism and despondency, he was more than ever
haunted by these feelings after his repeated victories over
Napoleon.

When the last soldier of the French army had retreated
over the frontier, Alexander published a manifesto, in
which he took a vow to erect a great cathedral at Moscow, dedicated to the Saviour.

Plans for this church were invited from all quarters,
and there was a great competition of artists.

Alexander Vitberg was then a young man; he had been
trained in the art schools at Petersburg and had gained
the gold medal for painting. Of Swedish descent, he was
born in Russia and received his early education in the
School of Mines. He was a passionate lover of art, with a
tendency to eccentricity and mysticism. He read the Emperor's manifesto and the invitation for designs, and at
once gave up all his former occupations. Day and night
he wandered about the streets of Petersburg, tormented
by a fixed idea which he was powerless to banish. He
shut himself up in his room, took his pencil, and began to
work.

The artist took no one into his confidence. After working for several months, he travelled to Moscow, where he
studied the city and its surroundings. Then he set to work
again, hiding himself from all eyes for months at a time,
and hiding his drawings also.

The time came for the competition. Many plans were
sent in, plans from Italy and from Germany, and our own

academicians sent in theirs. The design of this unknown youth took its place among the rest. Some weeks passed before the Emperor examined the plans, and these weeks were the Forty Days in the Wilderness, days of temptation and doubt and painful anxiety.

The Emperor was struck by Vitberg's design, which was on a colossal scale and remarkable for religious and artistic feeling. He stopped first in front of it and asked who had sent it in. The envelope was opened; the name inside was that of an unknown student of the Academy.

Alexander sent for Vitberg and had a long conversation with him. He was impressed by the artist's confident and animated speech, the real inspiration which filled him, and the mystical turn of his convictions. "You speak in stone," the Emperor said, as he looked through the plans again.

The plans were approved that very day; Vitberg was appointed architect of the cathedral and president of the building committee. Alexander was not aware that there were thorns beneath the crown of laurels which he placed on the artist's head.

§3

THERE is no art more akin to mysticism than architecture. Abstract, geometrical, musical and yet dumb, passionless, it depends entirely upon symbolism, form, suggestion. Simple lines, and the harmonious combination and numerical relations between these, present something mysterious and at the same time incomplete. A building, a temple, does not comprise its object within itself; it differs in this respect from a statue or a picture, a poem or a symphony. The building needs an inhabitant; in itself it is a prepared space, a setting, like the shell of a tortoise or marine creature; and the essential thing is just this, that the outer case should fit the spirit and the inhabitant, as closely as the shell fits the tortoise. The walls of the temple, its vaults and pillars, its main entrance, its foundations and cupola, should all reflect the deity that dwells within, just as the bones of the skull correspond exactly to the convolutions of the brain.

To the Egyptians their temples were sacred books, their obelisks were sermons by the high road.

Solomon's temple is the Bible in stone; and so St. Peter's at Rome is the transition, in stone, from Catholicism to a kingdom of this world, the first stage of our liberation from monastic fetters.

The mere construction of temples was at all times accompanied by so many mystical rites, allegoric ceremonies, and solemn consecrations, that the medieval builders ranked themselves as a kind of religious order, as successors to the builders of Solomon's temple; and they formed themselves into secret companies, of which freemasonry was a later development.

The Renaissance robbed architecture of this essentially mystical note. The Christian faith began to contend with scepticism, the Gothic spire with the Greek façade, religious sanctity with worldly beauty. This is why St. Peter's at Rome is so significant; in that colossal erection Christianity is struggling to come alive, the Church turns pagan, and Michael Angelo uses the walls of the Sistine Chapel to depict Jesus Christ as a brawny athlete, a Hercules in the flower of youth and strength.

After this date church architecture fell into utter decadence, till it became a mere reproduction, in varying proportions, either of St. Peter's or of ancient Greek temples. There is one Parthenon at Paris which is called the Church of the Madeleine, and another at New York, which is used as the Exchange.

Without faith and without special circumstances, it was hard to build anything with life about it. All modern churches are misfits and pretentious anachronisms, like those angular Gothic churches with which the English ornament their towns and offend every artistic eye.

§4

BUT the circumstances in which Vitberg drew his plans, his own personality, and the Emperor's temperament, all these were quite exceptional.

The war of 1812 had a profound effect upon men's minds in Russia, and it was long after the liberation of Moscow before the general emotion and excitement subsided. Then foreign events, the taking of Paris, the history of the Hundred Days, expectations and rumours, Waterloo, Napoleon on board the *Bellerophon,* mourning for the dead and anxiety for the living, the returning armies, the warriors restored to their homes,—all this had a strong effect upon the least susceptible natures. Now imagine a young man, an artist and a mystic, endowed with creative power, and also an enthusiast spurred on by current events, by the Tsar's challenge, and by his own genius.

Near Moscow, between the Mozhaisk and Kaluga roads, a modest eminence dominates the whole city. Those are the Sparrow Hills of which I spoke in my early recollections. They command one of the finest views of all Moscow. Here it was that Ivan the Terrible, still young and unhardened, shed tears at the sight of his capital on fire; and here that the priest Silvester met him and by his stern rebuke changed for twenty years to come the nature of that monster and man of genius.

Napoleon and his army marched round these hills. There his strength was broken, and there his retreat began. What better site for a temple in memory of 1812 than the farthest point reached by the enemy?

But this was not enough. It was Vitberg's intention to convert the hill itself into the lowest part of the cathedral, to build a colonnade to the river, and then, on a foundation laid on three sides by nature herself, to erect a second and a third church. But all the three churches made one; for Vitberg's cathedral, like the chief dogma of Christianity, was both triple and indivisible.

The lowest of the three churches, hewn in the rock, was a parallelogram in the shape of a coffin or dead body. All that was visible was a massive entrance supported on columns of almost Egyptian size; the church itself was hidden in the primitive unworked rock. It was lighted by lamps in high Etruscan candelabra; a feeble ray of daylight from the second church passed into it through a transparent picture of the Nativity. All the heroes who fell in 1812 were to rest in this crypt; a perpetual mass was to be said there for those who had fallen on the field of battle; and the names of them all, from the chief commanders to the private soldiers, were to be engraved on the walls.

On the top of this coffin or cemetery rose the second church, in the form of a Greek cross with limbs of equal length spreading to the four quarters, a temple of life, of suffering, of labour. The colonnade which led up to it was adorned with statues of the Patriarchs and Judges.

At the entrance were the Prophets; they stood outside the church, pointing out the way which they could not tread themselves. Inside this temple the Gospel story and the Acts of the Apostles were represented on the walls.

Above this building, crowning it, completing it, and including it, the third church was to be built in the shape of the Pantheon. It was brightly lighted, as the home of the Spirit, of unbroken peace, of eternity; and eternity was represented by its shape. Here there were no pictures or sculpture; but there was an exterior frieze representing the archangels, and the whole was surmounted by a colossal dome.

Sad is my present recollection of Vitberg's main idea; he had worked it out in every detail, in complete accordance at every point with Christian theology and architectural beauty.

This astonishing man spent a whole lifetime over his conception. It was his sole occupation during the ten years that his trial lasted; in poverty and exile, he devoted several hours of each day to his cathedral. He lived in it; he could not believe that it would never be built; his whole life—his memories, his consolations, his fame—was wrapped up in that portfolio.

It may be that in the future, when the martyr is dead, some later artist may shake the dust from those leaves and piously give to the world that record of suffering, those plans over which the strong man, after his brief hour of glory had gone out, spent a life of darkness and pain.

His plan was full of genius, and startling in its extravagance; for this reason Alexander chose it, and for this reason it should have been carried out. It is said that the hill could never have supported such a building; but I do not believe it, especially in view of all the modern triumphs of engineering in America and England, those suspension-bridges and tunnels which a train takes eight minutes to pass through.

Milorádovitch advised Vitberg to have granite monoliths for the great pillars of the lowest church. Someone pointed out that the process of bringing these from Finland would be very costly. "That is the very reason why we should get them," answered Milorádovitch; "if there were granite quarries on the Moscow River, where would be the wonder in erecting the pillars?"

Milorádovitch was a soldier, but he understood the element of romance in war and in other things. Magnificent ends are gained by magnificent means. Nature alone attains to greatness without effort.

The chief accusation brought against Vitberg, even by those who never doubted his honesty, was this, that he had accepted the post of director of the works. As an artist without experience, and a young man ignorant of finance, he should have been content with his position as architect. This is true.

It is easy to sit in one's chair and condemn Vitberg for this. But he accepted the post just because he was young and inexperienced, because nothing seemed hard when once his plans had been accepted, because the Tsar himself offered him the post, encouraged him, and supported him. Whose head would not have been turned? Where are these sober, sensible, self-controlled people? If they exist, they are not capable of constructing colossal plans, they cannot make stones speak.

§5

As a matter of course, Vitberg was soon surrounded by a swarm of rascals, men who look on state employment merely as a lucky chance to line their own pockets. It is easy to understand that such men would undermine Vitberg and set traps for him; yet he might have climbed out of these but for something else—had not envy in some quarters, and injured dignity in others, been added to general dishonesty.

There were three other members of the commission as well as Vitberg—the Archbishop Philaret, the Governor of Moscow, and Kushnikov, a Judge of the Supreme Court; and all three resented from the first the presence of this "whipper-snapper," who actually ventured to state his objections and insist on his own opinions.

They helped others to entangle and defame him, and then they destroyed him without a qualm.

Two events contributed to this catastrophe, the fall of the Minister, Prince A. N. Golitsyn, and then the death of Alexander.

The Minister's fall dragged Vitberg down with it. He felt the full weight of that disaster: the Commission complained, the Archbishop was offended, the Governor was dissatisfied. His replies were called insolent—insolence was one of the main charges brought against him on his trial—and it was said that his subordinates stole—as if there was a single person in the public service in Russia who refrains from stealing! It is possible, indeed, that his agents stole more than usual; for he was quite inexperienced in the management of reformatories or the detection of highly placed thieves.

Alexander ordered Arakchéyev to investigate the affair.

He himself was sorry for Vitberg and sent a message to say that he was convinced of the architect's honesty.

But Alexander died and Arakchéyev fell. Under Nicholas, Vitberg's affair at once assumed a more threatening aspect. It dragged on for ten years, and the absurdity of the proceedings is incredible. The Supreme Court dismissed charges taken as proved by the Criminal Court, and charged him with guilt of which he had been acquitted; the committee of ministers found him guilty on all the charges; and the Emperor Nicholas added to the original sentence banishment to Vyatka.

So Vitberg was banished, having been discharged from the public service "for abusing the confidence of the Emperor Alexander and for squandering the revenues of the Crown." A claim was brought against him for a million *roubles*—I think that was the sum; all his property was seized and sold by auction, and a report was spread that he had transferred an immense sum of money to America.

I lived for two years in the same house with Vitberg and kept up constant relations with him till I left Vyatka. He had not saved even enough for his daily bread, and his family lived in the direst poverty.

§6

IN order to throw light on this trial and all similar trials in Russia, I shall add two trifling details.

Vitberg bought a forest for building material from a merchant named Lobanov, but, before the trees were felled, offered to take another forest instead which was nearer the river and belonged to the same owner. Lobanov agreed; the trees were felled and the timber floated down the river. More timber was needed at a later date, and

Vitberg bought the first forest over again. Hence arose the famous charge that he had paid twice over for the same timber. The unfortunate Lobanov was put in prison on this charge and died there.

§7

Of the second affair I was myself an eye-witness.

Vitberg bought up land with a view to his cathedral. His idea was that the serfs, when transferred with the land he had bought, should bind themselves to supply a fixed number of workmen to be employed on the cathedral; in this way they acquired complete freedom from all other burdens for themselves and their community. It is amusing to note that our judges, being also land-owners, objected to this measure as a form of slavery!

One estate which Vitberg wished to buy belonged to my father. It lay on the bank of the Moscow River; stone had been found there, and Vitberg got leave from my father to make a geological inspection, in order to determine how much stone there was. After obtaining leave, Vitberg had to go off to Petersburg.

Three months later my father learned that the quarrying operations were being carried out on a great scale, and that the peasants' cornfields were buried under blocks of stone. His protests were not listened to, and he went to law. There was a stubborn contest. The defendants tried at first to throw all the blame on Vitberg, but, unfortunately for them, it turned out that he had given no orders whatever, and that the Commission had done the whole thing during his absence.

The case was referred to the Supreme Court, which surprised everyone by coming to a fairly reasonable decision. The stone which had been quarried was to belong to the landowner, as compensation for the injury to his fields; the Crown funds spent on the work were to be repaid, to the amount of 100,000 *roubles,* by those who had signed the contract for the work. The signatories were Prince Golitsyn, the Archbishop, and Kushnikov. Of course there was a great outcry, and the matter was referred to the Tsar.

The Tsar ordered that the payment should not be exacted, because—as he wrote with his own hand—"the members of the Commission did not know what they were signing"! This is actually printed in the journals of the Supreme Court. Even if the Archbishop was bound by his cloth to display humility, what are we to think of the other two magnates who accepted the Tsar's generosity under such conditions?

But where was the money to be found? Crown property, we are told, can neither be burnt by fire nor drowned in water—it can only be stolen, we might add. Without hesitation a general of the Staff was sent in haste to Moscow to clear matters up.

He did so, restored order, and settled everything in the course of a few days. The stone was to be taken from the landowner, to defray the expenses of the quarry, though, if the landowner wished to keep the stone, he might do so on payment of 100,000 *roubles.* The landowner was not to receive special compensation, because the value of his property had been increased by the discovery of a new source of wealth (that is really a noble touch!)—but a certain law of Peter the Great's sanctioned the payment of so many *kopecks* an acre for the damage done to the peasants' fields.

The real sufferer was my father. It is hardly necessary to add that this business of the stone quarry figured after all among the charges brought against Vitberg at his trial.

§8

VITBERG had been living in exile at Vyatka for two years when the merchants of the town determined to build a new church.

Their plans surprised the Tsar Nicholas when they were submitted to him. He confirmed them and gave orders to the local authorities that the builders were not to mar the architect's design.

"Who made these plans?" he asked of the minister.

"Vitberg, Your Majesty."

"Do you mean the same Vitberg?"

"The same man, Your Majesty."

And so it happened that Vitberg, most unexpectedly, got permission to return to Moscow or Petersburg. When he asked leave to clear his character, it was refused; but when he made skilful plans for a church, the Tsar ordered his restoration—as if there had ever been a doubt of his artistic capacity!

In Petersburg, where he was starving for bread, he made a last attempt to defend his honour. It was a complete failure. He applied to Prince A. N. Golitsyn; but the Prince thought it impossible to open the question again, and advised Vitberg to address a humble petition for pecuniary assistance to the Crown Prince. He said that Zhukovski and himself would interest themselves in the matter, and held out hopes of a gift of 1,000 *roubles*.

Vitberg refused.

I visited Petersburg for the last time at the beginning

of winter in 1846, and there I saw Vitberg. He was quite
a wreck; even his wrath against his enemies, which I had
admired so much in former days, had begun to cool down;
he had ceased to hope and was making no endeavour to
escape from his position; a calm despair was making an
end of him; he was breaking up altogether and only waiting for death.

Whether the sufferer is still living, I do not know, but
I doubt it.

"But for my children," he said to me at parting, "I
would tear myself away from Russia and beg my bread
over the world; wearing my Cross of Vladímir, I would
hold out calmly to the passer-by that hand which the Tsar
Alexander grasped, and tell him of my great design and
the fate of an artist in Russia."

"Poor martyr," thought I, "Europe shall learn your
fate—I promise you that."

§9

My intimacy with Vitberg was a great relief to me at
Vyatka. His serious simplicity and a certain solemnity
of manner suggested the churchman to some extent. Strict
in his principles, he tended in general to austerity rather
than enjoyment; but this strictness took nothing from the
luxuriance and richness of his artistic fancy. He could
invest his mystical views with such lively forms and such
beautiful colouring that objections died on your lips, and
you felt reluctant to examine and pull to pieces the glim-
mering forms and shadowy pictures of his imagination.

His mysticism was partly due to his Scandinavian blood.
It was the same play of fancy combined with cool reflec-

tion which we see in Swedenborg;* and that in its turn resembles the fiery reflection of the sun's rays when they fall on the ice-covered mountains and snows of Norway.

Though I was shaken for a time by Vitberg's influence, my positive turn of mind held its own nevertheless. It was not my destiny to be carried up to the third heaven; I was born to inhabit earth alone. Tables never turn at my touch, rings never quiver when I look at them. The daylight of thought is my element, not the moonlight of imagination.

But I was more inclined to the mystical standpoint when I lived with Vitberg than at any other period of my life.

There was much to support Vitberg's influence—the loneliness of exile, the strained and pietistic tone of the letters I received from home, the love which was mastering my whole being with ever increasing power, and an oppressive feeling of remorse for my own misconduct.†

Two years later I was again influenced by ideas partly religious and partly socialistic, which I took from the Gospel and from Rousseau; my position was that of some French thinkers, such as Pierre Leroux.‡

My friend Ogaryóv plunged even before I did into the waves of mysticism. In 1833 he began to write a libretto for Gebel's oratorio of *Paradise Lost;* and he wrote to me that the whole history of humanity was included in that poem! It appears therefore that he then considered the paradise of his aspirations to have existed already and disappeared from view.

*Emmanuel Swedenborg (1688-1772), a Swedish mystic and founder of a sect.
†He refers to an intrigue he was carrying on at Vyatka.
‡A French publicist and disciple of Saint Simon, 1797-1871.

In 1838 I wrote from this point of view some historical scenes which I supposed at the time to be dramatic. They were in verse. In one I represented the strife between Christianity and the ancient world, and told how St. Paul, when entering Rome, raised a young man from the dead to enter on a new life. Another described the contest of the Quakers against the Church of England, and the departure of William Penn for America.

The mysticism of the Gospel soon gave way in my mind to the mysticism of science; but I was fortunate enough to escape from the latter as well in course of time.

§10

BUT now I must go back to the modest little town which was called Chlynov until Catherine II changed its name to Vyatka; what her motive was, I do not know, unless it was her Finnish patriotism.

In that dreary distant backwater of exile, separated from all I loved, surrounded by the unclean horde of officials, and exposed without defence to the tyranny of the Governor, I met nevertheless with many warm hearts and friendly hands, and there I spent many happy hours which are sacred in recollection.

Where are you now, and how are you, my snowbound friends? It is twenty years since we met. I suppose you have grown old, as I have; you are thinking about marrying your daughters, and have given up drinking champagne by the bottle and tossing off bumpers of *vodka*. Which of you has made a fortune, and which has lost it? Which has risen high in the official world, and which is laid low by the palsy? Above all, do you still keep alive the memory of our free discussions? Do those chords still resound that were struck so vigorously by our common friendship and our common resentment?

I am unchanged, as you know, for I suspect that rumour flies from the banks of the Thames as far as you. I think of you sometimes, and always with affection. I have kept some letters of those former days, and some of them I regard as treasures and love to read over again.

"I am not ashamed to confess to you," writes one young friend on January 26, 1838, "that my heart is full of bitterness. Help me for the sake of that life to which you summoned me; help me with your advice. I want to learn; make me a list of books, lay down any programme you like; I will work my hardest, if you will point the way. It would be sinful of you to discourage me."

"I bless you," another wrote to me just after I had left Vyatka, "as the husbandman blesses the rain which gives life to his unfertilized field."

I copy out these lines, not from vanity, but because they are very precious to me. This appeal to young hearts and their generous reply, and the unrest I was able to awaken in them—this is my compensation for nine months spent in prison and three years at Vyatka.

§11

THERE is one thing more. Twice a week the post from Moscow came to Vyatka. With what excitement I waited near the post-office while the letters were sorted! How my heart beat as I broke the seal of my letter from home and searched inside for a little enclosure, written on thin paper in a wonderfully small and beautiful hand!

I did not read that in the post-office. I walked slowly

home, putting off the happy moment and feasting on the thought that the letter was there.

These letters have all been preserved. I left them at Moscow when I quitted Russia. Though I longed to read them over, I was afraid to touch them.

Letters are more than recollections, the very life blood of the past is stored up in them; they *are* the past, exactly as it was, preserved from destruction and decay.

Is it really necessary once again to know, to see, to touch with hands which age has covered with wrinkles, what once you wore on your wedding-day?*

*These letters were from Herzen's cousin, Natálya Zakhárin, who became his wife in 1838.

CHAPTER X

The Crown Prince at Vyatka—The Fall of Tufáyev—Transferred to Vladímir—The Inspector's Enquiry.

§1

THE Crown Prince* is coming to Vyatka! The Crown Prince is travelling through Russia, to see the country and to be seen himself! This news was of interest to everyone and of special interest, of course, to the Governor. In his haste and confusion, he issued a number of ridiculous and absurd orders—for instance, that the peasants along the road should wear their holiday *kaftáns,* and that all boardings in the towns should be repainted and all sidewalks mended. A poor widow who owned a smallish house in Orlóv informed the mayor that she had no money to repair her sidewalk; the mayor reported this to the Governor, and the Governor ordered the floors of her house to be pulled up—the sidewalks there were made of wood—and, if that was insufficient, the repairs were to be done at the public cost and the money to be refunded by the widow, even if she had to sell her house by auction for the purpose. Things did

*Afterwards Alexander II.

not go to the length of an auction, but the widow's floors
were torn up.

§2

FIFTY *versts* from Vyatka is the spot where the wonder-
working *ikon* of St. Nicholas was revealed to the people
of Novgorod. When they moved to Vyatka, they took the
ikon with them; but it disappeared and turned up again
by the Big River, fifty *versts* away. The people removed
it again; but they took a vow that, if the *ikon* would
stay with them, they would carry it in solemn procession
once a year—on the twenty-third of May, I think,—to
the Big River. This is the chief summer holiday in the
Government of Vyatka. The *ikon* is despatched along
the river on a richly decorated barge the day before, accompanied by the Bishop and all the clergy in their full
robes. Hundreds of boats of every description, filled with
peasants and their wives, native tribesmen and shopkeepers, make up a lively scene, as they sail in the wake
of the Saint. In front of all sails the Governor's barge,
decorated with scarlet cloth. It is a remarkable sight. The
people gather from far and near in tens of thousands,
wait on the bank for the arrival of the Saint, and move
about in noisy crowds round the little village by the river.
It is remarkable that the native Votyaks and Cheremisses
and even Tatars, though they are not Christians, come
in crowds to pray to the *ikon*. The festival, indeed, wears
a purely pagan aspect. Natives and Russians alike bring
calves and sheep as offerings up to the wall of the monastery; they slaughter them on the spot, and the Abbot repeats prayers and blesses and consecrates the meat, which
is offered at a special window on the inner side of the

monastery enclosure. The meat is then distributed to the people. In old times it was given away, but nowadays the monks receive a few pence for each piece. Thus the peasant who has presented an entire calf has to spend a trifle in order to get a bit of veal for his own eating. The court of the monastery is filled with beggars, cripples, blind men, and sufferers from all sorts of deformity; they sit on the ground and sing out in chorus for alms. The gravestones round the church are used as seats by boys, the sons of priests and shopmen; armed with an ink-bottle, each offers to write out names of the dead, that their souls may be prayed for. "Who wants names written?" they call out, and the women crowd round them and repeat the names. The boys scratch away with their pens with a professional air and repeat the names after them— "Marya, Marya, Akulina, Stepanida, Father Ioann, Matrona—no, no! auntie, half a *kopeck* is all you gave me; but I can't take less than five *kopecks* for such a lot— Ioann, Vasilissa, Iona, Marya, Yevpraxia, and the baby Katherine."

The church is tightly packed, and the female worshippers differ oddly in their preferences: one hands a candle to her neighbour with precise directions that it is to be offered to "the guest," *i.e.*, the Saint who is there on a visit, while another woman prefers "the host," *i.e.*, the local Saint. During the ceremonies the monks and attendant acolytes from Vyatka are never sober; they stop at all the large villages along the way, and the peasants stand treat.

This ancient and popular festival was celebrated on the twenty-third of May. But the Prince was to arrive on May 19, and the Governor, wishing to please his august visitor, changed the date of the festival; what harm could it do, if St. Nicholas paid his visit three days too soon? The Abbot's consent was necessary; but he was fortunately a man of the world and raised no difficulty when the Governor proposed to keep the twenty-third of May on the nineteenth.

§3

INSTRUCTIONS of various kinds came from Petersburg; for instance, it was ordered that each provincial capital should organise an exhibition of the local products and manufactures; and the animal, vegetable, and mineral products were to be kept separate. This division into kingdoms perplexed our office not a little, and puzzled even the Governor himself. Wishing not to make mistakes, he decided, in spite of the bad relations between us, to seek my advice. "Now, honey, for example," he said, "where would you put honey? And that gilt frame—how can we settle where that belongs?" My replies showed that I had surprisingly exact information concerning the three natural kingdoms, and he proposed that I should undertake the arrangement of the exhibition.

§4

I WAS still putting in order wooden spoons and native costumes, honey and iron trellis-work, when an awful rumour spread through the town that the Mayor of Orlóv had been arrested. The Governor's face turned yellow, and he even seemed unsteady in his gait.

A week before the Prince arrived, the Mayor of Orlóv wrote to the Governor that the widow whose floors had been torn up was making a disturbance, and that a rich and well-known merchant of the town declared his intention of telling the whole story to the Prince on his arrival. The Governor dealt very ingeniously with this firebrand; he recalled with satisfaction the precedent of Petrovski, and ordered that the merchant, being suspected of insanity, should be sent to Vyatka for examination. Thus the matter would drag on till the Prince left the province; and that would be the end of it. The mayor did what he was told, and the merchant was placed in the hospital at Vyatka.

At last the Prince arrived. He greeted the Governor coldly and took no further notice of him, and he sent his own physician at once to examine the merchant. He knew all about it by this time. For the widow had presented her petition at Orlóv, and then the merchants and shop people had told the whole story. The Governor grew more and more crest-fallen. The affair looked bad. The mayor had said plainly that he acted throughout on the written orders of the Governor.

When the physician came back, he reported that the merchant was perfectly sane. That was a finishing stroke for the Governor.

At eight in the evening the Prince visited the exhibition with his suite. The Governor conducted him; but he made a terrible hash of his explanations, till two of the suite, Zhukovski* and Arsenyev, seeing that things were not going well, invited me to do the honours; and I took the party round.

*The famous man of letters (1783-1852) who acted as tutor to Alexander. Arsenyev undertook the scientific side of the Prince's education.

The young Prince had not the stern expression of his father; his features suggested rather good nature and indolence. Though he was only about twenty, he was beginning to grow stout. The few words he addressed to me were friendly, and he had not the hoarse abrupt utterance of his uncle Constantine.

When the Prince left the exhibition, Zhukovski asked me what had brought me to Vyatka; he was surprised to find in such a place an official who could speak like a gentleman. He offered at once to speak to the Prince about me; and he actually did all that he could. The Prince suggested to his father that I should be allowed to return to Petersburg; the Emperor said that this would be unfair to the other exiles, but, owing to the Prince's intercession, he ordered that I should be transferred to Vladímir. This was an improvement in point of position, as Vladímir is 700 *versts* nearer Moscow. But of this I shall speak later.

§5

In the evening there was a ball at the assembly-rooms. The musicians, who had been summoned for the occasion from one of the factories of the province, arrived in the town helplessly drunk. The Governor rose to the emergency: the performers were all shut up in prison twenty-four hours before the ball, marched straight from prison to the orchestra, and kept there till the ball was over.

The ball was a dull, ill-arranged affair, both mean and motley, as balls always are in small towns on great occasions. The police-officers bustled up and down; the officials, in full uniform, squeezed up against the walls; the ladies crowded round the Prince, just as savages mob a traveller from Europe.

Apropos of the ladies, I may tell a story. One of the towns offered a "collation" after their exhibition. The Prince partook of nothing but a single peach; when he had eaten it, he threw the stone out of the window. Suddenly a tall figure emerged from the crowd of officials standing outside the building; it was a certain rural judge, well known for his irregular habits; he walked deliberately up to the window, picked up the stone, and put it in his pocket. When the collation was over, he went up to one of the important ladies and offered her the stone; she was charmed to get such a treasure. Then he went to several other ladies and made them happy in the same way. He had bought five peaches and cut out the stones. Not one of the six ladies could ever be sure of the authenticity of her prize.

§6

WHEN the Prince had gone, the Governor prepared with a heavy heart to exchange his satrapy for a place on the bench of the Supreme Court at home; but he was not so fortunate as that.

Three weeks later the post brought documents from Petersburg addressed to "The Acting Governor of the Province." Our office was a scene of confusion; officials came and went; we heard that an edict had been received, but the Governor pretended illness and kept his house.

An hour later we heard that Tufáyev had been dismissed from his office; and that was all that the edict said about him.

The whole town rejoiced over his fall. While he ruled, the atmosphere was impure, stale, and stifling; now one could breathe more freely. And yet it was hateful to see the triumph of his subordinates. Asses in plenty raised their heels against this stricken wild-boar. To compare small things with great, the meanness of mankind was shown as clearly then as when Napoleon fell. Between Tufáyev and me there had been an open breach for a long time; and if he had not been turned out himself, he would certainly have sent me to some frontier town like Kai. I had therefore no reason to change my behaviour towards him; but others, who only the day before had pulled off their hats at the sight of his carriage and run at his nod, who had smiled at his spaniel and offered their snuffboxes to his valet—these same men now would hardly salute him and made the whole town ring with their protests against the irregularities which he had committed and they had shared in. All this is an old story and repeats itself so regularly from age to age, in all places, that we must accept this form of baseness as a universal trait of human nature, and, at all events, not be surprised by it.

§7

His successor, Kornilov, soon made his appearance. He was a very different sort of person—a man of about fifty, tall and stout, rather flabby in appearance, but with an agreeable smile and gentlemanly manners. He formed all his sentences with strict grammatical accuracy and used a great number of words; in fact, he spoke with a clearness which was capable, by its copiousness, of obscuring the simplest topic. He had been at school with Púshkin and had served in the Guards; he bought all the new French books, liked to talk on serious topics, and gave me a copy of Tocqueville's* *Democracy in America* the day after he arrived at Vyatka.

It was a startling change. The same rooms, the same furniture, but, instead of the Tatar tax-collector with the face of an Esquimo and the habits of a Siberian, a theorist with a tincture of pedantry but a gentleman none the less. Our new Governor had intelligence, but his intellect seemed to give light only and no warmth, like a bright day in winter which ripens no fruit though it is pleasant enough. He was a terrible formalist too, though not of the red-tape variety; it is not easy to describe the type, but it was just as tiresome as all varieties of formalism are.

As the new Governor had a real wife, the official residence lost its ultra-bachelor characteristics; it became monogamous. As a consequence of this, the members of the Council became quite domestic characters: these bald old gentlemen, instead of boasting over their conquests, now spoke with tender affection of their lawful wives, although these ladies were past their prime and either angular and bony, or so fat that it was impossible for a surgeon to draw blood from them.

§8

SOME years before he came to us, Kornilov, being then a colonel in the Guards, was appointed Civil Governor of a provincial town, and entered at once upon business of which he knew nothing. Like all new brooms, he began by reading every official paper that was submitted to him. He came across a certain document from another Govern-

*Alexis de Tocqueville, a French statesman and publicist (1805-1859).

ment which he could not understand, though he read it through several times.

He rang for his secretary and gave it to him to read. But the secretary also was unable to explain the matter clearly.

"What will you do with this document," asked Kornilov, "if I pass it on to the office?"

"I shall hand it to Desk III—it is in their department."

"So the chief of Desk III will know what to do?"

"Certainly, Your Excellency; he has been in charge of that desk for six years."

"Please summon him to me."

The chief came, and Kornilov handed him the paper and asked what should be done. The clerk ran through it hastily, and then said a question must be asked of the Crown Court and instructions given to the inspector of rural police.

"What instructions?"

The clerk seemed puzzled; at last he said that, though it was difficult to state them on the spot, it was easy to write them down.

"There is a chair; will you be good enough to write now?"

The clerk took a pen, wrote rapidly and confidently, and soon produced the two documents.

The Governor took them and read them through; he read them through again; he could make nothing of them. "Well," he used to say afterwards, "I saw that it really was in the form of an answer to the original document; so I plucked up courage and signed it. The answer gave entire satisfaction; I never heard another word about it."

§9

THE announcement of my transference to Vladímir arrived before Christmas. My preparations were quickly
made, and I started off.

I said a cordial good-bye to society at Vyatka; in that
distant town I had made two or three real friends among
the young merchants. They vied with one another in showing sympathy and friendship for the outcast. Several
sledges accompanied me to the first stopping-place, and,
in spite of my protests, a whole cargo of eatables and
drinkables was placed on my conveyance. Next day I
reached Yaransk.

After Yaransk the road passes through endless pine-
forests. There was moonlight and hard frost as my small
sledge slid along the narrow track. I have never since seen
such continuous forests. They stretch all the way to Arch-
angelsk, and reindeer occasionally find their way through
them to the Government of Vyatka. Most of the wood is
suitable for building purposes. The fir-trees seemed to
file past my sledge like soldiers; they were remarkably
straight and high, and covered with snow, under which
their black needles stuck out like bristles. I fell asleep
and woke again—and there were the armies of the pines
still marching past at a great rate, and sometimes shaking
off the snow. There are small clearings where the horses
are changed; you see a small house half-hidden in the
trees and the horses tethered to a tree-trunk, and hear
their bells jingling; a couple of native boys in embroidered
shirts run out, still rubbing their eyes; the driver has a
dispute with the other driver in a hoarse alto voice; then
he calls out "All right!" and strikes up a monotonous song

—and the endless procession of pine-trees and snow-drifts begins again.

JUST as I got out of the Government of Vyatka, I came in contact for the last time with the officials, and this final appearance was quite in their best manner.

We stopped at a post-house, and the driver began to unharness the horses. A tall peasant appeared at the door and asked who I was.

"What business is that of yours?"

"I am the inspector's messenger, and he told me to ask."

"Very well: go to the office and you will find my passport there."

The peasant disappeared but returned in a moment and told the driver that he could not have fresh horses.

This was too much. I jumped out of the sledge and entered the house. The inspector was sitting on a bench and dictating to a clerk; both were half-seas over. On another bench in a corner a man was sitting, or rather lying, with fetters on his feet and hands. There were several bottles in the room, glasses, and a litter of papers and tobacco ash on the table.

"Where is the inspector?" I called out loudly, as I went in.

"I am the inspector," was the reply. I had seen the man before in Vyatka; his name was Lazarev. While speaking he stared very rudely at me—and then rushed towards me with open arms.

It must be remembered that, after Tufáyev's fall, the officials, seeing that his successor and I were on fairly good terms, were a little afraid of me.

I kept him off with my hand, and asked in a very serious voice: "How could you order that I was to have no horses? What an absurdity to detain travellers on the high road!"

"It was only a joke; I hope you won't be angry about it." Then he shouted at his messenger: "Horses! horses at once! What are you standing there for, you idiot?"

"I hope you will have a cup of tea with some rum in it," he said to me.

"No, thank you."

"Perhaps we have some champagne"; he rushed to the bottles, but they were all empty.

"What are you doing here?" I asked.

"Holding an enquiry; this fine fellow took an axe and killed his father and sister. There was a quarrel and he was jealous."

"And so you celebrate the occasion with champagne?" I said.

The man looked confused. I glanced at the murderer. He was a Cheremiss of about twenty; there was nothing savage about his face; it was of purely Oriental type with narrow flashing eyes and black hair.

I was so disgusted by the whole scene that I went out again into the yard. The inspector ran out after me, with a bottle of rum in one hand and a glass in the other, and pressed me to have a drink.

In order to get rid of him, I accepted. He caught me by the arm and said: "I am to blame, I admit; but I hope you will not mention the facts to His Excellency and so ruin an honest man." As he spoke, he caught hold of my hand and actually kissed it, repeating a dozen times over, "In God's name, don't ruin an honest man!" I pulled away my hand in disgust and said:

"You needn't be afraid; what need have I to tell tales?"

"But can't I do you some service?"

"Yes; you can make them harness the horses quicker."

"Look alive there!" he shouted out, and soon began tugging at the straps himself.

§11

I NEVER forgot this incident. Nine years later I was in Petersburg for the last time; I had to visit the Home Office to arrange about a passport. While I was talking to the secretary in charge, a gentleman walked through the room, distributing friendly handshakes to the magnates of the office and condescending bows to the lesser lights. "Hang it! it can't surely be him!" I thought. "Who is that?" I asked.

"His name is Lazarev; he is specially employed by the Minister and is a great man here."

"Did he serve once as inspector in the Government of Vyatka?"

"He did."

"I congratulate you, gentlemen! Nine years ago that man kissed my hand!"

It must be allowed that the Minister knew how to choose his subordinates.

CHAPTER XI

The Beginning of my Life at Vladímir.

§1

WHEN we had reached Kosmodemyansk and I came out to take my seat in the sledge, I saw that the horses were harnessed three abreast in Russian fashion; and the bells jingled cheerfully on the yoke worn by the wheeler.

In Perm and Vyatka they harness the horses differently —either in single file, or one leader with two wheelers.

My heart beat fast with joy, to see the Russian fashion again.

"Now let us see how fast you can go!" I said to the lad sitting with a professional air on the box of the sledge. He wore a sheepskin coat with the wool inside, and such stiff gloves that he could hardly bring two fingers together to clutch the coin I offered him.

"Very good, Sir. Gee up, my beauties!" said the lad. Then he turned to me and said, "Now, Sir, just you hold on; there's a hill coming where I shall let the horses go." The hill was a steep descent to the Volga, along which the track passed in winter.

He did indeed let the horses go. As they galloped down the hill, the sledge, instead of moving decently forwards, banged like a cracker from side to side of the road. The driver was intensely pleased; and I confess that I, being a Russian, enjoyed it no less.

In this fashion I drove into the year 1838—the best and brightest year of my life. Let me tell you how I saw the New Year in.

§2

ABOUT eighty *versts* from Nizhni, my servant Matthew and I went into a post-house to warm ourselves. The frost was keen, and it was windy as well. The post-master, a thin and sickly creature who aroused my compassion, was writing out a way-bill, repeating each letter as he wrote it, and making mistakes all the same. I took off my fur coat and walked about the room in my long fur boots. Matthew warmed himself at the red-hot stove, the post-master muttered to himself, and the wooden clock on the wall ticked with a feeble, jerky sound.

"Look at the clock, Sir," Matthew said to me; "it will strike twelve immediately, and the New Year will begin." He glanced half-enquiringly at me and then added, "I shall bring in some of the things they put on the sledge at Vyatka." Without waiting for an answer, he hurried off in search of the bottles and a parcel.

Matthew, of whom I shall say more in future, was more than a servant—he was my friend, my younger brother. A native of Moscow, he had been handed over to our old friend Sonnenberg, to learn the art of book-binding, about which Sonnenberg himself knew little enough; later, he was transferred to my service.

I knew that I should have hurt Matthew by refusing, and I had really no objection myself to making merry in the post-house. The New Year is itself a stage in life's journey.

He brought in a ham and champagne.

The wine was frozen hard, and the ham was frosted over with ice; we had to chop it with an axe, but *à la guerre comme à la guerre*.

"A Happy New Year," we all cried. And I had cause for happiness. I was travelling back in the right direction, and every hour brought me nearer to Moscow—my heart was full of hope.

As our frozen champagne was not much to the taste of the post-master, I poured an equal quantity of rum into his glass; and this new form of "half and half" was a great success.

The driver, whom I invited to drink with us, was even more thoroughgoing in his methods: he poured pepper into the foaming wine, stirred it up with a spoon, and drank the glass at one gulp; then he sighed and added with a sort of groan, "That was fine and hot."

The post-master himself helped me into the sledge, and was so zealous in his attentions that he dropped a lighted candle into the hay and failed to find it afterwards. He was in great spirits and kept repeating, "A Happy New Year for me too, thanks to you."

The "heated" driver touched up the horses, and we started.

§3

At eight on the following evening I arrived at Vladímir and stopped at an inn which is described with perfect accuracy in *The Tarantas*,* with its queer menu in Russian-French and its vinegar for claret.

"Someone was asking for you this morning," said the waiter, after reading the name on my passport; "perhaps he's waiting in the bar now." The waiter's head displayed that dashing parting and noble curl over the ear which used to be the distinguishing marks of Russian waiters and are now peculiar to them and Prince Louis Napoleon.

I could not guess who this could be.

"But there he is," added the waiter, standing aside. What I first saw was not a man at all but an immense tray piled high with all sorts of provisions—cake and biscuits, apples and oranges, eggs, almonds and raisins; then behind the tray came into view the white beard and blue eyes belonging to the bailiff on my father's estate near Vladímir.

"Gavrilo Semyónitch!" I cried out, and rushed into his arms. His was the first familiar face, the first link with the past, that I had met since the period of prison and exile began. I could not look long enough at the old man's intelligent face, I could not say enough to him. To me he represented nearness to Moscow, to my home and my friends: he had seen them all three days before and brought me greetings from them all. How could I feel that I was really far from them?

§4

THE Governor of Vladímir was a man of the world who had lived long enough to attain a temper of cool indifference. He was a Greek and his name was Kuruta. He took my measure at once and abstained from the least attempt

*I.e., *The Travelling Carriage,* a novel by Count Sologub.

at severity. Office work was never even hinted at—the only duty he asked me to undertake was that I should edit the Provincial Gazette in collaboration with the local schoolmaster.

I was familiar with this business, as I had started the unofficial part of the Gazette at Vyatka. By the way, one article which I published there nearly landed my successor in a scrape. In describing the festival on the Big River, I said that the mutton offered to St. Nicholas used to be given away to the poor but was now sold. This enraged the Abbot, and the Governor had some difficulty in pacifying him.

§5

PROVINCIAL Gazettes were first introduced in the year 1837. It was Bludov, the Minister of the Interior, who conceiv:d the idea of training in publicity the land of silence and dumbness. Bludov, known as the continuator of K: ¯amzín's History—though he never added a line to it—and as the author of the Report on the Decembrist Revolution—which had better never have been written—was one of those doctrinaire statesmen who came to the front in the last years of Alexander's reign. They were able, educated, honest men; they had belonged in their youth to the Literary Club of Arzamas;* they wrote Russian well, had patriotic feelings, and were so much interested in the history of their country that they had no leisure to bestow on contemporary events. They all worshipped the immortal memory of Karamzín, loved Zhu-

---

*Zhukovski and Púshkin both belonged to this club. It carried on a campaign against Shishkóv and other opponents of the new developments in Russian style.

kovski, knew Krylóv* by heart, and used to travel to Moscow on purpose to talk to Dmítriev† in his house there. I too used to visit there in my student days; but I was armed against the old poet by prejudices in favour of romanticism, by my acquaintance with N. Polevói, and by a secret feeling of dissatisfaction that Dmítriev, being a poet, should also be Minister of Justice. Though much was expected of them, they did nothing; but that is the fate of doctrinaires in all countries. Perhaps they would have left more lasting traces behind them if Alexander had lived; but Alexander died, and they never got beyond the mere wish to do the state some service.

At Monaco there is a monument to one of their Princes with this inscription. "Here rests Prince Florestan"—I forget his number—"who wished to make his subjects happy." Our doctrinaires also wished to make Russia happy, but they reckoned without their host. I don't know who prevented Florestan; but it was our Florestan‡ who prevented them. They were forced to take a part in the steady deterioration of Russia, and all the reforms they could introduce were useless, mere alterations of forms and names. Every Russian in authority considers it his highest duty to rack his brains for some novelty of this kind; the change is generally for the worse and sometimes leaves things exactly as they were. Thus the name of 'secretary' has given place to a Russian equivalent in the public offices of the provinces, but the duties are not changed. I remember how the Minister of Justice put for-

---

*Krylóv (1768-1844), the famous writer of fables.

†Dmítriev, a poet once famous, who lived long enough to welcome Púshkin.

‡*I.e.*, the Emperor Nicholas.

ward a proposal for necessary changes in the uniform of civilian officials. It began with great pomp and circumstance—"Having taken special notice of the lack of uniformity in the cut and fashion of certain uniforms worn by the civilian department, and having adopted as a principle . . . ," etc.

Beset by this itch for novelty the Minister of the Interior made changes with regard to the officers who administer justice in the rural districts. The old judges lived in the towns and paid occasional visits to the country; their successors have their regular residence in the country and pay occasional visits to the towns. By this reform all the peasants came under the immediate scrutiny of the police. The police penetrated into the secrets of the peasant's commerce and wealth, his family life, and all the business of his community; and the village community had been hitherto the last refuge of the people's life. The only redeeming feature is this—there are many villages and only two judges to a district.

§6

ABOUT the same time the same Minister excogitated the Provincial Gazettes. Our Government, while utterly contemptuous of education, makes pretensions to be literary; and whereas, in England, for example, there are no Government newspapers at all, every public department in Russia publishes its own organ, and so does the Academy, and so do the Universities. We have papers to represent the mining interest and the pickled-herring interest, the interests of Frenchmen and Germans, the marine interest and the land-carriage interest, all published at the expense of Government. The different departments contract for articles, just as they contract for fire-wood and candles, the only difference being that in the former case there is no competition; there is no lack of general surveys, invented statistics, and fanciful conclusions based on the statistics. Together with a monopoly in everything else, the Government has assumed a monopoly of nonsense; ordering everyone to be silent, it chatters itself without ceasing. In continuation of this system, Bludov ordered that each provincial Government should publish its own Gazette, and that each Gazette should include, as well as the official news, a department for history, literature and the like.

No sooner said than done. In fifty provincial Governments they were soon tearing their hair over this unofficial part. Priests from the theological seminaries, doctors of medicine, schoolmasters, anyone who was suspected of being able to spell correctly—all these were pressed into the service. These recruits reflected, read up the leading newspapers and magazines, felt nervous, took the plunge, and finally produced their little articles.

To see oneself in print is one of the strongest artificial passions of an age corrupted by books. But it requires courage, nevertheless, except in special circumstances, to venture on a public exhibition of one's productions. People who would not have dreamed of publishing their articles in the *Moscow Gazette* or the Petersburg newspapers, now began to print their writings in the privacy of their own houses. Thus the dangerous habit of possessing an organ of one's own took root, and men became accustomed to publicity. And indeed it is not a bad thing to have a weapon which is always ready for use. A printing press, like the human tongue, has no bones.

§7

My colleague in the editorship had taken his degree at Moscow University and in the same faculty as myself. The end of his life was too tragical for me to speak of him with a smile; but, down to the day of his death, he was an exceedingly absurd figure. By no means stupid, he was excessively clumsy and awkward. His exceptional ugliness had no redeeming feature, and there was an abnormal amount of it. His face was nearly twice as large as most people's and marked by small-pox; he had the mouth of a codfish which spread from ear to ear; his light-grey eyes were lightened rather than shaded by colourless eye-lashes; his scalp had a meagre covering of bristly hair; he was moreover taller by a head than myself,* with a slouching figure and very slovenly habits.

His very name was such that it once caused him to be arrested. Late one evening, wrapped up in his overcoat, he was walking past the Governor's residence, with a field-glass in his hand. He stopped and aimed the glass at the heavens. This astonished the sentry, who probably reckoned the stars as Government property: he challenged the rapt star-gazer—"Who goes there?" "Nebaba,"† answered my colleague in a deep bass voice, and gazed as before.

"Don't play the fool with me—I'm on duty," said the sentry.

"I tell you that I am Nebába!"

The soldier's patience was exhausted: he rang the bell, a serjeant appeared, the sentry handed the astronomer

*Herzen himself was a very tall, large man.
†The word means in Russian "Not a woman."

over to him, to be taken to the guard-room. "They'll find out there," as he said, "whether you're a woman or not." And there he would certainly have stayed till the morning, had not the officer of the day recognised him.

§8

ONE morning Nebába came to my room to tell me that he was going to Moscow for a few days, and he smiled with an air that was half shy and half sentimental. Then he added, with some confusion, "I shall not return alone." "Do you mean that . . . ?" "Yes, I am going to be married," he answered bashfully. I was astonished at the heroic courage of the woman who was willing to marry this good-hearted but monstrously ugly suitor. But a fortnight later I saw the bride at his house; she was eighteen and, if no beauty, pretty enough, with lively eyes; and then I thought him the hero.

Six weeks had not passed before I saw that things were going badly with my poor Orson. He was terribly depressed, corrected his proofs carelessly, never finished his article on "The Migration of Birds," and could not fix his attention on anything; at times it seemed to me that his eyes were red and swollen. This state of things did not last long. One day as I was going home, I noticed a crowd of boys and shopkeepers running towards the churchyard. I walked after them.

Nebába's body was lying near the church wall, and a rifle lay beside him. He had shot himself opposite the windows of his own house; the string with which he had pulled the trigger was still attached to his foot. The police-surgeon blandly assured the crowd that the deceased had suffered no pain; and the police prepared to carry his body to the station.

Nature is cruel to the individual. What dark forebodings filled the breast of this poor sufferer, before he made up his mind to use his piece of string and stop the pendulum which measured out nothing to him but insult and suffering? And why was it so? Because his father was consumptive or his mother dropsical? Likely enough. But what right have we to ask for reasons or for justice? What is it that we seek to call to account? Will the whirling hurricane of life answer our questions?

§9

AT the same time there began for me a new epoch in my life—pure and bright, youthful but earnest; it was the life of a hermit, but a hermit thoroughly in love.

But this belongs to another part of my narrative.